W9-ABH-428

In Memory of

Bobbie Reeves
(and his faithful
dogs, Rex and
Duchess).

"Hunting quail
without a dog is
like painting
without a brush."

Quail Hunting in America

Quail Hunting in America

Tactics for finding and taking bobwhite, valley, Gambel, mountain, scaled, and Mearns quail by season and habitat

Tom Huggler

Stackpole Books

Copyright © 1987 by Tom Huggler

Published by
STACKPOLE BOOKS
5067 Ritter Road
Mechanicsburg, PA 17055

All rights reserved, including the right to reproduce this book or
portions thereof in any form or by any means, electronic or mechanical,
including photocopying, recording, or by any information storage and
retrieval system, without permission in writing from the publisher. All
inquiries should be addressed to Stackpole Books, 5067 Ritter Road,
Mechanicsburg, PA 17055.

Maps reprinted by permission of the publisher from the book *Easy-to-Make Maps . . . Using Your Office Copier* © 1985 by Caddylak Systems, Inc., 201 Montrose Road, Westbury, NY, 11590.

Maps illustrated by Debra R. Courts.

Cover photo by Tony Mandile

Printed in the U.S.A.

Library of Congress Cataloging-in-Publication Data

Huggler, Thomas E.
   Quail hunting in America.

   Includes index.
   1. Quail shooting—North America. I. Title.
SK325.Q2H84   1987   799.2'48617   86-14590
ISBN 0-8117-1277-X

To autumn sun,
To golden ale,
To rod and gun,
To wily quail.

White Horse Tavern
Flint, Michigan

Contents

Acknowledgments

Many people had an influence on this book. Unfortunately, there is not enough space to thank them all.

Several fellow writers and photographers—members of the Outdoor Writers Association of America—invited me into their homes; let me use their word processors, telephones, showers and freezers; allowed my dogs to all but destroy their shrubbery; cut red tape with fish and game departments; gave me good advice, and kept up my spirits. They are Larry Brown, Thayne Smith, Paula Del Giudice, Mike Pearce, Tony Mandile, Bob Hirsch, Jesse Williams, Chuck Cadieux, Steve Bodio, Steve Grooms, Dennis Phillips, Jim Reid, and David Morris.

Others, many of whom I met for the first time while on the road, helped show the way. They include Harry Rutherford, Greg Koch, Jim Wooley, Colonel Gerald Graham, Rick Jameson, Lawrence Smith, David Denayer, Hoyd Patty, Floyd Mansell, and Floyd Preas.

Most state fish and game department personnel were helpful. Some went out of their way, sacrificing personal time to make sure I got the right information. Richard Bishop, Willy Suchy, Roger Wells, Gerald Gates, San Stiver, and Al Stewart all deserve thanks.

I would like to compliment my associates—Randy Carrels for his yeoman work in the studio and darkroom, Debra Courts for her research assistance and painstaking work with the quail distribution maps. I appreciated, too, the proofreading suggestions by Steve Smith, Gerry Bethge, Laura Albrecht, and Steve Bodio.

George Conrad and Rocky Evans of Quail Unlimited lent advice and enthusiastic support.

And a special thanks to Judith Schnell of Stackpole Books for believing in this idea from the onset, then helping me see it through to completion.

Foreword

As I write this, my suitcase and guns are still packed up, and my boots are still covered with Georgia red clay. Tom Huggler and I just got back from a three-day shoot at a plantation in northern Georgia, where the birds were plenty, the dogs excellent, and the companionship exemplary.

Tom will tell you about that experience a little later in this book, but I can tell you—because he won't—that a bobwhite in the open, or in the woods, for that matter, doesn't have even a fifty-fifty chance if Tom and his 20 gauge stroll by to pay a visit. Fact is, having spent a fall and winter doing little else except shooting and shooting at quail, Tom Huggler has come to know these birds—these quails in their many and varied forms—as well as any upland hunter could. He's had the chance, without time getting things all sort of fogged up, to compare, scrutinize, chase, collect, talk about, sort out, eat, and get stuffed the quails of America. He's asked questions, interviewed the experts, and looked at a lot of birds from behind a camera lens and over a gun barrel. Sadly, this book will contain only a small fraction of the knowledge he has and the experience he's gained.

But that fraction is one which makes this book so valuable, not only to the quail hunter, but to the person who just loves a good story written by a fine writer about a task undertaken—Huggler's Grand Slam.

Tom has gone to a lot of trouble and expense to make this book as accurate as possible. It's not only a book of the present; it's one of the future—a book you can use as a guide, as a piece of literature, and as a work which is accurate. That's because Tom Huggler just may be the best "digger" in the outdoor-writing business, a man whose personal integrity will not allow a fact to go unchecked, a statement to remain unproved.

So because you didn't buy this book to read what I have to say, I'll turn you over to Tom Huggler and his friends, the quails of America.

I think you're going to like the trip.

Steve Smith
Gun Dog Magazine

Introduction

As to the species of exercise, I advise the gun.
Let the gun, therefore, be the constant companion of your walks.

Thomas Jefferson

I love to hunt birds, yet I had an overwhelming desire to hunt quail. In Michigan, where I live, bobwhites are scarce, and so hunting for them is not allowed. Pheasants are hurting, too. In recent years I had been going to South Dakota, Kansas, and Iowa to hunt farmland game.

It was Ron Spomer's suggestion that I hunt birds across America. We were driving home from Alaska after six weeks of gathering stories and photographs for our work as full-time freelance writers. Ron planted the seed that fall of 1984. I spent the winter writing letters, researching, asking a lot of questions. I discovered that to hunt all the gamebirds in North America was next to impossible in a single hunting season. I would have to limit that goal somehow.

The quails were likely candidates. I could find bobwhites in any one of more than 30 states. The five Western species, however, I had never seen and knew next to nothing about hunting. No one state is home to all five but, with luck, I might find them in as few as three.

Hunting quail across America seemed like a good thing to do. I could tell you that being single at age 40, I was in a midlife crisis and

13

needed to take to the road. But that isn't true. I went because I wanted to learn and to share an adventure at the same time. So I sold my old Chevy truck and converted the $800 into gasoline for a borrowed Winnebago motorhome. I packed it with shotguns and ammunition, five pairs of hunting boots, and plenty of clothing for all weather conditions. I put in a word processor and portable typewriter so that I might keep up with magazine assignments and correspondence.

On a balmy Halloween Eve, 1985, I loaded my setters into an over-the-road kennel and headed out on the first leg of my journey. I dropped off Holly, my yellow Labrador, at a trainer's in southern Michigan, hoping to have a polished retriever when I returned. I found out later she had come into her heat the day after we left. The trainer could not work with her, nor with his other dogs as they were too interested in Holly. She would have enjoyed the trip had I taken her. When the setters and I entered Michigan again on Thanksgiving Day, snow swirled across the highway like campfire smoke. We had hunted bobwhites in Iowa, Kansas, Oklahoma, and Missouri and had seen our first scaled quail—fascinating birds—in the grasslands of southwestern Kansas.

Late in the evening of Christmas Day, I left home again, this time adding Holly to the dog trailer. It had struck me that, as far as I knew, no one had ever shot all six species of quail on a single trip. Robert Elman and Charley Waterman, both fine writers and sportsmen, are two of perhaps many who have bagged all the quails. But I don't think they did it on one trip. Anyway, it seemed like a good idea to at least try.

As I write this, I am looking at six mounted cock quail on a skeleton of cholla cactus that I picked up in the Sonoran Desert. I was lucky to be able to shoot bobwhites in Oklahoma again, then scaled and Gambel quail in New Mexico and Arizona, Mearns quail in Arizona, and the mountain and valley species in Nevada. I wheeled the motorhome back into my driveway on Super Bowl Sunday. Altogether, I had hunted seven states, driven 13,000 miles, and—as near as I can figure it—walked about 300 miles behind my dogs.

In a letter to Ron Spomer, I told him I had just spent the best three months of my life.

Then in March I booked a commercial flight to Atlanta and hunted Georgia bobwhites to at least get a taste of quail hunting, Southern style.

True, those experiences helped get me in shape and even took an inch off my paunch. But they hardly qualify me as an expert on the subject of quail hunting. I will vigorously take issue with anyone who

At a campground in New Mexico, the author works on correspondence while Holly enjoys the winter sun. The following day he shot his first Gambel quail.

calls this book the "complete guide to hunting quail" or insists that I am an expert on these remarkable little gamebirds. No one person knows everything about anything, and no book is ever complete.

Still, I hope you will find much valuable information on these pages. I attempted to balance my experiences and observations, with what others—some of whom have hunted quail all their lives—have told me. There is some natural history and biological research in this book, too, and that is because I believe today's discriminating sportsman wants to know *why* along with *how to* and *where to*.

I love to hunt birds, yet I had an overwhelming desire to hunt quail.

Tom Huggler
Otisville, Michigan
June 1, 1986

1

The Quails of America

Quail are among our most popular gamebirds. Only mourning doves, with an annual harvest of 50 to 55 million nationwide, figure more importantly in terms of numbers killed. Paul Johnsgard, in his book on quail and grouse, estimated that in 1970, hunters shot about 35 million bobwhites and 7.4 million Western species of quail. In 1980, according to the National Survey of Fishing, Hunting, and Wildlife-Associated Recreation, hunters bagged about 22 million bobwhites.

The apparent harvest decrease of 13 million bobwhites between 1970 and 1980 is a reflection of several things: habitat loss, population swings of the species, and fewer hunters. Even so, the estimated 3.6 million quail hunters that participated in 1980 spent twice the number of days afield than did mourning dove hunters. The quail hunters also lead all gamebird hunters in terms of effort. The 22 million bobwhites they shot far surpassed the roughly 9.8 million pheasants and 5.8 million grouse bagged.

Wild-bred bobwhites are currently legal targets in 35 states and Ontario. Several other states and provinces allow shooting for pen-reared quail. Eight Western states—not necessarily the same ones—each host seasons for valley, scaled, and Gambel quail. In British Columbia, valley quail may also be hunted. Mountain quail are legal targets in four states of the Northwest, and Mearns quail can be taken in two states of the Southwest.

The Evolution of Quail

Quail hunting in America began soon after Man the Settler arrived on the East Coast. The lack of quail bones in most excavations of native American living sites suggests that early hunters targeted bigger game worth the effort to pursue. But quail were certainly here, probably long before Man the Hunter arrived. Birds, possibly in rough form of feathered reptiles, are thought first to have appeared in North America some 140 million years ago during the Jurassic Epoch. The forerunner of today's quails dates to the Oligocene Epoch of some 25 to 38 million years ago. According to evidence presented in Johns-

After mourning doves, quail are the country's most popular gamebird in terms of harvest statistics. In recent years, hunters have bagged between 20 and 35 million quail annually.

The bobwhite is legal to hunt in 35 states, plus he is a popular gamebird at shooting preserves across the country. *Michigan Department of Natural Resources photo.*

gard's book, quail and their close cousins—the grouse—probably evolved from common ancestors beginning at this time. *Lophortyx,* or top-knot quail, and *Colinus,* the bobwhite, developed progressively during the Pliocene Epoch of a million or more years ago. The evolution of these gamebirds into the 15 species found above southern Mexico today, no doubt has occurred because of changing environment over thousands of years.

Johnsgard argues pursuasively that "New World quails had their center of evolutionary history and speciation in tropical America, whereas the grouse are a strictly Northern Hemisphere group . . ." Thus, quail moved north and grouse moved south to populate what is now the United States.

The bobwhite lives throughout the eastern U.S., as far north as southern New England and the lower reaches of the upper Midwest.

Home is as far west as eastern New Mexico, Colorado, and South Dakota. Introductions of bobwhites in Washington, Oregon, and Idaho have been successful enough to offer limited hunting opportunities in those states. Bobwhites prefer grasslands interspersed with brush and forests.

The five species of quail living in the West have specific habitat needs yet often overlap and sometimes — although rarely — interbreed to produce hybrid young that are usually sterile. Four of the five sport feathered plumes or crests. Only the Mearns quail, which can be traced to the oscellated quail of old Mexico and which moved north into southern Arizona and New Mexico, lacks a topknot or crest. Valley quail live in foothills and valleys of the far West. Mountain quail inhabit higher altitudes of the same region. Gambel quail, which look very much like the valley species, prefer lowland desert regions of brush. Scaled quail can be found in sage and desert grasslands of the Southwest, sometimes living near bobwhites.

Nine other species of quail live in old Mexico. Those which most recently could be hunted include Yucatan, barred and Douglas or elegant quail. About 15 more species of quail are native to South America.

A Wealth of Research

Due to their popularity and wide distribution, quail are the most intensively studied gamebird on the continent. The U.S. Fish & Wild-

The scaled or blue quail was the author's favorite among the five Western species that may be legally hunted in the U.S. Scaled quail are known for their sprint style of walking.

Gambel or desert quail are legal targets in eight Western states. Also a runner, the Gambel is a tricky, fast-moving gamebird.

life Reference Service in Maryland has hundreds of bobwhite research projects on microfiche and microfilm, along with several dozen more for the Western quails. Walter Rosene said that he drew from the best of 1,400 published works for his excellent book on bobwhite management. And Rosene's book is nearly 20 years old. Many more quail studies have been conducted since its printing.

Herbert L. Stoddard's studies in the Southeast in the 1920s paved the way for much of this outpouring of research. Prescribed burning on 90 percent of the woodland at Tall Timbers Research Station in northern Florida has been going on for some 85 years, along with other research aimed at benefitting quail. As this is written, Alabama researchers are studying how radio-tagged quail react to a recently burned environment. At Tall Timbers and at key hunting plantations in the Southeast, a study is underway to determine the differences between "good" and "bad" hunting courses. Maryland researchers want to know the effect that Treflan, a pre-emergent herbicide, has on nesting bobwhites. Oklahoma investigators are looking at the effects of land management practices on use, productivity, and survival of bobwhites in a grassland-brushland habitat. Tennessee researchers are studying minimum-till farming practices to see if they might benefit bobwhites. Texas investigators recently determined that the cost to put a pen-reared quail into the game bag of a hunter is prohibitive at $18.65 per bird. That is because only 20 percent recovery can be expected.

Biologists and university researchers know how many times bobwhites breed in a day, week or month; how many giant ragweed seeds they had for lunch; the thickness of quail-egg shells; the average travel distance from the dinner table to the bedroom; how an adult bird needs 64,600 calories to stay warm on a day when the temperature is five degrees above zero. More than 50 years ago, Aldo Leopold advanced the theory that population saturation occurs at one bobwhite per acre of habitat. Researchers today not only accept Leopold's arguments, they know the precise living conditions that bobwhites and other quail need in order to survive, indeed, thrive. They can, and are frequently asked to, give prescriptions to landowners who want to hear and see more quail on their property. And the methods work.

In short, there is a wealth of information available on quail, especially bobwhites. The bible, according to most, is Herbert L. Stoddard's *The Bobwhite Quail: Its Habits, Preservation and Increase* (Charles Scribner's Sons, 1931, reissued in 1978). Based on his research and studies in the Southeast, Stoddard laid down principles of bobwhite management followed yet today. Aldo Leopold's *Game Management* (Charles Scribner's Sons, 1933) advances many of the theories that have become more popularly known through *A Sand County Almanac* (Oxford University Press, 1949).

There are at least three more recent books that summarize available research at their respective times of publication. Each is packed with information. I highly recommend them for the quail hunter who wants to broaden his knowledge. Walter Rosene's *The Bobwhite Quail: Its Life and Management* (Rutgers University Press, 1969) is written in an informative, easy-to-read style. Paul Johnsgard's *Grouse and Quails of North America* (University of Nebraska Press, 1973) offers excellent individual accounts of the various quail species, including those of Mexico. Val W. Lehman's *Bobwhites of the Rio Grande Plain of Texas* (Texas A&M University Press, 1984) involves 40 years of painstaking record keeping on the daily lives of quail. It, too, is fascinating reading.

These authors spent the better part of their lives studying quail and other gamebirds. They were also hunters who knew firsthand how a covey rise stirs the sportsman's heart. Listen to this excerpt from Rosene's book:

"The number of birds brought to bag is only one thing remembered. To most hunters, it is old boots with broken and tied laces,

Mearns or Harlequin quail reminded the author of Russian easter eggs. It is difficult to capture the birds in focus because they dig for tubers and invertebrates with those long toes.

that particular sound of khaki hunting clothes, the taste of a dog whistle unused since last year, scratched hands and legs from a wade through a big briarpatch, and cold, stiff fingers. At noon, it is the sandwich, and the smell of old coffee on a thermos cork. In the afternoon, it is heat from freshly killed quail in a game pocket. On the way back home it is that tired, sweaty feeling, and the smell of wet bird dogs, burned powder, and gun oil. Tomorrow it is always a talk with a friend about yesterday's broken points, wild flushes, coveys, singles, the steady dog, and the young puppy and his first find."

If you want to know more, these writers can lead you to other good books and additional research. The research helps hunters and nonhunters alike to better understand quail and know how to improve the world in which they live. That is important because bobwhites, in particular, are in trouble today.

Current Status of the Gamebird

In the past 20 years, quail harvests in Georgia have tumbled from 4 million per year to 1 million. In 1960, Texas hunters shot 9.8 million quail. In 1982, they bagged 3.3 million. In nearly every state where they live, bobwhites are not faring as well as they might. The situation is even more grim in states along the bird's northern limits. In northern New Jersey and northern Indiana, quail are either extirpated or so few in number as to be nearly so. Populations in Pennsylvania have been so low the past 15 years that the state closed the season. In 1969, Ohio biologists estimated that 7.3 million quail lived in the Buckeye State. The grim winter of 1977–78 wiped out 90 percent of the population, and birds have not yet been able to fight back. Minnesota hunters last enjoyed a quail hunting season in 1958. Michigan's most recent season occurred in 1977.

The reasons for reduced populations are several and complex. Most, though, are related to habitat. Weather variables that make it too hot, too cold, too dry, or too wet can spell doom at various times of

Mountain quail proved to be the toughest to bag of the six American quails. The author found them in Nevada between 6,000 and 7,000 feet altitude. *(John Higley photo)*

Valley, or California, quail live throughout the West and are similar to the Gambel quail in appearance. When the author finally shot a rooster for mounting, he left Nevada for his Michigan home. *(John Higley photo)*

year. Predators and disease may exact a heavy toll of eggs, nesting hens, juvenile birds, and adults too weak from hunger to protect themselves. Even though researchers understand population swings of quail, there may be little they can do about it.

Farming and other land-use practices are other considerations altogether. The tearing out of hedgerows, early and late alfalfa mowing, prescribed burning when hens are nesting, fall plowing, double cropping, fencerow-to-fencerow planting, and excessive livestock grazing are all practices that can hurt quail.

The key to producing more quail in this country lies in habitat restoration. That means showing landowners its importance as well as explaining to them how to do it in a cost-effective way. Money is usually the bottom line.

The Future for Quail

In spite of the doomsday evidence, the future for quail in America is far from hopeless. In fact, the glass is half-full, not half-empty. Three positive happenings underway at this writing are already helping quail. Given enough opportunity, they could help restore high numbers and improved hunting.

One is *Quail Unlimited*. Patterned after the successful Ducks

Unlimited and copied in turn by the Ruffed Grouse Society and Pheasants Forever, Quail Unlimited seeks to raise funds for habitat restoration.

That's where the answers lie and where our emphasis is, said Rocky Evans, who founded Quail Unlimited in 1981 and serves as executive director to its 20,000 members in 200 chapters in 38 states. *We buy seed, fertilizer, and specialized equipment, such as tractors and root plows. These we either give or loan to landowners who want to improve living conditions for quail.* At this writing, Quail Unlimited's annual budget has soared to $800,000, no mean sum.

Evans said that with the recent collapse of the International Quail Foundation, Quail Unlimited is also helping to fund key research projects. These include no-till farming, delayed toxicology of herbicides and insecticides on sprayed birds, and diet-related studies. Youth programs to encourage food-plot plantings and other habitat improvements also figure into the organization's plans.

We are definitely not involved with the raising of pen-reared quail. Evans emphasized. *Time and again, the introduction of pen-reared quail has proved to be a financial fiasco. Pen-reared birds don't make it in the wild, and the return is cost-prohibitive. Just a year ago at Tall Timbers, for example, 38 pen-raised bobwhites suffered 100 percent mortality within 50 days. Only three of 38 wild birds in similar habitat died during that period, and that was due to problems adjusting to the radio transmitters with which they were equipped. The answer to more quail lies in improving habitat for wild birds to propagate themselves.*

Evans said that 20 percent of the money raised by each Quail Unlimited chapter must go to respective state fish and game departments willing to earmark the funds for habitat use. Those and other efforts, according to Evans, have raised the consciousness level of state agencies to do something for quail.

They have heard plenty from the deer and turkey hunters in recent years, Evans said. *Now they are hearing from quail hunters.*

Quail Unlimited has annual, charter, sponsor, and life memberships available at staggered rates. Membership benefits include a subscription to the group's bi-monthly magazine, which contains hunting, dog training and habitat-related articles in each issue. In cooperation with Tall Timbers Research Station, Quail Unlimited has a 40-page booklet available, "Bobwhite Quail Management: A Habitat Approach," available at printing cost. For details on the booklet, as well as membership, contact Quail Unlimited, PO Box 10041, Augusta, GA 30903 (803-637-5731).

The second good-news item is the *Conservation Reserve Program.*

Part of the federal government's *1985 Farm Act*, this program has the potential to remove as much as 40 to 45 million acres of highly erodable land from cultivation for at least 10 years. In addition to checking erosion and helping to adjust surplus stocks of wheat, corn, soybeans, and other foods, idling the acres has tremendous benefits for quail and other wildlife. That is because enrolled landowners also agree to plant perennial grasses, wildlife plantings, windbreaks, or trees.

The benefits to gamebirds could be similar to those during the hiatus years of the old Soil Bank program. Improved nesting, rearing, roosting, and security habitat could result. Not only is the U.S. Department of Agriculture providing annual rental payments for idled land, it will also cover half the expense of establishing permanent

Quail Unlimited, founded in 1981, already has grown to 200 chapters in 38 states. Membership is currently 20,000. The organization is dedicated to the improvement of habitat.

Bobwhite quail are the most researched gamebird in North America. Here, a biologist prepares a rooster for radio-telemetry studies. *(Iowa Conservation Commission photo)*

cover on the land, plus offer technical assistance. For details on this and other government cost-share programs, landowners can contact their county office of the Soil Conservation Service.

Third, the increasing use of *minimum tillage,* where farmers rely on methods other than moldboard plowing to prepare their land for planting, is another potential bright spot for quail. In 1983, the Soil Conservation Service estimated that about 100 million acres, or about one-fourth of the nation's cropland, was being tilled with conservation methods. The shift from conventional plowing has been so dramatic that one USDA administrator, Terry B. Kinney, Jr., predicts that "plowless farming" will be in full swing on virtually all U.S. cropland by the year 2,000.

Quail could benefit from that. So could quail hunters.

2

The Bobwhite: A Remarkable Gamebird

The bobwhite quail is a likely candidate for America's most resilient gamebird. Hunters, predators, poor habitat, tough winters, diseases, parasites, and lack of food can combine to reduce its numbers by 75 percent from fall to spring. Yet when all goes well from April through September, it bounces back to formerly high numbers. Cut the breeding stock by 90 percent and the comeback takes two years, sometimes more. It depends on many factors. By itself, hunting is among the least significant.

History of Bobwhites and Bobwhite Hunting

As mentioned in the last chapter, weather and land-use patterns dictate bobwhite numbers. When European explorers reached the shores of North America, they found a huge expanse of mature forest broken, no doubt, here and there with some openings. In these openings—probably caused by fire—and along wooded waterways, they found bobwhites. No one really knows how many quail lived in the new land. As early as 1614 though, John Smith reported an abundance of quail. In 1637, a man named Morton noted "quailes . . . bigger than the quailes in England. They take trees also: for I have numbered 60 upon a tree at a time. The cocks doe call at the time of the yeare, but with a different note from cock quailes of England."

As Man the Settler cleared the forests for his small farms, bobwhites increased dramatically. Fencerows and hedgerows were to his liking. So were hayfields and cropfields of corn, wheat, oats and barley. As the pioneers expanded to the west, so moved the bobwhites.

Quail hunting also had its origins during this colonial period. William Penn, who led the first settlers to Pennsylvania, claimed that the bobwhite was an important food species there. It seems unlikely, however, that the early settlers would waste precious gunpowder on so small a target. They probably trapped the quail in nets as there are references elsewhere in our history to this practice of catching birds. Even so, hunting for sport grew rapidly. Those that could afford it used dogs and experimented with European pointing breeds in an effort to develop animals suited for hunting American quail.

Game laws followed. In 1820, New Jersey hunters could not shoot quail, except on their own land, from February 1 to September 1. By 1838, the hunting season in that state was shortened to the period November 1 to January 10. A New Hampshire law in 1842 afforded quail some protection. Other states established hunting laws regulating quail harvest.

Bobwhite populations historically experience highs and lows, especially in states on the fringe of their broad distribution. In his book, Walter Rosene concludes that numbers in the North peaked about 1860, then began a gradual decline. In New Jersey, the season was closed for three years, beginning in 1869. In the bird's Southeast stronghold, numbers increased until about 1900, remained stable until World War II, then began to slip in an overall decline that continues yet today. The number of hunters that go afield and their success rates nearly always correspond to the bobwhite's rising and falling populations.

Life Needs of the Bobwhite

According to a publication called *Game on Your Land*, put out by the South Carolina Wildlife and Marine Resources Department, there are five reasons for the decline of bobwhites in that state:

1. a change to cleaner and more mechanized farming methods.

2. intensive cultivation in unbroken fields formed by joining small farms.
3. the development of pastures for livestock and hay production.
4. intensified timber production.
5. dense, mature woodlands and not enough use of prescribed burning to improve habitat.

Virginia is one of many states where habitat loss and lack of quality has been carefully documented. In 1940, 64 percent of Virginia was in farmland. By 1982, the figure was only 37 percent. During that period, the amount of cropland left idle fell by 76 percent, and the number of cattle increased by 90 percent to 1.7 million. The use of

The number of quail hunters rises and falls with bobwhite populations. This is Jim Oursler, a young hunter from Newton, Kansas, with a pair of bobwhites.

chemicals increased by 129 percent between 1969 and 1982 alone. Irrigation and drainage, double cropping, increased field size, and the replacement of native grass pastures with widespread monoculture have reduced the diverse habitat that quail need. Cropfields, for example, that halt at woodlines create little or no edge or plant diversity. Bush-hog mowing and hay baling on marginal ground further destroy habitat. Routinely mowed electric fences have replaced brushy fence-rows.

These and other land-use patterns make it tough for bobwhites, whose ideal environment is an equal mixture of cropland, idle land, brushland and woodland—all interspersed. Put another way, bobwhites prefer areas where about half the ground is exposed and the other half contains upright growth of woody and nonwoody vegetation. Studies in Nebraska, Wisconsin, and other states prove that populations increase as the amount of *edge cover*—particularly in the form of brushy hedgerows—increases. As mentioned in the chapter on how to hunt bobwhites, edge cover is the transition between two types of habitat.

Besides the edge, bobwhites need *nesting cover,* usually one- to two-year-old clumps of grass offering just enough overhead protection from hawks but not too dense to walk through. Further, nesting sites must be within 50 feet or less from an opening or edge.

Bobwhites thrive in an environment of mixed habitat that affords plenty of edge cover. Fencerows and hedgerows are especially important. *(Iowa Conservation Commission photo)*

Hunting the edge—in this case, where crop field meets weed field—can be productive. Quail often can be found near old buildings and junk piles.

Roosting cover should furnish some overhead protection but not enough to hamper flight if the covey must take to wing in the dark. There should be some opportunity for warmth—the base of a pine tree or perhaps a southern exposure—on cold nights. *Loafing cover* is brush, shrubs, vines, and small trees a few feet off the ground. Yet the ground cover must not be too heavy to walk through. Dusting areas should be nearby so that birds can control external parasites such as mites. *Screening cover* protects quail when they are feeding or traveling. It, too, must contain canopy protection from winged predators. Thick hedgerows, because they are linear, offer good screening cover. *Escape cover* is heavy-duty stands of brush, grass, weeds, and woods into which quail can duck to elude predators.

All these cover types must be within fairly close proximity as studies show that bobwhites will not move beyond 900 yards to find something to eat. Indeed, most quail spend their lives within a half-mile or so of where they were hatched.

Food needs of bobwhites are most easily met in summer and early fall. Insects are high-protein foods needed by chicks soon after hatching. Adult birds also depend on insects to some degree in summer and early fall, but as plants mature, the birds target seeds, buds, fruits, and leaves. In fact, quail eat a huge variety of foods. A recent summary of 27 food habit studies involving 20,000 bobwhites in several southeastern states revealed that over 650 different types of seeds figured importantly in their diets.

Not all the foods that bobwhites eat, however, are beneficial. This is especially true in winter when fat reserves alone will not see them through a nasty period of bad weather. Laboratory tests show that during a cold snap, bobwhites can starve in just three or four days when they can't find food. Pheasants, on the other hand, can survive up to three weeks without eating.

A high metabolic rate and relatively large surface area mean that a quail must eat several times daily during bitterly cold temperatures. High-energy foods such as Western ragweed and sunflower often shatter and their seeds become unavailable under inches of snow and ice. Quail simply don't have the ability to scratch for something to eat as do pheasants. Foods such as lespedeza, smartweed, and milo may be more available, but they are also low in metabolizable energy. Thus, they may not sustain starving birds, no matter how much they eat.

I'm convinced that during a tough winter, quail can starve to death on top of a milo pile, biologist Roger Wells told me when I hunted with him in Kansas. Wells should know. As a graduate student working with famed quail researcher Dr. Robert Robel at Kansas State University, Wells studied the bobwhite's energy needs.

A bobwhite requires an average of 44,700 calories a day during the winter just to stay warm and even more if he has to dodge many predators, search for food, or move any distance from food to roosting cover, Wells said. *At five degrees above zero, the same quail will use 64,600 calories a day to maintain his body temperature. Seeds from the sunflowers, ragweeds and dogwood (all preferred, high-energy foods) supply 4,000 useable calories per gram. A bobwhite's crop will hold a little more than two grams of seeds, so he has to find enough of these wild seeds to fill his crop six times a day to get the 44,000 calories he needs to stay alive during normal winter weather. A bobwhite empties out his crop in an hour and one-half. On a short winter day then, he will spend nearly all his time eating.*

Winter often plays the grim reaper then. Early spring before greenup occurs is another demanding time for quail. Even though the weather might have relaxed its icy grip on the land, food may still be scarce. What little fat reserves are left, if any at all, are needed for breeding and nesting. When quail are stressed, they may actually delay nesting by several weeks until food is more plentiful and they can restore their strength.

A bobwhite's need for *grit* may not be as demanding as originally thought. Wells said that a recent study indicates that the birds do not necessarily need grit on a regular basis. In fact, grit may be retained in the gizzards of quail for as long as six months.

Winter often plays the grim reaper with quail. Without food, a bobwhite can starve to death in only three or four days. One reason late-season hunting is justified is that it is compensatory. *(Iowa Conservation Commission photo)*

More than half a bobwhite's body weight is *water*. According to Rosene, bobwhites need water, either free-running or as dew, and the bird will only thrive where rain is adequate for its needs. Hens will stop laying eggs entirely when there is no source of water.

The Bobwhite's Life Cycle

With few exceptions, bobwhite males, and most females, are monogamous. Unlike pheasant hunting, where the hens are protected because one polygamous rooster can service many females, both cock and hen bobwhites are legal targets. It is a good law because on the covey rise, hunters would have a tough time distinguishing the white face markings of cocks from the similar buff-yellow ones of hens. Suppose you could always identify the cocks. Still, it would be hard not to kill hens that got caught in the crossfire.

Even though the sex ratio is similar at hatching, males seem to be a bit hardier than females. By fall, the ratio can be 1:10 to 1; by spring, 1:25 to 1 in favor of males. As we shall see, nature's purpose for that may well come into play when hens are forced to renest.

Depending upon the latitude where they live, quail begin nesting in late March through May with breeding and egg laying going well into September. The downy yellow-and-black newborn chicks look

like big bumblebees. When the young are completely dry, mother and
father bobwhite lead their brood into surrounding cover to find insects. Juvenile plumage that begins to replace the down within a
couple of weeks makes the birds less vulnerable to cold and wet
weather. They forage immediately on their own and soon can fly short
distances. In about two months, when adult plumage appears, the
chicks will have reached half their adult weight. By early fall, they are
no longer dependent on their parents, and the covey starts to break
up.

The phenomenon known as the *fall shuffle* begins in late September, peaks during October, and often lasts into November. This is a
period of tension and hostility, especially among the adult males. Old
myths die hard. Some people continue to believe that hunting helps
to break up family units. The fall shuffle is simply nature's way of
reorganizing bobwhite groups to be more evenly distributed in terms
of size and the available habitat. Coveys are usually well defined by
the time most hunters go afield. Coveys average 10 to 15 birds, but
some of them may contain 20 to 30 quail.

Over a period of nearly 40 years, Val Lehman counted an amazing
5,316 coveys of Texas bobwhites. Three of the coveys contained 50
quail each. Most, however, fell within the range of 10 to 15 birds. In
1936, the initial year of his studies, covey size averaged 11.7 birds. In
1962, the year Lehman retired, the average covey held 11.3 birds.

**Jerry Hedges and Rick Jameson found Oklahoma bobwhites in soapweed where the
birds were loafing at midday. Oklahoma is one of the country's best states in terms of
quail harvest.**

Escape cover for this Oklahoma covey was a weedy thicket along the edge of woods. Jim Reid of Wichita, Kansas, moves in. Dog in center of photo has the birds pinned. Author's male, Chaucer, is backing.

In the how-to-hunt chapter, I describe the daily routine in a bobwhite's life during the hunting season. By late winter or early spring, warm days and increasing light from longer days trigger sexual growth in testes of the males and ovaries of the females. Roosters start to square off in mock or real combat. Mate selection begins. Within a month, the winter coveys break up, and mated pairs begin to build their nests. The birds scrape out an area in the soil a few inches in diameter, which they then fill with dead leaves and grass. Overhead grasses are bent to form a roof of sorts over the nest to conceal it from enemies. The hen lays an egg every day or so until her clutch averages 14 eggs. Then she sits on them for 23 days until they hatch.

Therefore, an undisturbed period of about 40 days is needed in order for nesting to be successful. Because of the constant threat from predators, plows, bad weather, and other variables, it is not uncommon for 60 to 70 percent of the nests to fail.

Generally, the female handles incubation chores, but in some cases the roosters sit on the eggs, too. Although double clutching occurs in captivity, the evidence is unclear whether or not it happens in the wild. If so, it is rare, and what many observers think are second and third hatches of birds is actually one successful nesting attempt after two or three tries. Most hens will renest if they lose their first clutch, and according to Johnsgard, probably rely on unmated males still in top breeding condition, to refertilize them for a second or third try.

The familiar *bob-bob-white* whistles we so love to hear from farm fields in the spring are actually lonely males looking for mates.

Bobwhite Subspecies

Investigators both agree and disagree as to the number and types of subspecies or different races of bobwhite quail. Nineteen to 22 subspecies live in North America, mostly in Mexico. There are five to seven subspecies living in the U.S., depending on whether or not you count the Mexican and New England races as one with Eastern bobwhites. At a minimum, then, the five include Eastern, plains, Texas, Florida, and masked bobwhites. All but the masked bobwhite are in good supply and are similar in appearance. The masked bobwhite is a special bird with a special story.

Masked Bobwhite

Good quail habitat is often fragile and always changing. For an example of what can happen when it is destroyed, we need look no farther than the masked bobwhite, which became extinct in the U.S. shortly after it was discovered living in southern Arizona. When I saw and photographed captive birds at the Desert Museum in Tucson, I noticed that the females look just like ordinary hen bobwhites. The males, on the other hand, are striking in appearance with their robin-red breast, black head and throat with white above the eye.

First identified in 1884, the last masked bobwhite was collected near Calabasas in 1897. The birds' original range was in southcentral Arizona and northcentral Sonora, Mexico, where it was associated with broad level valleys and plains and grassy river bottoms containing 10 to 12 or more species of grasses and forbs. The decline of masked bobwhites coincided with the huge influx of cattle, which literally ate away the quail's home. In 1870, there were 5,000 cattle in Arizona. Ten years later, the number swelled to 135,000 and, by 1890, to 927,000.

Fragile grasslands in this dry part of the world are easily overgrazed. When scrub cover replaced the grass, scaled and Gambel quail replaced the masked bobwhites. Wild populations still lived in Sonora; however, the spread of cattle there in the 1930s quickly threatened their existence, too. When I checked with the U.S. Fish & Wild-

The masked bobwhite was extinct in the U.S. before 1900. Trap-and-transfer projects involving wild Mexican birds are finally paying off after many failures. The U.S. now has a resident population of 130 adult masked bobwhites on a national wildlife refuge near Sasabe, Arizona.

life Service in Albuquerque, officials told me the number of masked bobwhites left in old Mexico was thought to be less than 300.

By the time you read this, they are likely to be extinct in that country.

But all is not lost. Over the past 50 years, several expeditions by American biologists and naturalists to Mexico spurred multiple attempts to reintroduce this handsome bird in the U.S. The efforts have finally paid off. Twenty years ago, the USF&WS got involved through the endangered species act. Recently, the government was able to overcome much local opposition—mostly from people afraid of losing their jobs—to purchase the 118,694-acre Buenos Aires Ranch. This property, located near Sasabe on the Mexican border 65 miles southwest of Tucson, is now a national wildlife refuge. In the summer of 1985, biologists released 853 two-week-old masked bobwhite chicks

Bobwhite Quail Distribution

hatched at the Patuxent Wildlife Research Center in Maryland. The chicks were released with sterilized Texas bobwhite males in the hope that the foster parents could teach them survival skills.

Apparently they are. As this is written, 130 mature masked bobwhites are making it on their own and are even expanding their range beyond the 3,000 acres originally set aside within the refuge. The government's recovery plan includes establishing three or more self-sustaining populations in Arizona and one or more in Mexico. A self-sustaining population is an average of 200 or more singing males each year for five years.

Masked bobwhites are fighting back from near extinction. We can make every effort to ensure that the more plentiful races of bobwhites will never have to.

3

The Tactics for Hunting Bobwhites

When I was 13 and in the eighth grade, I wore crane legs in a basketball uniform and owned a skinny body that seemed to go in different directions whenever I dribbled the ball. As awkward as I was, for some reason I could hit game—at least that year—on the wing. Earlier, my dad had presented me with a new Mossberg 16 gauge shotgun with a Poly-Choke. The stock of that gun was clear-grain wood the color of burnt almond. It shined like the lacquered knotty pine in my aunt's cabin Up North, as we downstate Michiganders referred to anywhere above Bay City.

I loved that gun and shot my first pheasant, duck, and quail with it.

One day after school, I took Dad's setter, Queenie, in the fields behind our home for some bird work. Actually, Queenie took me for she was a running fool—a habit that later cost her life when a local farmer, a man named Saxson, shot her. Or so we thought but could never prove. Anyway, Queenie went on point along a slope of weed stubble, and five or six bobwhites blasted out. I shot one and when the report put some more in the air, dropped a second bird. A third bunch went up; a third bird went down. Three quail, dead, all in a row.

I was as proud as if I had swished 10 for 10 from the foul line.

That year I learned many things about hunting. One was never to rub motor oil on the stock of a new shotgun in an effort to keep the wood shiny and waterproof. When Dad saw me doing that, he got so angry, the veins on his forehead stuck out like clothesline rope. A second enlightenment was that quail often flush in waves instead of one big explosion. Third, they were (and are) illegal to shoot in Genesee County, Michigan. I suppose I *did know* that but played dumb before Dad. He probably figured that anyone stupid enough to rub motor oil on a new gun had likely not read the game law digest.

To this day, I have yet to shoot another quail in Michigan, and 20 years passed before I began passionately hunting them in other states.

A New Breed of Bird

Wherever you find him — in a ragweed slough in Iowa, on peanut ground in South Carolina, in a clover field in Kentucky — the bobwhite is one cool, tough customer. He is challenging to hunt and just plain hard to hit on the wing, unless you catch him in the open. Even then, he will only be a short *brrrrrrrrrrrr* from heavy cover, where he will instinctively go when put into the air. In fact, from what I'm told, quail hunting has changed tremendously in the past 25 years. Gone, for example, are many of the gentleman coveys that held patiently for the dogs while you and a partner discussed the wind, the conformation of a shorthaired pointer, and your mothers-in-law.

The bobwhite may be an ideal gamebird, but he does not usually behave in an ideal manner. There is nothing gentlemanly about him at all, and I rather think of him as a veteran of guerrilla wars. Hunt him for a few times for yourself, and you will learn to take him where he is found. That may well be the most inhospitable cover in the region.

Those quail hunters with something besides dead air space in their game bags don't all wear cotton-twill pants and lightweight leather boots. Not at all. Some prepare for the field as if they were jousting knights-in-training, slapping on brush-busting trousers and punctureproof hunting coats. One fellow I know even wears hip boots at times to meet elusive bobs on their own terms.

Most hunters think of the sport the way it is often shown in paintings: golden afternoons of shirtsleeve weather, starch-stiff points from a spanking-clean pointer, a hunter who whistles a tune as he wends his way home, sweatless, the backs of his hands unmarred by

Bobwhites usually head for the toughest cover they can find. This Oklahoma covey ran from grass into a heavy plum thicket. Rick Jameson prepares to move in over point.

scratchberry canes. *It ain't always so.* It also happens less often, at least with wild birds, than many people think.

Just like today's pheasant, today's bobwhite has more survival skills at his disposal than a commando. He may dash for cover at the sound of hunters' voices, a car door slamming, or a dog whistle. He finds escape cover so thick it can rival bamboo. On the wing, he can zigzag through the thick stuff with the ease of any ruffed grouse, and because he is one-fourth the size of those noble birds, he is harder than any to hit. He will hide under thorny walls of multiflora rose, defying all efforts to get him off the ground. He may run away from the dogs, then flush twice out of range. He knows when to freeze, when to run, and how to sidestep the multi-hunter drive.

David Denayer, a friend of mine from Missouri, hunts bobwhites in abandoned, strip-pit coal mines grown back to a profusion of brush. Flushed quail bounce back and forth between these densely covered hills. After putting birds up, you must find a window of daylight for a snap shot as that is all the chance you will get. One time Denayer witnessed a covey rise in tangles so thick that one bird impaled itself on a locust thorn and died—fluttering.

Today's bobwhite will even go *underground* to escape detection by hunters and their dogs. Richard Bishop has many years of experience hunting quail in his native Iowa. One day his Brittany bitch locked up along a stream bank, then began digging a hole in the soft earth. Figuring she was after a varmint of some sort, Bishop called her off.

But when the dog backed out of the hole, she had both dirt and a quail feather stuck to her nose. Bishop and his friends couldn't believe there was a bobwhite in the hole, so Dick began probing it with a long stick. Out rattled a quail, surprising everyone so much that they missed the bird. The dog pointed again; a second bird rocketed up and away. More misses ensued, although they did manage to bag one of two others that popped out, then took to the air.

David Morrison, a farmer with whom I hunted in Missouri, told me a similar story. The only difference was that Morrison and his friends hit their birds. I'm not suggesting that Show Me State hunters are better shots than those from Iowa (even though both can readily humble this fellow from Michigan).

Hunting pressure, perhaps coupled with an increase of predators—mostly raptors and coyotes—has no doubt contributed to the making of a new breed of bobwhite. He is smarter with survival skills

Richard Bishop and his Brittany, Duchess, often find Iowa bobwhites in thick cover. Bishop walks in on one of Duchess' points in wooded escape cover.

that are pin-prick sharp. Biologists call this culling of the less intelligent the *process of natural selection*. Quail that survive the hawk's stoop and the hunter's gun pass on their genes to their offspring. In the world of huntable game, this phenomenon has produced races of brainy bucks, super pheasants and, to some degree, savvy quail. I say "to some degree" because as long as there are bobwhites, the covey will form the basic unit of interaction. The covey helps the species to survive, but it can also be the bird's Achilles heel.

Forcing the Flush

Quail know there is safety in numbers. Roosting in rosette formation—heads pointing out and tails aimed to the center—bobwhites generate life-giving heat for each other on cold nights. The roosting covey also has all the security of 100-eyed Argus. When one bird spooks, the others usually bust out with it. However, some quail—the smarter ones—delay their flush or don't take to the air at all. These are the birds that often survive to pass on their superior intelligence.

When you think about it, it is dangerous, perhaps even unnatural, for bobwhites to flush. Unlike valley quail, which roost in the

Quail flush as a last means of escape, relying on surprise and the roar of wingbeats to gain a split-second advantage over predators, including hunters. *(Kentucky Department of Fish and Wildlife Services photo)*

thickest cover they can find, bobwhites will accept some canopy protection but not so much that it impedes their flight. Bobs (along with other ground-roosting quail such as the scaled and Mearns species) still rely on the element of surprise—the roar of hundreds of wingbeats in a second—to help them make a fast getaway. Even so, the smarter ones know that taking to the air means exposure to a leaping fox, a dive-bombing owl, a load of No. 8 shotgun pellets.

If he does not have to flush, he may not have to die. Getting a bobwhite into the air, then, is the hunter's main weapon. Doing it in the open is his best chance to score.

The Determined Hunter

To be sure, a lot of quail are shot by hunters seeking pheasants, grouse, rabbits, and squirrels. Many more bobwhites, however, go into the game bags of seasoned sportsmen—men and women who walk through quail covers even in their sleep, kicking awake their spouses at each covey rise.

Identifying prime habitat and then hunting it effectively is the key to becoming a primary, rather than an incidental, hunter of quail. The ability is something not easily explained. It is something you do, almost intuitively, and it comes from a combination of hundreds— maybe thousands—of mental photographs of what productive habitat looks like. You gain that knowledge by hunting countless covers that do not hold birds and by remembering those that do.

Looking for the right habitat at the right time is the place to start.

Where to Look

The wise hunter looks at the cover before him in much the same way that a bass fisherman looks at a lake. At any given time of year, bass will likely be in a small portion of the lake, perhaps only five to 10 percent of the available habitat. The same is true for bobwhites. *Edge cover*, the intersection of two types of habitat, is generally the best place to find quail, especially if the types are *roosting, feeding, loafing* or *escape* (also called *security*) *cover*. A weed field abutting some acres of soybean, milo, or corn is one example. Weed stubble next to brush is another. A wood pile, sumac stand, or woodlot in the middle of a pasture is yet another. Edge cover can be linear—a brushy fencerow along a farm lane or cropfield—or irregular—a snakelike slough, fingering cattail marsh, or pie-shaped chunk of untillable ground.

Hunting the edge. Larry Brown strides through foxtail patch bordering a crop field in Iowa. Note pheasant tail feathers in Larry's game bag—pheasants and bobwhites are often found together in southern Iowa. Brown shoots a 16-gauge Sauer double barrel and often carries it on a sling.

Rarely will you find bobwhites in the middle of a sea of corn or in a heavy woods more than a short jump from the edge.

The more appropriate edge cover you can find, the better your hunting opportunities will be.

The importance of edge is hardly new. Aldo Leopold advanced the theory 50 years ago, yet it is often neglected, especially by quail hunters without dogs (good dogs instinctively know about the edge). But not all edges contain quail. Ideal bobwhite cover is usually a mixture of roosting, feeding, loafing, and escape covers. When these ingredients are offered in small, broken doses featuring plenty of edge, bobwhites usually thrive. Farmers such as the Amish, who, for the most part, do not practice clean farming (shunning the use of herbicides and depending largely on organic fertilizers) do bobwhites—and bobwhite hunters—an immense favor. Some of the finest quail hunting I have experienced came from Amish farms, and, not surprisingly perhaps, abandoned farms that had gone to seed.

Roosting Cover. Bobwhites prefer grassy beds with a southern exposure, especially if the weather is bad. Look for them in roadside ditches containing bromegrass, along edges of alfalfa or wheat stubble fields, in heavy edge cover of brush, and in native grass fields. Bluestem, Indiangrass, canarygrass, switchgrass, buffalograss, and cordgrass are likely places to find plains-area bobwhites. Foxtail barley is popular throughout the Midwest. In the South and East, look for broomsedge.

Feathers and small piles of green-and-white droppings are telltale clues as to roosting sites. I have heard that the size of scat piles is strong evidence as to the size of coveys. There may be some truth to that, but then some people will believe anything. One story I heard in my travels was about two hunters who pooled their mischievous natures to dupe a third member of their party. The pair scooped together droppings from several roosting sites, then dumped them in a huge pile where their friend would find it.

The man swore he located the mythical hundred-bird covey or what is known as the Quail Hunter's Heaven on Earth.

Feeding Cover. As mentioned in the last chapter, bobwhites eat a wide variety of grains, wild seeds, legumes, forbs, and nuts. In the East and South, partridge pea, lespedeza, chickweed, acorns, and beggar lice are important. In the Midwest, crop fields of milo, soybeans, and corn figure importantly, along with sunflower seeds, acorns, and lespedeza. In the Southwest, deervetch, filaree, and thistles are key foods.

Loafing Cover. Loafing cover is anything that gives quail some protection from predators and weather yet affords the opportunity to bask in the sun, preen and delouse themselves through dust baths. Feathers, small depressions in the grass, and three-toed tracks are

Piles of green-and-white droppings are evidence of quail roosting sites.

Quail tracks in the sand near loafing areas are clues that birds passed through or used the area for dusting.

clues to loafing quail. Loafing cover may, indeed, also be feeding cover, and the two usually are found not far apart. Good loafing grounds anywhere include meadow area, cropped fields of alfalfa or grain, pastures, mown orchards, and farm lanes with spits of sand. In the Southwest, soapweed is preferred; in the South, broomsedge.

Escape or *Security Cover.* Always close to food and loafing grounds will be escape cover. When threatened, bobwhites merely have to run or fly a short distance to security. Brushlands created from recent timbering are ideal, especially if they contain a mixture of ground cover and canopy. Examples are dogwood thickets, blackberry tangles, weed fields, grapevine clusters, cranberry patches, and hardwood saplings interspersed with low conifers. Escape cover can also be mature hardwoods a hundred yards deep and is often a brush-choked fencerow, brush pile, creek bottom, stand of scrub oak, heavy slough, wild orchard, property line of multiflora rose or autumn olive.

I surprised Mike Marcotte and myself when we hunted his farm near Concordia, Kansas, and moved a covey of bobwhites sitting under a plum thicket at the edge of a milo field. *How did you know they'd be here?* Mike asked.

They were here two years ago, the last time I stopped by, I said.

I am often amazed at the nasty cover that quail duck into when jumped. One time in Iowa, my setter stuck a large covey in sloughy horseweeds over which massive cottonwoods stood guard. After a 10-minute search, I found her, thanks to trembling tips of the man-high horseweeds. Upon flushing, the blurred targets disappeared before I could shoulder my shotgun.

Another time, while hunting along the South Soloman River in Kansas, I moved four coveys from big bluestem stands that weaved in and out of timbered bottomlands. On each rise the birds managed to put ponderous black swamp oaks as solid as the butt of a Belgian horse, between me and safety. My game bag was considerably lighter than I had anticipated when I walked, birdless, back to the car.

The edges of such escape cover can provide fantastic shooting but few scores. An added problem is that it is often difficult to mark singles from a busted covey when you are immersed to your ear lobes in cover. We experienced the ultimate in frustration one November afternoon in Kansas when Ken Lowe's setter, Shakespeare, nailed a covey of bobs in a hellish swath of cockleburs on state land. On the far side was a wall of river-bottom hardwoods. Of course, the exploding birds cut low for the timber, sailing across the river to safety. Ken was still picking cockleburs from Shakespeare three days and 1,000 miles later when we arrived home.

A final comment on escape cover: When you drop birds in the shintangle, mark them well, then walk immediately to that spot and do not take your eyes from it. I toss a hat or handkerchief to the ground or drape it over a bush about where I think the bird went down. Even with these precautions, I invariably mark short. Without them, I would lose several birds each season, even though I have dogs and even though they are supposed to help me search.

Sizing Up the Cover

Finding good habitat means little if hunters do not size it properly and then hunt it in a way to force the flush. Knowing the lay of the land is the first key to taking it on. If you know, for example, that at the end of a hedgerow is a plowed field, then you can expect that quail will flush from that edge when you arrive, assuming that they held for your dog.

Many hunters looking for good habitat mistakenly think that bigness is always best. Some of my best days in the field have come from targeting small strands of crops or weeds, what I call *pocket cover*. Crop field corners out of reach of the combine or irrigation system, abandoned railways, small sloughs, cattail pods in small marshes, grassy terraces, dirty fencerows, brushy waterways, weedy roadside ditches, and thickets of plum, kochia, sunflowers, and dogwood are examples of pocket cover.

Some of these choice quail covers are found in suburbia itself near abandoned buildings, in vacant fields, and in strip cover behind backyard lawns. Safety, of course, is paramount when hunting in such areas, and, in fact, discharging firearms may even be illegal. Always check the state game laws and local ordinances first. Also, be sure you know who owns the property.

With a good dog, you can quickly hunt these pocket covers for quail. If you have a half-dozen spots in mind, some are bound to pay off. To me, it makes more sense to hunt the small places where you figure quail might hang out, rather than spend valuable hunting time tramping a farm with marginal habitat or covers too large for you to handle.

The wise hunter marks his hits, then walks immediately to that spot without taking his eye from it. Hanging a hat on a tree will help. If you are balding, like the author, use a handkerchief to avoid sunburn.

Hunting It Effectively

Once you have identified and sized the cover for the number of hunters and dogs in your party, you must learn to hunt it effectively. Again, the objective is to force the flush, then be ready when it occurs. Ways to anticipate the flush and to position yourself for the best shots are covered in the chapter on guns and loads. Here we will deal with trying to make the flush happen.

Let Your Dog Work at His Own Pace. Hunters that goose step along push their dogs, resulting in sloppy field work, incompleted objectives, and missed birds. A good dog—one that casts out, works the wind to his favor, and constantly reports back or at least always knows where you are—will check out promising cover in his own time and way. As explained in the chapter on dogs, each animal works at his own pace. The wise hunter knows that, then paces *himself* to allow it. In the case of a too-fast dog, taking your own time will cause your partner naturally to slow down.

Watch the dog constantly for clues that he is becoming birdy. With a flushing breed, the time to move fast is when the dog grows excited. A pointing breed, of course, will hold birds, hopefully, until you arrive to put them up. Not surprisingly, that may be at a spot where birds have run out of places to hide or run. It might also be in the open where they were caught off guard.

Slow Yourself Down, Too. Because so much of the prime bobwhite habitat is linear, such as hedgerows, the temptation is to squeeze birds at the other end by moving them there as quickly as possible. Move too fast, though, and you'll walk right over quail. In Missouri one foggy morning, my setter, fresh from a day of rest, scooted down a hedgeapple row. She grew birdy at one spot, but nothing went up. So I waited there for her to finish out the line, which ran for another 200 yards. Do you know about those seemingly interminable waits? A farm dog barks in the distance, and you can hear the *click, click* of freight-train wheels pounding a loose tie on the Kansas City Southern Railway. Five minutes later, when Macbeth returned, she stiffened to a point right at my feet. A bobwhite promptly flushed and I promptly missed it.

There are times, though, when hunting fast has merit. Closing quickly the vise between you and another hunter or the vacancy of cover is one way to be there when birds flush. Another is when your dog is closing fast on scented bobs, especially if they have been edgy.

Keep Your Head Up. Learn to look ahead while you walk because quail will often run through open woods and down fencerows to reach the safety of connecting cover such as a stream bank choked with brush or a slough. They will dash through the scantiest fingers of weed stubble to disappear into unmown alfalfa. They will sprint across roads because they know there is a ditch filled with bromegrass on the other side.

Hunting Alone or with a Partner.   Usually, the single quail hunter will do just as well, if not outperform, individuals in a group. But hunting with a partner adds flavor to the tang of gunpowder, the tinkling of dog bells, the whir of a covey rise.

A pair of hunters can work adjacent sides of fence rows and shelter belts. They can position themselves over dog points to post the escape routes, and they can more effectively mark and hunt up singles. Further, they can split off to work connecting cover. Besides, hunting with a partner usually helps each of you to try for birds and to bear down on shots. The best partner will praise your kills and offer scandalous arguments for your misses, too.

Hunters should pace themselves according to the available habitat and type of dog they are using. This hunter is moving in fast to seal off possible escape route.

Hunting quail with a partner is fun and sometimes advantageous. Lead hunter in photo will take this shot. Rear hunter will back him up. The hunters are Greg Koch and Jim Reid.

Two or more hunters can take turns posting and driving for each other, pinching birds and making them take to the air.

Hunt Quietly. A fellow I know once complained that he couldn't get near a certain covey of shot-over quail because they always jumped the gun ahead of his shorthair's points. A blocker might have shot some of those smart bobs as long as it wasn't this man.

The guy's jaws flap like the collective mouth of a seventh-grade study hall. He simply does not know how to be quiet. Yelling at his dogs, laughing loudly, and slamming shells into his pump gun serve ample warning that trouble walks upright and carries a thunderstick. Quail have an uncanny ability to hear. That is why blockers and flankers should tiptoe into position, stay put, and keep quiet. Those following the dogs should also keep noise to a minimum. The earlier you alert quail to danger, the longer they will have to dig into escape cover.

Hunt the Daily Timetable

Unless pressured by hunters or altered by foul weather, a bob-white's daily regimen is rather predictable. About a half-hour before sunup, birds will generally whistle a time or two while still in the roost. The reason is to report their location to strays that might not have made it to the roost the evening before. Shortly after sunup, the covey will walk and sometimes fly to the nearest feeding area. When food is plentiful, a quail can stuff his crop in a matter of minutes. When it is scarce, he may spend most of the day looking for something to eat. Once morning appetites are satisfied, birds turn to loafing areas, especially if the weather is nice. Here they lounge about for several hours or until hunger prods them to visit the dining table again. After filling their crops once more, they seek the roost. Roosting calls generally begin around sundown.

Knowing this timetable, I am always surprised to see hunters working the wrong habitat at the wrong time. The first time I hunted in Kansas, I learned to expect bobwhites in a food plot of milo planted by the fish and game commission at Webster Reservoir near Stockton. Ron Spomer, a fellow freelancer who lived in Kansas at the time, and I caught a 15-bird covey in the milo at 4:15 one afternoon. They were there the next day, too.

Many quail hunters keep so-called banker's hours, again contributing to the outdated notion that the bobwhite is a gentleman's bird. Sure, he will accommodate you by leaving plenty of scent for the dogs when you stroll out for a midmorning hunt. But wild birds, at least those on public hunting ground—and even on private land when they get pressured—can also be hunted effectively soon after daylight. True, if six hours of hunting is all you want in a day (and that is quite a bit), then 10 a.m. until 4 p.m. is ideal. Nonresidents, however, who have driven a thousand miles don't all want to sit in a restaurant when they could be hunting. The bobwhite will measure up to expectations.

Early morning hunting in the roost or in travel corridors (fence rows, road edges, stream bottoms, weed fringes, and so on) between the roost and feeding site pays dividends. Open the crop on your first bird in the bag to see what it has been eating, if anything. One time when hunting in Iowa, a bird I shot from a small weed field had a crop bulging with corn. The nearest cornfield was 300 yards away. I took my dog there, and we worked the outer rows and fringe cover of brush and weeds. She put up two more coveys.

Check the crops on birds you shoot from loafing cover as well because the evidence will help guide you to feeding sites to try in the afternoon or the following morning. Remember, too, that roosting, feeding, and loafing habitat may very well be close together, and sometimes are one and the same. Bobwhites are not stupid—they are not going to risk exposure to enemies if they don't have to. So they may very well be content to sleep, eat, and rest in the same location when conditions require or allow it.

Most states have defined bobwhite shooting hours which often shorten in length as the season progresses. The reason is to give birds a chance to recovey for the night. Those left out are subject to predation and exposure and could die before morning. Many hunters have self-imposed time limits on afternoon hunting—say 4 p.m. if sundown is slated for 4:40.

Calling Quail. Sometimes quail will call at night and nearly always at first light when they are still in the roost. The calls are not the typical *bob-bob-white* heard in spring by the males but are a mixture of different notes. Birds might whistle only a couple of times, or they may sing out frequently. Again, they are calling to locate missed members of the covey before heading out to feed.

Hunters who position themselves near roosting sites at dawn can often pinpoint a covey. Some hunters use manufactured quail calls to get birds to respond, too, a tactic that can also work during the day when coveys are scattered, and again at dusk to mark birds for the following day. Use a compass or your wristwatch to determine the

Manufactured quail calls can be helpful in locating both coveys and singles separated from the covey. Colonel Gerald Graham shows how it works.

exact location of whistling birds. Then strike a line to the point on the compass or hour on the watch so that you can walk right to them.

Whenever I hunt quail, I ask myself the question, *Where would birds be now?* Using the daily timetable, at least as a starting point, has proved most helpful in reducing the amount of cover to the best type, depending upon the time of day.

Hunting the Seasonal Timetable

Because the bobwhite is a gamebird of the farmland edge, his world is ever changing, most dramatically at spring planting and fall harvest times. Fall is actually the greatest time of upheaval for two reasons. One is that in addition to harvest, modern farming practices call for chisel plowing, late cuttings of alfalfa, and double cropping with winter wheat. The other reason is due to the onset of winter. Trees denude their leaves, ground covers wither and die, grasses and other canopies break down under snow and ice. As hunters, we can see the kaleidoscope of change easily enough from six feet above ground. Imagine what it looks like to a bird six inches from the ground.

Early Season. Depending on your state, this could be October or November. It is perhaps ironic that the season of greatest change is also the year's greatest time of bounty. Preferred quail foods are never more abundant than in fall. Nature's reason, of course, is that bobwhites are among many wild creatures that must put on fat reserves to help see them through winter. There are a couple of other reasons, too, as to why quail are most abundant in early fall. The hunting season is just getting underway, and family units are still intact. Plus predators are less of a problem than at other times of year, thanks to the spread of protective cover. That is also why hunters' scores are often low in the early season.

Bobwhites could be just about anywhere, and that is why many hunters don't bother looking for them. They prefer to hunt pheasants or grouse in the early season, then shift to bobwhites later when conditions are more favorable. Hunters who scout their area, however, looking for sign or listening at dawn or dusk for bobwhite calls, can get a fix on their whereabouts. A good dog is a must, especially early and late in the day when scenting conditions are best.

Midseason. Again, depending upon your state's season, this period could be as early as late November or as late as early January. Most farm crops are in the elevator or a railroad car. The leaves are gone, and woods have changed to gunsmoke gray. Snow may cover

Early season hunting finds heavy cover and birds sometimes still in family groups. Jack Coffee of Iowa moves in on a point by the author's setter, Chaucer, while hunting in Iowa. Note pheasant in Jack's game bag.

fields. The cold wind picks at your clothing, makes your nose weep, tightens fingers so that you might need to wear a shooting glove.

I liken the midseason to a grocery store going out of business. Shelves that once bulged with food are showing empty. To give at least the impression of plenty and perhaps to make it easy for shoppers, the grocer concentrates what is still available in one or two aisles instead of a dozen. Preferred quail habitat and food plots likewise shrink to concentration.

By midseason, bobwhites may find their favorite roosting ground of wheat stubble turned into chisel-plowed chunks of earth that look like polished anthracite. Gone, too, might be the food patch of shattercane, but a quarter-mile away is the ragweed slough and there is always the soybean field next door. However, loafing cover, orchard-grass along the farm lane, is gone for this year. Cattle have trampled it beyond all possible use to quail.

This is the period that sees the greatest amount of hunting activity. Birds are reasonably predictable and easy enough to find. And they have not been shot over to the point where they vanish at the sound of a dog whistle. Coveys are bird full, the individual members mature, strong fliers. The midseason period was designed with hunter in mind.

Late Season. This period covers the final weeks of the hunting season. Most gunners are home watching football bowl games on television or looking for their pike tip-ups so they can go ice fishing. The few that venture out in January, February, and even March in some cases, can find very good hunting.

Winter quail habitat is a whole new consideration. Protective cover further shrinks as remaining crops go into storage, residues are plowed down, winter storms ravage the countryside. This tends to concentrate bobwhites, where they compete for available food and become vulnerable to starvation and predators. Small wonder that hawks and owls perch on powerlines overlooking grassy ditches or on fencerow trees where they can survey the buffet table below.

Late-season birds that are dog-wise and hunter-shrewd head for the densest cover they can find where food, but especially security, is available. This is the most challenging time of all to hunt quail.

Does late season hunting hurt bird numbers? It can if hunters shoot down coveys too low. Smart hunters—those who hope to find targets the next year—reduce birds by no more than half, knowing that if 25 to 35 percent of fall populations remain to breed in spring, there likely will be enough to repopulate for next year. Some hunters stick by the six-bird covey rule. In other words, they leave at least six

The November 20 opener in Oklahoma is actually a midseason type of hunting. Trees are barren of leaves and birds are strong, capable fliers. Mike Pearce and guide Grant Irwin flush a single.

birds in a covey. The fallacy of that logic, however, is that coveys often mix throughout the fall and winter. If a hunter keeps shooting them down to six birds each, he may wind up with one covey of only six birds.

The best advice is to know how many coveys exist and how large each is. The best way to do that is to inventory your hunting grounds earlier in the fall.

Hunting is entirely compensatory, at least we hope so, Roger Wells, a former quail specialist with the Kansas Fish & Game Commission and now a field representative with Quail Unlimited, told me when I hunted with him near Emporia, Kansas. *Each bird taken by a hunter allows that much more food for those remaining.* Wells said the real danger is in shooting down coveys too low because a higher percentage of late season bobwhites are spring breeders.

Why do some states, then, allow hunting well into winter? *Because few hunters go out then,* Wells said. *Our surveys showed* [when Wells worked for the Kansas Fish & Game Commission] *that 88 percent of the hunting pressure occurs in November and December and that only 12 percent occurs in January.* (The Kansas season typially ends January 31.)

Indeed, in 1983–84, Maryland extended its hunting season to 120 days with no effect on populations. Even so, as seasons lag on, and the nesting season approaches, an increasing number of bobwhites are potential breeders. Shooting individual coveys down too low can make a difference in the number of quail available for the next hunting season.

Hunting in Foul Weather

Quail are not only creatures of habit, they are creatures of comfort. Successful hunting in foul weather means knowing what quail do under certain conditions, then applying special tactics.

A high wind makes most gamebirds jumpy because they cannot readily hear danger. Wind also distorts sounds. Because quail are gregarious and depend on the covey for their safety, strong winds further serve to put the birds on a hair trigger. Then, quail flush seemingly without warning or provocation. They can be tough to hit, especially when moved along by a tailwind. Hunting into the wind instead of with it will help to conceal your approach. You should also be ready for the flush at any time.

Rain keeps bobwhites in the roost later than normal plus on really bad days, birds may not leave the roost at all. Further, rain greatly inhibits their desire to forage and move around. Coupled with an inhaling earth, which sucks up scents, rainy days make it tough for the dogs to smell birds. In the absence of wind, flushes will probably be close. Hunting tips: Target the middle hours of the day, stick to thick cover, and slow your hunting pace.

Cold and *snow conditions.* Bitterly cold days can also hold birds in the roost longer and in heavy cover once they leave their beds. Coveys may hold exceptionally well in snow—especially after the first storm or two—requiring the toe to get them into the air. Or they may spread out to feed and therefore be jumpy because they realize their vulnerability. As mentioned, later in the season, hunting pressure adds to the spookiness factor. Then, hunters should work at being extra quiet, even communicating with hand signals if necessary.

They should also consider hunting only the middle portion of the day because the birds need much more time to feed. A bobwhite out of the covey on a cold winter night probably won't be alive the next day.

Prestorm conditions can make birds less cautious as they concentrate on filling their crops. Then again it can also make them nervous. Perhaps the lull that often precedes bad weather sharpens their hearing. They may also realize increased vulnerability when feeding in the open. Again, keeping noise to a minimum and working with hand signals are good ideas.

These Nebraska bobwhites were caught foraging for spilled grain in a cornfield during the winter. Hunters should be careful not to shoot coveys down below half of preseason counts. They should also give birds plenty of opportunity to recovey before nightfall. *(Nebraska Game Commission photo)*

Finding a Place to Hunt

Finding good places to hunt is a fun part of the success formula for putting bobwhites in the game bag. Plus, it can give you an early indication of fall populations. It is also crucial if you are short on time.

Local Scouting. You can find quail in your area by taking male singing counts in spring. Using a county map and felt marker, pick a travel route through areas where birds are likely to be setting up housekeeping. Then, at each stopping place, X the map accordingly. Wildlife biologists usually time their stops (at the same places year after year) for one to three minutes, noting the number of singing males. The information is important for establishing short and long-range breeding indices and, in some states, for determining hunting season dates. A hunter who knows where quail are in spring has all summer and part of the fall to determine who owns the land to seek permission for hunting later.

You can avoid local hunting pressure by finding quail habitat half a mile or more from county roads, by seeking heavy covers that turn back those hunters less determined, and by ferreting out smaller,

Kansas hunter Harry Rutherford shot this bobwhite as it flushed from a stand of sumac.

little-known public game areas and the fringes of bigger ones. The larger public grounds often contain small, nearby parcels unattached to the main unit. New acquisitions, in particular, may not be posted or even be found on the usually free maps. Pinning down state or federal wildlife personnel is the best way to find the best places. That is because wildlife experts who are reluctant to make public a sensitive area are less cautious about telling a single hunter, especially if the sportsman has taken time to seek him out.

Out-of-State. Besides quail, I have been hunting pheasants in other states because numbers of both birds in Michigan have badly slid. Over the years I have developed some successful tactics for finding birds far from home and for getting permission to hunt them.

Once I pick my state, I write to the respective wildlife agency for population densities, estimates, and where-to-go information. Those early bird-number estimates can change faster than video games in a downtown arcade, and that is why I keep checking back, including a day or two before leaving home.

For example, a mild winter recently had Kansas biologists in spring hoping for a record harvest of quail and pheasants in fall. But a cold spring contributed to wide, first-time nest failure, and then summer drought conditions stressed young birds that did hatch. In September, biologists began to hedge their bets but still looked for a good season. A week after the November 12 opener, the word was out—bird numbers were actually down by about 30 percent.

Late planning also means checking with a district or regional biologist where you hope to hunt. If bird numbers are hurting, ask him to suggest another part of the state, and try to get a name and phone number of a contact to clue you in. In other words, be flexible with your plans. When planning to hunt late in the season, be sure to talk with returning sportsmen. They may offer the most reliable estimates you will get.

Another point about those quail density maps put out by the game agencies: Remember that every hunter who requests information will get one. That is why I often target the fringe areas or adjacent counties of the so-called hotspots. If you must hunt the black-shaded areas, pick a spot miles from the nearest town.

Careful planning also means buying your license through the mail so that you don't have to chase all over the county trying to find an agent with nonresident paperwork. Failure to follow my own advice cost us an extra $40 each in Oklahoma when the game warden, who met us on opening day to sell us licenses, had only season—and not five-day—permits with him.

Public Land.   The public lands, those that offer an oasis of food
and cover for nesting as well as for wintering birds, are good places to
hunt. They can be red-hot early in the season and again late in the
year when crop harvest and bad weather tend to reduce habitat and
concentrate quail. But they often get burned-off early. The best bobwhite hunting almost invariably occurs on private land.

Private Land.   How do you line up private hunting land, especially in an area you have never visited? You must learn to think
creatively and be willing to do some homework. Contacting the friend

**Public hunting areas are often best early and late in the season. The hunter is Willy
Suchy with his wirehaired pointer, Hershey.**

Missouri hunters David Denayer and Gary Sears heading out to hunt abandoned strip-mining cover. It rained daily during the author's visit to the Show Me State.

of a friend of a friend is the formula that has worked well for me— whether the goal is finding a place to hunt bobwhites or the best spot to go for silver salmon in Alaska. Yes, it may be easier to get information when you are an outdoor writer, but I relied on "networking," or so the business people call it, long before I began putting pen to paper for my living. You can, too.

Start by making a list of who you know in the state where you want to hunt. A friend, relative, Army buddy, or business associate, for example, could offer where-to-go leads. Call or write a letter (a self-addressed, stamped envelope often hastens a reply) to the local chamber of commerce or regional tourist agency (your public library has directories), and ask for help in setting up a hunt. Check with farmers in your own state for leads to farm organization contacts where you hope to hunt.

Consider reciprocity. For example, in Michigan we are blessed with outstanding grouse and woodcock hunting, plus Great Lakes salmon and trout fishing. I have learned to repay favors and pave the way for invitations elsewhere by inviting friends from quail hunting states for a try at our fish and game. Don't know anyone in the area you wish to hunt? Take out an ad in a big-city newspaper and offer reciprocal consideration. The number of things you can do to find a place to hunt is limited only by your imagination and determination.

Also, make your contacts in person, if at all possible, long before the season opens. I once used part of a family vacation to South Dakota in June to line up key hunting areas for October. It worked.

Freelancing. So you do all this homework, only to arrive at your Shangri-la and find out that the place changed hands and the new owner has put up a yard sign that reads, "Large Dog Lives Here: Hunters Will Be Eaten." What do you do? Simple. Use your creative wits to turn an eleventh-hour disaster into the hunt of a lifetime.

This situation can be disguised opportunity. Often the best hunting land is in absentee ownership anyway, and that is because the farm failed, is now abandoned, and the title holder lives somewhere else. Spend a couple hours at the county courthouse, poring over a plat book to see who owns the land. Then, get on the telephone or make personal contacts to find out if you can hunt. Opportunities for getting on private land improve as the season wears on. Many times signs that say *No Hunting or Trespassing* can be amended to read *Without Permission*, provided you have made a courteous request.

What is a courteous request? It includes inviting the farmer along, and when he can't go, sharing a cleaned bird or two with him. Friend Larry Brown and I had a great hunt for pheasants and quail on an Iowa farm during the first leg of my travels. Next day, I swung by to give the owner five dressed bobwhites and, later that day, a ringneck. I think she'll remember me when I knock on her door again this fall.

Learn to ask questions like, "Are there livestock around? Standing crops off limits? Fences to be locked?" And here's another tip: Leave the Blaze Orange bandoleer in the car and keep your hunting parties small in size. Take time out to talk to the farmer, too.

A battered John Deere cap also breaks the ice nicely.

4

The Scaled Quail

very classroom, it seems, had one. Danny Rogers. A bright kid whose temples fairly throbbled with intelligence but who wore a devilish smirk on his face, a mischievous glint in his eye. I don't mean the vicious kids, those smart-mouthed incorrigibles who scratched out graffiti on their desk tops with ink pens they borrowed from you. Who thanked you for the bathroom pass by flushing cherry bombs down the toilet. Those charges you wanted to, well, snuff out.

The Danny Rogers were different. Bold and impetuous, they always had the answer. Even when it was wrong. Unpredictable and irrascible, they made huge demands on your time, challenged you to make class purposeful. While the rest of the students labored with noun clauses, the Danny Rogers read *Penthouse Forum* under cover of an open textbook. Pure imps, they both frustrated and brightened my years in public education.

Scaled quail remind me of kids like Danny Rogers.

The first bird I ever saw stuck out his pointed head from behind a yucca plant in southwestern Kansas and watched my female setter, Lady Macbeth, holding a point as solid as a Sherman tank. She did not know the quail had already sidestepped her. A hellish light gleamed in the bird's eye. Could he have talked, he might have said, *Hey, you big dummy, I'm over here. Bet you can't catch me, hee, hee!*

And you can't, of course, unless you can run a four-minute mile.

A flushing dog can outrun a covey of scaled quail, but the birds will be well out of shotgun range when they flush with a collective roar of wings. Bust the covey, though, and the singles—assuming they scattered—will hold. You can also waylay scaled quail as they walk or fly into the roost or head for water or food. Sometimes, plotting hunters can surround a covey or cut them off at the pass, so to speak. When legal, others ride shotgun in trucks, then leap out when they spot a covey and load their guns on the fly. Some Texans and New Mexicans are especially fond of this guerrilla tactic.

Other considerations, although illegal, are grenade launchers, poison, and flamethrowers.

Scaled quail play the game of hide and seek to perfection. Here is a gamebird that likes to make fools of hunters and their dogs. Chase a covey at track-dash speed for a quarter-mile, and they will either flush too far for a shot, or they will simply disappear altogether. Rock-hard points may produce nothing, then a moment later while you and the dog are ambling along, a bird will flush from cover so scant it wouldn't conceal a pack rat hole. You just never know about scaled quail. One time in New Mexico, my male setter, Chaucer, cocked his leg on a cholla cactus (a potentially painful thing to do as he would discover later in Arizona), and a quail came whirring out as though on fire.

By human standards, scaled quail are likely insane. Look at a photograph, any photograph, of a live scaled quail. The head will probably be up, the bird tensed to run or fly. They have an edgy,

America's fastest-running quail is the scaled quail, found in grasslands of the Southwest. Jesse Williams of New Mexico moves in on a half-hearted point by a tired Lady Macbeth.

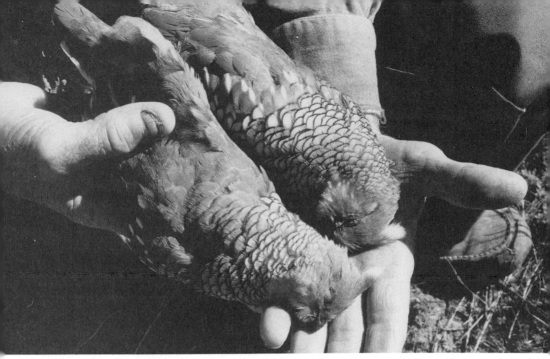

Sexes of the scaled quail are similar to all except the practiced eye. These birds were shot in southwestern Kansas.

hyperactive personality, and that is one reason I love this bird, my favorite among the five Western species.

The way they look is a second reason. True, there is nothing special about the overall color, a dusky blue-gray. Both sexes look that way except that adult males have clear-buff throats whereas adult females' throats are gray and dark-streaked. Of interest, though, is that breast and abdomen feature buff-colored feathers tipped with contrasting brown. This imparts a scalloped or scaled effect and gives the bird its name. The scaling is repeated to a smaller degree on the upper back although the feathering there is gray-brown rather than buff.

A subspecies living in southern Texas and in northern Mexico has a chestnut belly and is often referred to as the chestnut-bellied scaled quail.

Both sexes of scaled quail sport punk-rocker hairdos—crestlike shocks of gray-brown, tipped with white. Michael Pearce, a Kansas resident who hunted these birds with me in the southwestern corner of his home state, said scaled quail remind him of a kid with a big cowlick he knew in seventh grade. It is an apt description.

Scaled quail are also known as blue quail, scalies, cottontops, and blue racers. To Mike and me, they were also coneheads.

LEBANON JUNIOR HIGH LIBRARY
500 NORTH ADAMS
LEBANON, MISSOURI 65536

The birds live in the southwestern United States and deep into Mexico. A quail of semi-arid desert grasslands, the blues' habitat more or less conforms to the Chihuahuan desert and adjacent desert grasslands. On the other hand, the distribution of the Gambel quail centers on the Sonoron desert. In New Mexico and Arizona where I hunted them, the ranges of both birds overlap considerably, with scaled quail being more readily found near grass habitat in flat plains areas and Gambel quail occupying the arroyos and stream bottoms. Mesquite, cholla cactus, and creosote bush are characteristic of Gambel habitat. Yucca, century plant, sagebrush and various grasses make up the scalie's home range.

Most of the 200,000 quail shot in New Mexico during an average hunting season are cottontops. They are most abundant in the southern half of the state. Southeastern and south-central Arizona hunters kill 50,000 to 125,000 each year. Southeastern Colorado yields 40,000 blues in a typical season. They are also legal targets in Oklahoma and are most common in Cimmaron County but live in the southwestern and panhandle regions, too. In the Texas Panhandle and in western Texas, there are huntable numbers, and they are legal game in Kansas and the Mexican states of Chihuahua, Coahila, Neuvo Leon, San Luis Potosi, and Zacatecas.

Release programs of scaled quail in central Washington's Yakima County and in eastern Nevada have been moderately successful. In the sandhills of Nebraska, they failed.

Hunters have little impact on populations of scaled quail. An intensive study in New Mexico several years ago concluded that this gamebird could receive more hunting pressure, even during years when numbers are low, without any harm to the resource. Population ups and downs have more to do with land-use practices—such as cattle grazing and farming—and weather factors of drought, precipitation and winter severity. But even those are not fully understood. For example, a three-year Oklahoma study showed that in spite of increasingly severe drought, brood size, juvenile-to-adult age ratios, and rate of hunting success all increased.

Mike Pearce, who is also a freelance writer, and I had been chasing pheasants and bobwhites near his home in eastern Kansas. Like me, Mike had never seen a scaled quail. If it hadn't been for Lawrence Smith of Elkhart, we might not have seen any either, at least in Kansas where the birds live side by side with bobwhites, lesser prairie chickens and pheasants on the 100,000-acre Cimmaron National Grassland.

Fifty years ago the dust bowl rearranged both the land and peo-

Grass habitat in flat plains areas is the place to look for scaled quail. These New Mexico hunters found birds on Bureau of Land Management land near Deming in the Florida Mountains area.

ple's lives in this tabletop-flat country. Their once-productive topsoil blown away, the landowners moved on. The federal government bought the vacated land for as cheaply as $3 an acre. Forest service plantings of Johnson grass, bluestem and sand love have helped to check erosion. Although the soil is still sandy in many places, there is some cropping, with the help of irrigation, for milo and wheat and even a little corn. Native plants are mostly sagebrush, tumbleweeds, and yucca.

Lawrence Smith, 60, came to this country from Missouri as a young man. In 34 years he drove over a million miles delivering mail for the U.S. Postal Service. A self-taught naturalist and avid hunter, Lawrence and his wife, Ruth, are active Audubon members with a difference. Both must see the bird species before including it on their lists. The Smiths' life list, begun only three years before Mike and I met them, already contained 401 species. A mutual friend put us in touch with Lawrence, and he agreed to take us hunting.

Unless a person had unlimited time, it would be difficult to find many coveys of scaled quail here. Over the years, Lawrence has helped U.S. Forest Service personnel with management programs on the grasslands. These included the installation of 85 guzzlers—tin-roofed sheds built low to the ground and designed to catch rainwater and snow melt to provide drinking water for wildlife. The captured water runs into a holding tank that is 18 inches wide, 18 inches deep, and eight feet long. Shade from the low roof helps keep the water from evaporating. Average annual precipitation in the grasslands is only 15 inches, but a minimum of five inches is enough to keep the guzzlers full for wildlife.

Quail tracks are usually everywhere near the guzzlers and in nearby tepee-shaped brushpiles, which are designed to provide shade for quail and other wildlife. Most of the oases are about an acre in size and are usually fenced by barbed wire. A hunter with a good pair of binoculars could find those near service roads. Asking a ranger or local sportsman where they are located is another good idea.

I liked the grasslands. They reminded me of South Dakota where I have hunted pheasants and quail in the plains country and in draws of the Missouri River breaks. The wind is a common denominator wherever you hunt plains habitat. It begins in mid-morning and doesn't stop until nightfall. You can hear it sift through tumbleweeds and whine around oil and natural gas wells. Sometimes it carries the bawl of a Hereford steer or the *clack-clack-clack* of windmill vanes. Grass sways to and fro like ocean swells, and you can see heat waves, even on a 20-degree temperature day. Tumbleweeds will startle you as they skip along.

As I mentioned, both blue quail and bobwhites live on the grasslands. Lawrence said in a solid week of hunting, he could probably move 30 coveys, an equal number of bobwhites and scalies. To me, scaled quail seemed to move out faster than bobwhites, but that may be due in part to their wild habit of flushing on the edge of range. With regard to their weight, they are about the same as bobs. Lawrence assisted the U.S. Forest Service in weighing 50 of each species. The bobwhites averaged 195 grams (about 7 ounces), and the blue quail averaged 210 grams (about 7½ ounces). At 10 to 12 inches in length, however, scaled quail are longer than bobwhites.

Although the two species don't actively mix, coveys often feed side by side. On a couple of occasions, we put up bunches of blues that appeared to have bobwhites mixed in with them. In actuality, the flush of the scaled quail probably spooked the bobwhites into flight, too.

Picking the ideal gun for blue quail can be difficult. Lawrence relies on a 12-gauge Browning automatic, choked improved cylinder, and he likes No. 7½ or No. 8 shot in a target or skeet load. Mike used a Ruger Red Label in 12 gauge with barrels of improved cylinder and modified. I was using a 20-gauge Winchester 101 with improved cylinder and modified, but there were times when I wished I had screwed in the full-choke tube.

Home range for grasslands scaled quail is probably a quarter-mile radius from a guzzler or other gathering point such as dilapidated buildings, abandoned cars or farm machinery, or barbed-wire heaps. Weeds usually grow up around such objects, as well as along fence-rows and in gullies and blowouts. Research shows that blue quail strongly favor the use of man-made structures, and that is why some landowners erect such shelters and other cover for them. Although many landowners will allow hunting elsewhere on their property, they protect such "home coveys" with the tenacity of a sow bear with cubs.

According to a study in Oklahoma, the average area of 10 winter-home ranges was about 52 acres with extremes from 24 to 84 acres. Interchange between established winter coveys was common, too. A west Texas study showed covey movements to average 160 acres, but there are times when scaled quail make mass fall dispersals. Little is known of this phenomenon, but it involves both sexes and young-of-the-year birds. In southeastern New Mexico and western Texas, for example, hunters recovered leg bands from birds that had moved from 10 to 25 miles. In one instance, a scaled quail journeyed 60 miles.

Mike Pearce and Lawrence Smith get a closeup-look at scaled quail. In the grasslands of southwestern Kansas, scaled and bobwhite quail live side by side.

Nobody seems to know with certainty if scaled quail need free-running water to survive, but it is a proved fact that they frequent watering sites. Curiously, according to the study in Oklahoma, the birds are found closer to water in winter than at any other time. Hunters should never pass up the opportunity to check out a watering location such as cattle tanks, irrigation ditches, ponds, and streams.

Scaled quail begin nesting in May and continue throughout the summer into September or even October as far north as Oklahoma. Egg laying is keyed somewhat to summer rains because in periods of drought, scaled quail may not even attempt to nest. Their nests, containing 12 to 14 eggs, are usually in a shady area under a shrub.

Blues eat a wide variety of seeds including mesquite, hackberry, catclaw, sunflower, Russian thistle, and ragweed. Deervetch, filaree, lupine and locoweed are also important. Apparently, they also eat the juice or seeds of prickly pear. Bob Hirsch, with whom I hunted Gambel quail in his native Arizona, said he and some friends one time shot several red-headed scaled quail. A closer look showed that the birds had been burrowing into ripe prickly pear and staining their crests red. According to Floyd Mansell, with whom I hunted in New Mexico, the seeds of cholla cactus flower are also favored.

Although flushed birds will travel a half-mile, especially in a tailwind, they usually set down again after a hundred yards or so. For some reason, blues sometimes fly higher than the other species. It is not uncommon to swing on them when they are 50 to 100 feet above the ground.

I hit one such scalie on a high crossing shot after leading him the length of a full-sized Buick. The bird was hit but instead of crashing to the ground, he spiraled higher and higher, then caught the wind and sailed to earth 200 yards away. I have observed many gallinaceous species, when head shot, to corkscrew straight up, then fall to the ground, dead. There is likely a biological reason for this, but I don't know what it is.

That same experience taught me that scaled quail are difficult to find, especially when they fall near lookalike sagebrush. We were just about to call off searching when Macbeth, who had been hunting dead at heel, stiffened into a point. There was my quail, dead, its scalloped belly up and feet in the air. Because I could find no trace of blood, this bird carefully went into my game pouch. He would make an ideal mount.

Lawrence hunts quail only between the hours of 10 a.m. and 4 p.m. The birds' typical routine is to leave the roost soon after daybreak and fan out to forage nearby. The period from mid-morning through mid-afternoon finds them loafing, usually in an area providing shade and water. Now is when they rest, dust and preen themselves. Later in the afternoon they will eat once more, then walk or fly into the roost, usually in grassy areas on a hillside with a southern exposure.

He refuses to hunt after four o'clock, in order to give the birds ample time to covey up before nightfall. Singles left alone at night are more vulnerable to predation and can freeze to death during a cold snap. He also makes it a point to know how many quail are in the various coveys he hunts, then takes no more than 50 percent. Assuming natural mortality claims another 25 percent, he feels there will be enough birds left to repopulate the following year.

Mike had his crack golden retriever, Mysti, along and I had my pair of settters. Like many other scaled quail hunters, Lawrence prefers to hunt without a dog. *They are very sporting birds,* he told me, *especially if you don't have a dog. True, they don't sit as tightly as bobs, but*

Blue quail prefer a variety of foods, among them the seeds of cholla cactus flower. Floyd Mansell of Magdalena, New Mexico, shows what the seeds look like.

the singles—once you scatter the covey—do hold for walking hunters to get close enough to shoot.

The thicker the cover, the more tightly busted birds stick. A high wind, we learned, may make them spooky. Although the season had just opened a couple days before our arrival, apparently pressured birds also get jumpy and will flush at the slightest alarm, such as a car door opening.

Tracks, droppings, and feathers are clues to roosting, feeding, watering, and loafing areas. In winter, Lawrence often tracks the birds. Snowy conditions will also keep them at feeding sites longer than usual, sometimes for most of the day. It was in mid-November, for example, when Pearce and I visited the grasslands. One morning the temperature plunged 30 degrees overnight, and the temperature on an Elkhart bank seemed frozen at 23 degrees when we passed it in my Winnebago.

A northern wind, steady at 10 mph now, would triple in velocity by afternoon. Horizontal snow was already racing by the windshield, and by the time we reached our hunting site, a skiff of the white stuff covered the ground. That morning we shot at blue quail as they flew into a standing milo field to feed, and then we busted coveys of both scaled and bobwhite quail in tree and grass islands between picked fields.

I clearly remember this day because it was our last hunt for mixed-bag quail. Every time the sky stopped spitting snow, the sun made a valiant effort to show itself. The clean, cold light added an intensity to the normally washed-out earthtones of the grasslands. Suddenly, taupe, dun, and mauve took on new brilliance. Even the dark-green yucca had a new cast, that, for want of a better description, reminded me of lima beans.

While I don't like lima beans, I would certainly miss the grass-lands. And it would be several weeks and another trip altogether before I encountered scaled quail again.

The place was southwestern New Mexico. The time, early January. I had already tramped the northern fringe of the upper Sonoran desert in the region of Magdalena, New Mexico, and refer you to the chapter on Gambel quail for details of that experience. Now I was 200 miles southwest of there in the Deming area, not far from the Florida Mountains. Some of the plants were the same, but there were new varieties. In fact, there are three levels of vegetation here, in terms of height.

Tall-growing ones include three kinds of cholla cactus, mesquite—a brushy shrub that is naked gray in winter and that features crab-

Author's setter, Lady Macbeth, retrieves a scaled quail from desert grassland habitat in New Mexico. This state has generous bag limits, plenty of public land, and excellent hunting for scaled quail.

treelike thorns—barrel cactus, Spanish bayonet, and a type of yucca with a 10-foot-long spire that grows from what appears to be a brown, rotted stump. There are no trees, other than an occasional juniper. The tallest vegetation is the century plant with its sharp spears of green and purple edged with sawlike teeth. Spires of the century plant reach 20 feet.

The next level of vegetation is the brushes. These include smaller tangles of mesquite; two types of rabbit brush (one low and one high-growing); snakeweed, which reminded me of wild mustard—only shorter—back home in Michigan; four-wing saltbush; Mormon tea; creosote bush, which is a bright-green plant with leaves similar to cedar; and a nasty foot-stabber named lechequella. Locoweed is a bone-colored member of the pea family, favored by quail, with flowers of purple that come on in winter. Along waterways grows Apache plume.

Several short grasses that grow in this part of the desert are also favored by scaled quail. They include side-oats grama grass, which grows in mountain saddles and on hillsides; tabosa grass, a light-green/gray grass that springs up in flats; and sacaton, a straw-colored grass of the plains. Scaled quail use the grasses as nesting and escape cover. Sometimes they roost in it, forming a circle—like bobwhites—

with heads pointing outward so they can scatter if danger approaches. In the crops of several birds we shot was filaree, a low-growing forb available throughout the winter.

I was hunting with Jesse Williams and Gerald Gates of the New Mexico Fish and Game Department and with Eddie Munoz, a former chairman of the State Game Commission. I didn't figure I would have any problem keeping up with my friends, all in their late 50s. I was wrong. Hunting scaled quail, New Mexico-style, means hoofing it. We walked miles every day, up and down thirsty mountainsides, through bone-dry arroyos and powdery washes into alkaline flats cut by two-track roads. I live within a day's drive of 99 percent of the country's surface fresh water. I do not say that to boast, but to tell you how thirsty a Midwestern man can get in New Mexico.

Scaled quail hunters need to be ready at all times for unexpected flushes. Hunting with gun half-way up and the index finger extended near the trigger is good advice.

I learned to watch for the now familiar, three-toed tracks of quail. I listened for *chip-chew, chip-chew* notes of birds separated from the covey. I kept a sharp eye on the pockets of shrubs, grasses, and cacti ahead of me for running blues. And I learned to keep my gun halfway up with my index finger extended and near the trigger.

The daily bag limit in New Mexico is a liberal 15 quail. Hunters will have no problem having the opportunity, at least, to shoot that many if they hunt with determination in the right areas. As I have said elsewhere, the best places are grassy plains containing a mixture of cover. Incidentally, all of the areas we visited were public land open to hunting. They included Bureau of Land Management holdings and state-owned parcels.

Hitting scaled quail is quite another matter. You have to shoot fast. I didn't try for doubles because it is hard to find downed birds unless you mark your hits well and walk immediately to that spot, then toss out a handkerchief or your hat. Without a dog you will probably lose 50 percent of the birds you knock down. Even a good dog won't find all the cripples, and that is because the heat and lack of humidity will stifle your partner's ability to scent game.

My New Mexican hosts favor Brittanies that are trained to hunt close. Close means within 20 yards. Even though the habitat is sparse and a dog—especially my hard-running setters—may want to range wide, a good wingshot with a sharp pointer or flushing breed underfoot can earn a reputation among his friends. That is because close flushes improve the shooter's box score, and when birds fall near the dogs, they are more easily able to find them.

Gerald Gates shot a limit of birds every day I hunted with him, sometimes pocketing his 15th quail by mid afternoon. One day he treated me to a shooting exhibition on the southern side of a slope where blues had been roosting, or so a couple dozen piles of droppings suggested. Gates' Britts, Sam and Candy, alternated pointing a broken covey as we moved its members down the hill. The hillside was mostly scree with patchy growths of a thin grass that was about four inches high and here and there a clump of cholla.

One thing you want to remember, Gerald told me, *is that a scaled quail only needs a rock for cover, and Lord knows there are enough rocks in this country.*

Blues in this region follow the usual pattern of feeding, loafing, feeding, and roosting. Many hunters rest their dogs for a few hours at midday, when the heat—even in midwinter—can be uncomfortable. They concentrate on the morning and late afternoon, hunting perhaps two or three hours at a stretch. It's a leisurely way to hunt, I suppose,

Brittanies are favored for hunting scaled quail in New Mexico. The best dogs hunt close and are trained to retrieve.

but after I got my walking legs and became a little more acclimated to the altitude, I didn't mind all-day hunts. I will admit, though, to looking forward to the pop-and-sandwich breaks.

Actually we didn't move out all that fast, and for good reason. Walking slowly and allowing the dogs to sniff out the cover is the best method. The harder you push scalies, the faster they run anyway. Take your time, saving your energy for those mad dashes when you do spot quail. A good tip is to begin hunting in early morning on the north side of slopes because moisture from the night will be retained the longest there. Also, before daytime thermals rise, scenting conditions will be better.

The time to walk fast is when you have a line of hunters moving in a horseshoe shape across the desert. We tried this method one afternoon when we came across my hosts' friends—Dick Allgood, his son Lance, and two nephews. They were cleaning scaled quail from the morning hunt.

We didn't get 'em all, Dick said, reading my thoughts. *I'll wager there are a hundred or more within a square mile out there.* He motioned with his knife to bleak landscape of midday green and gray. Heat waves shimmered across it. Later, we formed a six-man line with 10 Brittanies zigzagging through the cover in front of us. I don't know how many birds we shot that afternoon, but I know I was down to three shells when we returned to the trucks for a second cleaning of quail.

Studies show that winter coveys may average 30 birds, and we saw several bands with that many quail. I won't soon forget riding in the back of Eddie's truck one afternoon when he crested a small hill, and there, off to the side of the road, were 40 to 50 blues. They didn't stand around to discuss what to do with us. Instead, like a flock of nervous barnyard pigeons, they headed for the security of a hillside.

Jesse and I jumped out. Eddie and Gerald took the truck around in an effort to cut them off or at least flush them back to the road where we posted as flankers. As so often happens with scaled quail,

Blue quail hunting, New Mexico-style, means resting men and dogs at midday. That's a good time to get opinions on how to improve your shooting. The author's friends had plenty of advice for him. Gerald Gates has a look at Lance Allgood's pump gun.

Scaled Quail Distribution

the ruse didn't work. The birds flushed early in successive waves, but we did manage to get some shooting and, if I remember correctly, Gates finished out his limit when some singles flushed from the other side of the hill.

Another tactic we used successfully was to drive slowly along a dirt trail leading to a windmill and stock watering tank. New Mexican law prohibits parking within 300 yards of a cattle watering tank, but well before we got there, Gerald banged on the cab roof as a signal for Eddie to stop. There, in the roadway, were what appeared to be hundreds of fresh quail tracks. A state highway sign announcing *Quail Crossing* could not have offered more of a clue. Fifty yards away we found them, a covey of perhaps 75 Gambel quail. When they erupted in panicked flight, they apparently triggered a covey of two-dozen blues into the air. We had some fine shooting there as the sun worked its way down the Western sky.

The last time I saw a covey of scaled quail, they were running across the top of a small hill on BLM land in Arizona. The morning sun backlighted their crests. When one bird turned sideways to steal a quick look at me, there was a sparkle in his eye.

It made me think of Danny Rogers.

5

The Gambel Quail

You would never guess from a dozen-bird flush—a blur of gray with flecks of rufous—that Gambel quail are such handsome birds. The rooster I now held in my hands was unlike any other gamebird I had seen. Bar markings of white began at the cape and swept upward to each side of the eyes. The upper breast was gray, the belly a buff color with a black patch at midsection. Under each wing lay a pattern of chestnut streaked with white. Nape plumage was slightly, though intricately, scaled.

True, the gray-brown back was common enough. But the bird's headgear—coal-black beak, black forehead, rust-colored crown, and those sculpted bar markings—lent him a royal look. The colors were especially warm in this rich light of late afternoon. Flourishing over all was an inch and one-half ebony tassel with a club on the upper end. It looked like a lazy apostrophe, a rather large one at that. At first glance, this forward-drooping plume appeared to be a single feather. Closer inspection revealed hundreds of tiny hairlike feathers.

A remarkable bird, I said aloud. *Such a concentration of beauty in something so small.*

Look behind you, Steve Bodio said. *There's an afterglow on the Magda-lenas.*

Far away to the north and east, the sun's low rays were warming several mountain peaks. They looked like cardboard cutouts spray-painted gold. A swirl of violet lay above them. It was New Year's Day. Back home in Michigan, I might be hunting rabbits in the snow, maybe watching the Rose Bowl Parade on television. Here, in west-central New Mexico, my friends and I were chasing Gambel quail.

The rooster I admired was one Steve had shot. But not without a price. Over three days of hunting, we had treked 20 miles, maybe more. My three dogs—the setters Lady Macbeth and Chaucer, and Holly, the yellow Labrador—had probably covered three times that distance. It was a long way to walk for a bird, but I had never hunted these fast-footed quail of the desert and hadn't even seen one until now.

Black topknot that looks like an apostrophe is characteristic of Gambel roosters. The Gambel is a bird of the Southwestern and Western deserts. He is often referred to as the desert quail.

In New Mexico, better Gambel country lies mostly to the south-west in the Deming area. I was going there the next day. Here, in the upper Sonoran desert, the birds occupy stringers of habitat along drainage systems, which, at this time of year, were mostly dry washes and dusty arroyos. There are probably more scaled quail in this semi-arid region of grassland and yucca with occasional clumps of cholla cactus. Two days earlier we had seen thousands of what I assumed were scaled quail tracks (they look like Gambel's or even bobwhite's for that matter) stitching their way across the sand flats.

Bodio and his hunting partner, Floyd Mansell, agreed that we had a better chance of jumping scaled quail than of getting a Gambel. Even though the scalies, or blue quail as they are often called, are my favorite among the five Western species, I desperately wanted to shoot a desert quail. Besides, I already had a scaled quail, along with a bobwhite, in the freezer at home from the earlier hunt in the Midwest. Because there are six huntable species of quail in America, collecting a Gambel would mean I was halfway toward a quail grand slam.

And I had had the chance, knocking down a single that flushed a moment too late after a covey of 12 birds had exploded from a patch of rabbit brush. A 20-minute search, some of it on hands and knees as the three of us carefully rearranged a cholla, failed to produce my bird. My dogs, exhausted and thirsty, were no help.

Maybe it ran into one of these pack rat holes, Floyd suggested.

That was entirely possible as the rodent borings were everywhere, and Gambels, like all quail, will employ every trick to get away. I don't like to leave lost game, but to search farther seemed fruitless. Before bagging my first desert quail, I learned plenty, not the least of which was that they can be hard to find, whether dead or alive.

Unusual circumstances had lead us to this last-chance covey in the shriveled stream bed. For three days we had been hunting the places—without luck—where either my hosts or their friends had seen bands of Gambels. Earlier that morning we had bounced around for 50 miles in Floyd's old Ford truck on corrugated gravel roads that lead us south of Magdalena where my friends live. At day's end, we had barely entered the dry wash when Floyd announced that he spotted fresh quail tracks.

Predator and prey alike concentrate along such fingers of plant growth in the sparse cover of the Southwest. A sharp-shinned hawk suddenly dive-bombed Floyd's head, mistaking it for something to eat, I suppose. In the next instant, Steve thought he heard quail talking. Rushing ahead, he saw a flick of movement in the dusty stream bed. Chaucer, my male setter, stretched into a fine, though brief, point. Then the rabbit brush came alive with gray-and-rust motion, and I knocked down my first Gambel quail.

After giving up looking for him, we moved on in hopes of putting up the covey again. Four hundred yards farther, Steve missed a single

Gambel and scaled quail often share the same habitat. These birds were taken in cholla cactus and mesquite country.

twice. Then a covey of 25 or 30 Gambels erupted, and Bodio dropped a leg on one. The bird landed near me. With the lost quail fresh in my mind, I ground-sluiced this bird before he could duck into the cover.

This was the little trophy I turned over in my hand while the sun glorified the Magdalenas. Some time ago I stopped measuring success only by bird weight in the bag. Steve's quail weighed a mere eight ounces, not much more than the pair of cotton gloves also in my game pouch where he came to rest. This one quail had made the long trip across six states worthwhile. Besides, I was just now entering the eastern range of the desert quail. There would be plenty of opportunities over the next several weeks.

The Gambel is a bird of the southwestern deserts. Its range includes bottomlands of the Rio Grande and other rivers of western Texas and southern New Mexico, southern and western Arizona, southeastern California, southern Nevada, and extreme south-central Utah. Gambels may be hunted in these states, as well as in Colorado where a few live in the southwestern corner. There are hunting seasons in the Mexican states of Baja California and Sonora, and small populations are legal targets on the islands of Hawaii, Lanai, and Kahoolawe. Although desert quail live in Idaho, there are not enough to warrant a hunting season at this time.

Arizona sportsmen have the best hunting, bagging from 1.1 to 2.6 million Gambel quail each year. About 20 percent of the statewide quail harvest in California, or 200,000 to 400,000 birds, are desert quail. Many of the 200,000 quail harvested in New Mexico each year are Gambels. Hunters do little to impact populations, wherever the Gambel is hunted, as studies in Arizona have proved.

Efforts to establish desert quail through releases in Pennsylvania, Massachusetts, Kentucky, Missouri, Oklahoma, Wyoming, Montana, and Washington have all failed. On the one hand, this bird—named for Dr. William Gambel, an explorer-naturalist who visited the Southwest in the 1850s—is tolerant of wide extremes in altitude and temperature. Gambel quail have been found near Mecca, California, where the elevation is 200 feet below sea level, to the top of 11,000-foot Charleston Peak in southern Nevada. The bird can survive temperatures of 120 degrees in the Arizona desert to lows of -40 degrees in Idaho.

On the other hand, Gambels have a limited toleration for plant-life forms that make up its habitat. And more critical than either elevation or temperature is the amount of precipitation, which is linked to the development of green plants. Studies in Arizona, for example, show that a minimum of five inches of rain in winter is necessary to produce a sufficient amount of green plants. Breeding success can be closely correlated since green plants contain vitamin A, which stimulates the reproductive cycle. Breeding activity of adult birds is related to spring crowing by cocks. By extension, then, biologists can often predict how good or bad fall hunting will be, based on the amount of rainfall the previous winter.

Gambel quail make nests at the base of desert shrubs or trees, which provide shade during the midday sun. In New Mexico, studies show that breeding occurs from April through June, and a typical clutch contains 12 to 14 eggs. Males perch on a cactus or shrub within a few yards of incubating females. Family coveys often come together to form groups of 10 to 30 birds by fall. These numbers may increase even more during the winter.

Before moving to Minnesota, famed grouse researcher Gordon Gullion studied Gambel quail while working for the Nevada Department of Wildlife. He found that the birds live in three main habitat types of the Southwest. Upland desert vegetation—such as the Mohave Desert region of Nevada, California, Arizona, and southwestern New Mexico and Utah—was dominated by catclaw, creosote bush, prickly pear, skunkbush, yucca, desert thorn, and burroweed.

From Texas west to southern California, Nevada, Utah, and northern Mexico, desert valley habitat included mesquite, saltbush, tamarisk, and desert thorn. In the colder Colorado River basin areas of New Mexico, Colorado, and Utah, vegetation included greasewood, rabbit brush, saltbush and sagebrush.

Gambels are as much at home in suburbia as they are in desert wilds. In fact, the birds may grow quite tame, nesting beneath backyard shrubbery and visiting bird feeders in winter.

Gambel quail will use standing water, when they can get it, even during the winter. Studies in Utah show that birds will make at least once-daily trips to water, often moving distances of two or three miles when necessary. Hunters who target the sources of water—stock watering tanks and ponds, streams and irrigation ditches—can do very well, but they should check the game laws to be sure there are no restrictions. In New Mexico, for example, parking within 300 yards of a stock watering tank is prohibited. If the water source is standing, a good hunting tactic—with or without a dog—is to walk around it, making larger and larger circles until you jump quail. If the water source is linear, such as a stream or irrigation ditch, hunt the bottomlands first, then progressively move up the slopes and flats areas. Do this on both sides of the waterway.

Another trick is to post watering holes from mid to late afternoon

Tackling the cover in New Mexico. Floyd Mansell and Chaucer step into heavy habitat south of Magdalena. Gambel quail head for the heavy stuff when danger threatens.

as Gambels will likely make short flights or walk to the supply. You can use the same tactic in early morning if you post that side of the water resource closest to roosting cover. This is usually low trees or high shrubs where the covey can get a few feet off the ground. Roosts, incidentally, are also good places to target for early morning or late afternoon hunts. You can find roosts by looking for feathers and droppings underneath limbs.

Other clues to Gambel whereabouts are triple-toed tracks in the sand and dusting spots along roadways and in washes. We used this tactic in southwestern New Mexico. After tracking birds from a watering tank to an arroyo a quarter-mile away, we jumped a big covey with the help of our dogs. Hunting the heavy cover along the arroyo and working up the sides of adjacent slopes gave us all the shooting we could handle one afternoon. I call it the crisscross-and-comb method.

Preferred Gambel's foods are deervetch, filaree, and other legumes. Food availability, however, may not be all that helpful to the hunter because Gambels are highly opportunistic when it comes to the supper menu. A study of 57 desert quail crops in New Mexico, for example, yielded 87 plant species representing 27 different families. In a California study of Mohave Desert birds, legumes—especially lotus, lupine, locoweed and filaree—made up 50 percent of the diet.

When their life needs are met, Gambels don't move far. In a Nevada study, for example, the home range of 10 coveys varied from only

19 to 95 acres. Hunting pressure, however, can make the birds at least seemingly disappear. A couple of weeks after visiting New Mexico, I was hunting in the San Pedros Mountains east of Tucson with Bob Hirsch, an outdoor writer from Cave Creek, Arizona. One day less than a week earlier, Bob and some other friends had shot 50 desert quail here. We found only two nervous coveys of maybe 15 quail each. On a long shot, I managed to drop one bird, a handsome male, perfect for mounting. He went into the small freezer in my Winnebago motorhome.

To be truthful, though, Hirsch and I hunted only an hour or so, and that was because we had trouble finding the place and because my dogs ran into nasty problems with a desert horror called teddy bear cholla. For the details of that experience, I refer you to the chapter on dogs.

I have traveled and hunted throughout much of the West, but never have I experienced such distance distortion as in New Mexico. It is not uncommon to see 100 miles in this wide-open land, a huge area of desert seas and island mountains, as other writers have called them. On the drive south of Magdalena on dusty washboard roads, I could see two-mile Mt. Baldy to the east and the San Mateo Mountains, miles away to the west. There are places in New Mexico that are 100 miles from pavement. We found an isolated spot in Red Canyon, a dry wash containing cottonwood trees, mullein, wild asparagus, and flowering spikes of yucca. All this was sandwiched among monolithic

Bob Hirsch and the author head back to the motorhome for a cold one after a dry afternoon of hunting for Gambel quail in the Sonoran Desert near Tuscon. The only bird they shot that afternoon, the author decided to have mounted.

canyon walls with juniper, oakscrub and pinyon scrambling up the slopes.

Land often looks alike until you hunt it on foot. Here, the canyon floor was littered with deer tracks and coyote scat, which was full of rust-colored juniper berries. On this windless afternoon, the sun bore at us from a blue sky unstreaked by jet tracks. As the sun rose higher, the shadows began to disappear and the canyon colors washed out into bland earth tones of brown and mauve and dull green. Here and there we could see a splash of yellow cholla flower, the blue flick from a flying mountain bluebird, the white rump patch of a western flicker.

A panel of warm musky odor from some winter-budding flower or fruit wafted down to us. The only sounds were the tinkling of the dog bells and the echoes of our voices reverberating from rock walls. Sometimes we could hear the loud crack of rock shards flipping over like tiddly winks as we scuffed them. The scene was like something from a Steinbeck novel. Appealing, yes, but there were no Gambels, other than the one Steve shot. I would have to go to the Deming area to bag my first desert quail.

The last blaze of light was gone from the Magdalenas by the time I lifted my tired dogs to the wire cages atop the flat bed of Floyd's old pickup. Floyd had built the cages for his several coursing dogs — ground-eating Salukis and greyhounds — which he uses to hunt coyotes. While Floyd drives backroads, just about anywhere in New Mexico, the gazehounds taste the air rushing by their cages. At the first sight of coyote, they go berserk. Floyd opens the cage by jerking on a rope over his head in the cab, and the dogs hit the desert running.

This sport sounded like fun the way Floyd and Steve had explained it earlier. Now, as we growled out of the canyon in low gear, headlights jumping all over the road, my friends must have read my thoughts.

I"d like you to see the dogs run, Floyd said. *Too bad you have to leave in the morning.*

I know.

You'll have to come back, Steve said.

I will.

Over the next several weeks, I would be doing this often, saying goodbye to new friends and old friends, not wanting to leave, yet feeling the pull of the road at the same time. There was no heater in Floyd's battered truck. Strange that I was not cold, even though the temperature was already in the low 40s and would dip below freezing before morning. Because his brakes were out, Floyd downshifted as

New Mexico has plenty of public land and good populations of both scaled and Gambel quail. Floyd Mansell and Steve Bodio enter national forest land for a morning of quail hunting.

the old truck rattled down the hills. Once or twice the canyon bottoms came up too fast, and we nearly fishtailed off the road.

Conversation on the drive back shifted between falconry and fine English doubles—two of Steve's many passions—to boxing and cock fighting—two of Floyd's. It was both ironic and fitting that these men had found each other in the hugeness that is New Mexico.

Steve Bodio is a young writer with Boston roots. He is the twentieth century equal to a man of letters and is a walking encyclopedia on topics as diverse as fine wine to a geologic history of the land. For the past eight years, he has written "Bodio's Review" for *Gray's Sporting Journal* and has recently published *Good Guns*, his second title from Nick Lyons Books (the first is *A Rage for Falcons*). When Bodio and his partner, Betsy Huntington, who is also a journalist, left Boston, they had no clear idea of where they would live.

After eight months on the road, they found New Mexico and Magdalena resident Floyd Mansell. Floyd, a wiry man in his late 50s, grew up in Arkansas and moved to New Mexico more than 30 years ago. He and his Navaho wife, Wanda, have nine children. Wanda is a nurse at the Indian reservation. Mansell teaches special education courses at the local high school and works for the National Forest Service in summer. He is a former mayor of Magdalena, a town of 1,000, which long ago was deserted by the timber and mining industries. Many of its citizens, about 80 or 90 percent of whom are of Spanish or Indian descent, are impoverished. Lucky ones have jobs with the forest service, the road commission, the local school, or on the reservation.

I knew Floyd liked me when he gave me the skin of a Western diamondback he had found in the desert. *Welcome to New Mexico*, he said. *Let's go hunt some quail.*

Everyone in Magdalena was friendly and open like Floyd and Steve. Their optimism was infectious, right down to the boarded-up warehouse I passed on my way out of town the next morning. A fading sign on that old building announced "Charles Ilfeld Company, Wholesalers of Everything."

Highway 60 west took me through the Plains of San Augustin where the road lay straight and black, like an endless typewriter ribbon. At Datil, I turned south-southwest on Highway 12. Here were the Gila Mountains, taupe-colored hills with a dusting of snow on their peaks. They made me think of the baked crust of a too-full apple pie, one generously sprinkled with sugar. The grocery store at Reserve had no apple pie, a condition for which my pancreas might be thankful. So I bought lunchmeat, bread, and a carton of chocolate milk.

I ate while crossing the Continental Divide near Saliza Pass, popping the motorhome in low gear and keeping a wary eye on the temperature gauge. At Glenwood, I noticed the hills took on an Arizona look—orange sandstone outcroppings deeply eroded by wind and water—and appearing as though some giant had raked his fingers down their sides. I stopped at the Aldo Leopold Vista to let the dogs urinate, but the setters were stiff and didn't want to leave their kennels in the trailer. Only Holly seemed to care enough that, under the prodding of Leopold, the National Forest Service was established with the 1924 Gila acquisition, its first. But even she didn't seem impressed when I told her that it was here in the Southwest that Leopold had developed his philosophy of land ethics and conservation.

Travel with your dogs long enough, and you almost expect them to join in your conversation. It was time to meet some new hunting friends. I crossed the Divide again just north of Silver City, slid the shift lever into neutral, and coasted into town.

Tomorrow I would hunt near Deming with Jesse Williams, the communications chief for the state wildlife department and a fellow member of the Outdoor Writers Association of America. Two of Jesse's friends, Gerald Gates of the department and Eddie Munoz, former chairman of the State Wildlife Commission, had already been hunting near Deming. I had a little trouble sleeping that night when I learned that they had each shot limits of 15 quail.

The next day the four of us pouched 46 birds, a mixed bag of scaled and Gambel quail. Incredible that we were shy of limits by 14 birds. As I mentioned before, I don't necessarily hunt for limits, but those three days of walking had made me hungry for action. I shot my 15th bird, a fine Gambel rooster, just before quitting time. That was thanks to a covey of 75 Gambels and a smaller group of nearby blue quail that we had scattered late in the afternoon.

There was no wind as the birds called to each other, and it was a simple matter to walk them up for flushes. Other writers say the Gambel makes a four-note sound with emphasis on the second syllable, *ka-KAA-ka-ka*, sometimes written as *chi-CA-go-go*. It doesn't sound like that to me, but then I don't claim to have super-auditory powers.

Three days of hunting near Magdalena, New Mexico, produced one Gambel quail for the author's hunting party. Freelance writer Steve Bodio shot the only bird at sundown.

To my ears, the notes are *huh-HEE-huh* and sometimes *huh-HEE-huh-huh*. The scaled quail, as I found out after shooting a couple, sounded like *chip-chew, chip-chip-chew*. Their notes contained two, three, or four syllables. I thought it unusual to hear both species so close together. My New Mexican friends say it is common because their habitats overlap.

Listening for the assembly calls of quail is an excellent way to hunt them, especially about 45 minutes before sundown when the birds are thinking of roosting. A Gambel out of the roost at bedtime is as jumpy as a kid trying to sleep with the lights out after watching a monster movie. He wants the assurance of his own kind nearby, and the same is true for Gambel or any quail for that matter. Based upon my limited experience, I believe the Gambel is more vocal than the blue quail. One evening near Wilcox, Arizona, my partner and I had stopped hunting and were ready to kennel the dogs when *huh-HEE-huh* came floating over the creosote bushes. We walked those birds up for some eleventh-hour sport.

Another tactic, legal in New Mexico, is to ride shotgun in the back of trucks while scouting the cover for Gambel or scaled quail. When someone spots a covey, he bangs on the truck roof as a signal for the driver to stop. The hunters then pile out and run after the covey, streaking away by now, in an effort to get the birds airborne. A scaled quail can outrun any Gambel and a Gambel can outrun any hunter. Sprinting speed for desert quail is a flat-out 15 mph.

If you can get the birds to flush, there is a good chance they will separate, especially if you put them into the air two or three times. The singles will hold for you or the dog. They will also call out for the covey. The heavier the desert habitat, the more tightly Gambels will hold, and that is because they don't know where you or the covey is.

We didn't run down any quail, but we did drive slowly along looking for birds and tracks in the road. The desert is not all cover; there are openings between plants. Binoculars may be helpful at times, but you don't really need them, at least to spot running desert quail. You will see their heads bobbing, the little apostrophe marks above the males. As long as you are moving, the covey will also keep moving.

When you mark a covey, three options become apparent: Run like hell to put them up as quickly as possible; surround them by dropping off hunters at strategic points, then pressure them with the kind of pincer movement that would bring tears to the eyes of Rommel; take advantage of a bluff or slope to mask your approach to an ambush spot.

To get running quail airborne, some hunters ground rake the cover behind them with a shotgun blast. Yelling or clapping hands may trigger the flush, too. I have heard of some hunters using a hawk call to stop birds temporarily in their tracks, thus allowing the hunter a precious moment or two to move within range. It is a tactic that I have never tried.

If the area you are hunting has received too much pressure, consider heading for an interior region far from roads. Most desert quail hunters stay on or near the roads. There are Gambel quail in the Southwest that never see a hunter, maybe don't even hear the report of a shotgun.

Dogs and hunters get thirsty. Sam Van Nostrand of Mutual, Oklahoma, and his dogs drink from a cattle-watering tank.

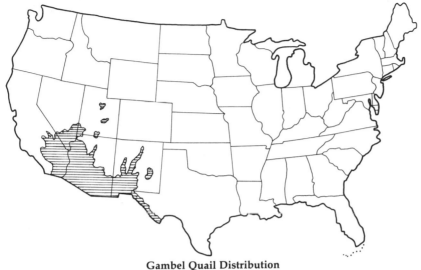

Gambel Quail Distribution

During three days of hunting in the Deming area, we successfully used most of these methods, as well as forming wedges of as many as six drivers. Gerald Gates' friend, Dick Allgood of Silver City, his son Lance and two nephews were also hunting in the area and joined us. These were all-out quail hunters, relying mostly on close-working Brittanies to find both live and dead game. The command these men most frequently use is *Back!* and they insist that their dogs work within 20 yards. The hunters move slowly, allowing the dogs to investigate thoroughly the cover. Most prefer shotguns choked improved cylinder or modified and low-brass loads in No. 7½, 8 or 9 shot.

Gambel quail hunting is great sport, and apparently there is no shortage of targets in the bird's primary range. Some quail gunners, such as Dick Allgood, who is retired, head for the desert nearly every day during the long hunting season.

Desert quail hunting can make you crazy, Gerald Gates told me, *but Dick is crazier than the rest of us. He hunts six days a week, with Mondays off for golf.*

6

The Mearns Quail

I'm telling you they sit so tight that you can throw a hat over them, Floyd
Preas insisted. *I picked up a live one once, and twice I've found dead
birds that cattle had stepped on.*

I must have been wearing my don't-give-me-that-crap-look because Floyd punched a finger on the table for emphasis. *You'll see in the
morning,* he said. *There's nothing like a Mearns. Why do you think they call
them fool quail?*

Floyd is a bird-hunting guide from Mesa, Arizona. He, I, and our
mutual friend—outdoor writer and photographer Tony Mandile from
Glendale—were drinking beer at the Stage Stop Inn in Patagonia,
Arizona. An hour earlier, the three of us had rendezvoused in the
dark at a rest stop east of Tucson. Then we had followed each other
south in our separate vehicles on Highway 83 to this little town on the
Mexican border. It was early January, and the air was cool. That didn't
bother me; back home in the Midwest it was snowing.

I don't like, however, coming into a strange town in the dark. It
throws my bearings off. I guessed I was close enough to Mexico to
hear a rifle fired there but didn't really know. See what I mean? Any-

way, I had driven a long way to hunt the mysterious Mearns quail. And if what Floyd said were true—that the little birds with the painted faces held like epoxy paint to a locker room wall—then it didn't matter much where I was or where I had to go to find them.

After running halfway across New Mexico, trying to get sprinting coveys of scaled quail to flush, it would be nice to have some leisurely hunting again. After all, Mearns were supposed to be a lot like bobwhites.

Which showed how much I knew about America's strangest quail.

The Mearns has more names than a crook on a post office wanted page. Take your pick: Montezuma quail, Harlequin quail, crazy quail, fool quail, painted quail, black quail, squat quail, massena quail. Those are his common names, mostly in English. He has more in Spanish.

Here is a bird with more eye shadow than a middle-aged streetwalker. A quail with a polka-dot breast of black and white that, when he squats low in the grass, looks amazingly like a Russian easter egg. A bird that builds a ground nest complete with roof and side door on hinges. A digger of bulbs, tubers and worms that—when scratching with his oversized feet and toenails—can blur a photo taken at $1/500$ second. A target that, without warning, pogo-sticks into the air, then zooms away at 45 mph.

Hunters who can't hit the elusive Mearns quail have many other names for them, too, but they can't be printed in this book. For a short time about 25 years ago, they couldn't be legally hunted either. Mearns quail were mistakenly placed on the original endangered species list. It took some good hunters from Tucson with crackerjack dogs to prove to the political powers-that-be that the Mearns wasn't as scarce as some people thought.

The bird is named for Edgar A. Mearns, lieutenant-colonel, U.S. Army doctor, and naturalist, who explored the Southwest one hundred years ago. Dr. Mearns hunted in Africa with Teddy Roosevelt and is mentioned in Roosevelt's classic, *African Game Trails*, as a superb shot. Mearns killed everything with a rifle, including birds, which suggests that he might have been as eccentric as the quail that bears his name. But that may be another story.

The Mearns is a subspecies, one of three of the Harlequin quail, a Mexican bird, actually, whose range lies from the northern states of Sonoro, Chihuahua, and Coahuila south to Oaxaca at altitudes from 3,000 to 10,000 feet. In the U.S. its range has shrunk considerably in the past 100 years. The largest supply of birds lives in southeastern and south-central Arizona. They occupy 3,500 to 9,000-foot oak and pinyon pine-grassland hills in the Huachucas, Whetstones, Santa Ritas, Rubys, Mules, and other ranges. Much of their home turf is in the Coronado National Forest, which is open to hunting.

In New Mexico, west of the Pecos River, Mearns live above 5,000 feet and in summer have been found as high as 12,000 feet altitude. Home base is the Capitan, Sacramento, and San Mateo ranges. There

Author shot this hen and cock Mearns quail in southern Arizona. His setters (Chaucer in photo) were a poor choice for this tight-sitting bird that lives in largely open habitat.

Mearns quail habitat in southeastern Arizona is oak and pine grasslands from 3,500 to 9,000 feet altitude. It reminded the author of photographs he had seen of East Africa.

are also some in the Mogollon and Black mountains. If there are any Harlequin quail left in Texas, they are living west of the Pecos River.

The Mearns is a shy, secretive bird that may spend its life within a few hundred yards of where it was born. Coveys are typically small, averaging six birds. Twelve is a big group. Dogless hunters don't find Mearns quail. These are reasons why the birds might appear scarce to all but the best hunters, and why others get discouraged from seeking them. Besides being a wonderful target, the Harlequin is a delicious bird to eat.

There are crazy quail in New Mexico for those that want to look hard for them. Hunting is also permitted in Chihuahua, across the border from Texas, and in the state of Tlaxcala near Mexico City. Until recently, Montezuma quail, as they are called in Mexico, were legal targets in Sonora and Coahuila. Most American hunters go to Arizona, though, keying their efforts in the triangle formed by Patagonia, Sonoita, and Durango. Arizona has a long quail-hunting season, beginning in mid-November and lasting until mid-February. Bag limits are a generous 15 birds daily and 30 in possession. Although hunters don't often kill limits, they do manage to bag 30,000 to 80,000 Mearns quail each year.

I wanted one, for sure, to get mounted. But I didn't realize how hard bagging a Mearns could be.

The next morning about 10 o'clock, Floyd, Tony, and I took my two setters and headed into the hill country outside Patagonia. The landscape looked like photos I had seen of east Africa—rolling savanna grasslands, parched brown, with green-leafed oaks of 10 to 25 feet tall interspersed throughout. Along dry washes and canyons, the oaks fold in to these depressions, which are further fringed with yucca, patches of buffalograss, and a nasty, low-growing gray bush called catclaw. Catclaw has small thorns that can puncture nylon-faced hunting pants. It leaves white marks along the skin, hence its name.

The canyon bottoms hold sand and rocks, plenty of rocks, from the size of cobblestones to Volkswagen buses. Growing everywhere, it seems, is the knee-high brown grass that Mearns quail need for survival. It has a small seed head and a brittle stalk and stems.

What kind is it? I asked Floyd.

Ass grass.

What do you call it? I repeated.

You'll know when it breaks off and creeps up your pant leg.

This is Mearns quail country. Tactics call for hunting along the grass and sand waterways, letting the dogs work the bottomlands and up the hillsides. You can split up, too, each hunter and dog team wandering up one of the many fingers of cover. Sometimes you will see the white flags of running Coues deer, the whitetail's smaller cousin. Once or twice I smelled the musky odor of javelina, which uproot the yucca plants to get at their tubers. This is big country; you couldn't hunt a square mile of it in a day. Maybe not even in a week.

After walking for a half-hour, we heard a quail flush on a hillside above us. On our move up, a second bird erupted, and I caught a flash of black and white. A little farther on, a covey of four exploded underfoot like black-and-white bombshells. Tony was out of range, I wasn't ready, but Floyd knocked down a bird that neither we nor the dogs could find.

It was 75 degrees and growing warmer. My long-haired dogs were panting with the heat, and there was no wind to help them scent game.

I should have brought my dogs, Floyd said. He wasn't being unkind. I've already stated that to hunt the Mearns effectively, you need dogs. But not just any dog will do. Close-working pointing breeds with super noses and that are as staunch as park statues are necessary. The

German shorthaired pointers, popular with bobwhite hunters, are also the dog of choice—along with Brittanies—of Mearns quail hunters. *(Iowa Conservation Commission photo)*

most successful Mearns quail hunters own Brittanies or German shorthairs that are trained to hunt underfoot. My dogs are trained— check that—my dogs are used to hunting the available habitat. Back home in Michigan woodcock cover, they work tightly. Then, when we're hunting sharptails in the Upper Peninsula or prairie chickens in Kansas they fan out, making casts of a quarter-mile, sometimes more.

The oak-grasslands are wide-open, an invitation to my dogs to run. And run they did, probably right over the top of more than one covey of quail. To the credit of Lady Macbeth, my five-year-old bitch, she later learned to work more tightly, but that was days later when I started killing game without her. A few days before my arrival in Patagonia, two hunters with 16 uninitiated dogs, mostly English pointers, visited the area. They did not kill very many quail.

Mearns quail are diggers. Those long legs and sharp toenails turn the ground to duff in their search for acorns, chufa (nutgrass) tubers and wood sorrel and sedge bulbs. After extracting the meat, they discard the hulls. The birds also eat sunflower seeds, beetles, worms and other invertebrates, along with buttercup tubers. There is some documentation, however meager, that they will eat corn and perhaps other cultivated grains when farm fields adjoin the lower end of their habitat.

Apparently the natural foods provide the Mearns' moisture needs as there is only one recorded instance of a bird sighted drinking. Richard Bishop, a friend of mine and with whom I've hunted bobwhites in his native Iowa, did his graduate research work on Mearns quail back in the 1960s. Bishop once saw a Harlequin drinking from a mud puddle.

Mearns quail don't wander far from day to day, and so the diggings are solid clues to their whereabouts. They usually scratch in the shade under oak trees, working their way up the hillside as a close group while day progresses, then down again as night approaches. Bishop has observed as many as eight birds feeding in a circle only 14 inches in diameter. Their foraging technique is to scratch with one foot for awhile, look around for danger, then scratch with the other foot. The diggings look like squirrels or, in some cases, wild turkeys have torn up little areas of the landscape.

During a water break back at the cars, we changed dogs, especially after Holly, my yellow Lab, insisted that she could outshine those hard-charging white setters. A hundred yards from the car, Holly and I went through an area of fresh diggings in sand patches under some oaks, but we didn't find any quail. I called Floyd over for a look.

Get ready, he said. *There's quail here. No doubt.*

Backtracking, I studied the ground as though looking for a lost contact lens but could see nothing that resembled even a feather. Just then, Holly swung in and padded close by. Suddenly, five quail, wings banging like a gang of roofers, erupted less than three feet from my boots. I felt the wind of one rooster in my face and got a closeup look at his clown's costume. A true art job of whitewashed face with swirls of black under the eyes and over the cheeks. His tan crest of feathers looked like long hair combed back. I thought of the "Joker" in those Batman comics I used to read as a kid. But the joke was on me; the bird went right over my own head.

I spun around, traced his speedy flight up the slope with my borrowed two-tube Winchester, and squeezed the trigger. *Click.*

I had forgotten to reload after the water break.

Floyd erased my mistake easily enough, though, and Tony knocked a second cockbird down, which we also found. Later that afternoon as we approached to within 20 yards of the cars, a covey of four birds flushed wild. I pulled feathers on one with my second barrel. Tony killed a hen for the third and final bird of the day.

Mearns quail have large feet and toenails, helpful for scratching for food. Their big feet and powerful legs also enable the birds to get into the air quickly.

While resting on a log, we marveled at the color pattern of these birds. *Harlequin,* my dictionary says, is *a droll character in comedy and pantomime, usually masked, dressed in parti-colored spangled tights and bearing a wooden sword or magic wand.* The male bird in my hand was droll at right, but he didn't carry any props. Didn't need to with that color scheme for attention. Besides their striking faces, Mearns males have upper sides of white spots on black and brown-black abdomens. Overall, hens are a light lavender to buff, much like the color of hen pheasants. The face is mottled brown with a white chin and throat.

You don't get much of a shooting chance with Mearns quail. Those strong legs (their thighs are the size of a man's thumb) and big claws help catapult them into the air. Their wings are proportionally larger to bodies than the other quail, too, except for perhaps the mountain species. Adult bobwhites, for example, average 9.5 to 10.6 inches in length and have a folded wing measurement that averages 98 to 119 millimeters. By comparison, the Mearns is more squatly built—8 to 9.5 inches long—but has a folded wing that tapes from 110 to 130 millimeters.

Mearns are artful dodgers, zipping in and out of hillside cover. Depending on where you flush them, they usually head either uphill or downhill. Shots have to be quick, often at little patches of daylight between trees or at skylined birds just before they clear the hilltop. I witnessed a couple quail rock left and right, much like prairie chickens do before setting their wings for a glide, but whether this was common or just a feint, I can't say.

Mearns don't fly far—50 to 100 yards—often settling to the earth like a helicopter. You should be able to saunter right over and put the boots to them again.

It is never that easy, though. How such a striking bird can completely vanish is beyond my understanding. Sometimes they will run off into heavy cover and hide. But just as often after hitting the ground, they will freeze in a turtlelike crouch. Mearns don't exude much scent that way, and when they've been air-washed from the flush, give off even less.

Gambel and scaled quail run from the scene of the crime. Mearns stay put. Late in the season, hunter-wise birds may flush wild, but early in the fall, they root to the ground. To get them into the air, try the old grouse zigzag trick, stopping and walking a few feet at intervals. When a Mearns quail gets nervous, he crouches. When he really gets nervous, especially with you standing over him, he flushes.

Close-working dogs, like these Brittanies, are necessary for hunting the up-and-down country of southern Arizona for Mearns quail. The hunter is Hoyd Patty of Patagonia, Arizona, with his dogs, Tray and Babe.

A few days after hunting with Tony and Floyd, I was standing at the base of a hill, waiting for another friend to pick up a bird he had shot and that had piled up in the catclaw. I didn't move from the spot where six birds had rocketed out a moment before. I was admiring a cockbird I had shot, one that my male setter, Chaucer, had returned to me. It looked like a good candidate for mounting.

Five minutes later, when my friend called for help, I went to take a step and another crazy quail buzzed up and away. Unless you learn to expect the unexpected, you won't fill a game bag with Mearns quail.

Hoyd Patty, an Illinois expatriate who has spent the last 22 years in sunny Patagonia, is a confirmed Mearns quail hunter. Hoyd and his pair of Britts—Babe and her son Tray—comb the oak-grass hillsides for Harlequin quail every chance they get. One time he saw a covey of about 25 birds go up in staggered flight, flushing so closely that he could have reached out and cuffed them. Each time Hoyd fired at one, another bird or two would leap from the grass. He killed eight quail without taking a step, and his dogs grew tired while running back and forth with the retrieves.

If you want to hit a Mearns quail, without going through a box of shells, you have to hunt hungry with your gun half-way up, Hoyd advises.

I decided that was my problem. Here I was—the complete outdoor writer—with two wide-strapped 35mm cameras crisscrossing my chest like bandoleers. A pencil and notebook in my hand half the time and asking enough questions to dizzy a quiz-bowl coach. Trying to keep an eye on a pair of setters that insisted on rambling over the next hill. And I was supposed to shoot a bird that moves out as though fueled by liquid oxygen?

On the other hand, no one ever accused me of not being able to explain my misses.

Floyd Preas had to return to Mesa on the afternoon of my first day's hunt, so Tony and I went out the next day on our own, with my dogs again. We never saw a quail. I like to think our poor luck had to do with the fact that a high wind tugged at our clothing all day and that the Mearns quail, at least in the immediate area, had been hunted pretty hard. One thing I do know for sure: Those hard climbs uphill, unsteady footing downhill, overall altitude, and unseasonal heat can fast wear out a flatlander.

When Tony had to go back to Glendale that evening, I was on my own to bag a Mearns quail. Thank God for Hoyd Patty.

The Stage Stop Inn hosts an interesting mix of people who come for breakfast and morning coffee. There was Henry, the 86-year-old retired cowboy with the kind of craggy face you see in those black-

Tony Mandile of Glendale, Arizona, shot this colorful cock Mearns quail near Patagonia in southern Arizona.

and-white photography books on the West. Each morning, Henry would claim his usual table, smoke a couple of cigarettes, and drink a cup of coffee into which he had dumped the contents of eight or 10 packets of sugar. Henry was interesting all right, but he was no quail hunter.

Hoyd Patty was. I met him one morning and we became friends. A couple of days later, he agreed to take me and another friend hunting.

I have never underestimated my ability as a predator, when I need to be one. I was ready now to bag a Mearns quail, so ready that I emptied my pockets of pencils and Kodachrome, kenneled my dogs, cased the borrowed Winchester 101 and broke out my own just-right-feeling Citori. Then I told Hoyd I was in his hands.

They'll fly uphill, he said. *Back off and get a good shooting lane.* We hadn't moved 125 yards from the Winnebago when Babe locked up in the shadows under a spreading oak. The old Britt's stub tail quivered. Her son, Tray, backed her from 10 feet away. Hoyd was like a movie director. *Move a little to your left,* he said to me. Then he advised Marilyn Underwood, my Tucson hunting partner, to position herself to the right.

Everybody ready? Hoyd asked. *OK, Babe.*

Strange how quail hunting and all its peripheries of planning, travel, dog training, and practice shooting is reduced to a single, explosive act of violence. I had my little 20-gauge half-way up when four quail detonated from the hillside. I smoked the first bird before it leveled off, followed right on through my swing, touching off the over barrel as I passed a second blur of black and white. That bird folded his tent, too.

My first Mearns quail turned out to be a two-cock double. *Wheeeoooooo,* Hoyd said. Then he made me feel pretty good when he added, *I've shot probably 500 of these little birds, but I've never gotten a double.*

Marilyn missed her target, but by the time the sun, now an orange ball of light, bumped the Western horizon, she had shot both a hen and a cock. We had eight birds between us, including a Gambel quail that Hoyd had collected. It is not uncommon to find both species, especially at lower altitudes near the desert floor.

Besides keeping an eye out for fresh diggings, hunters can locate Mearns quail by looking for their green-and-white droppings which are about twice the size of bobwhite scat. Unlike the other Western species, Mearns quail roost on the ground in a semicircle, usually next to a rock or clump of grass. Although they don't occupy the same spot night after night, they usually roost in the same general area.

Diggings and roost sites full of droppings are clues as to Mearns quail whereabouts.
Hoyd Patty checks for sign. Birds move up the hillside, digging in the moist, shaded
ground as day progresses.

Mid morning is the best time to start hunting because the birds
will be foraging, unless it is raining. Then they will stay in the roost or,
at best, won't travel very far. Daytime temperatures in southern Arizona can reach 80 degrees or more in the winter, but at night the
thermometer may plunge to below freezing. This tends to concentrate
the quail, and so the following morning, hunters may do well by
targeting sun-warmed patches that are first to thaw.

Usually, though, Mearns quail are birds of the moist shadows,
moving with the sun up hillsides and then back down in the course of
the day. During his research, Bishop found that the crop of a typical
Mearns was not filled until 3 p.m. That is probably not due so much to
a lack of food, but rather to their leisurely pace. While they eat, the
birds take time out to rest, dust, and preen themselves.

Mearns quail couple up in March or April with breeding active through May most years. Both sexes build the nest, using their strong claws to dig out a scrape in the ground, which might be two or three inches deep. They line the scrape with grass, leaves, and feathers and then roof the nest with grass. Hanging grass stems cover a side entrance which falls back in place after the parent birds enter or leave.

Average clutch size is 11 eggs, and both adults help with incubation chores. The young, which hatch during the summer, are able to forage on their own at two weeks. The covey unit is basically the family and, as I indicated earlier, averages six birds by hunting season. Coveys of four quail or less have probably been shot down. Groups of 10 birds and up are likely two or more families that have linked.

Mearns quail rely on visual signals associated with their riotous color scheme as much, if not more, than calls. That trait is likely due to the generally open country in which they live, where exposure can mean swift death from the usual parade of predators. These include

Arizonans Hoyd Patty and Marilyn Underwood admire color scheme of a Mearns quail that Marilyn shot. Mearns are not easy to hit as they dodge in and out of hillside cover at 45 mph.

Mearns Quail Distribution

hawks, owls, eagles, foxes, and coyotes. The call of the Mearns is a low quavering whistle that, according to the literature, is remindful of owl notes. I have never heard it myself.

Like other quail, the future of these unique gamebirds depends upon habitat preservation. At one time, the Harlequin lived throughout much of Texas and New Mexico, but extensive cattle grazing ruined its grassland habitat. For a long time, researchers believed that cattle competed for the foods that Mearns quail use, but more recent studies have proved that to be false. In fact, cattle grazing actually increases the amount of preferred quail foods, some of which is toxic to cattle anyway.

The real danger lies in destruction of escape, nesting, and roosting cover.

Thus far, hunting has not greatly affected Mearns numbers. A 1972 study conducted by the Arizona Game and Fish Department in Gardner Canyon—the state's most heavily hunted area—showed that prehunt populations of 87 coveys actually increased to 116 coveys over 12 months. This was in spite of the fact that hunters may have killed up to 78 percent of birds known to live there. What does the future hold for these one-of-a-kind quail? There will probably be huntable numbers in the immediate future. But the spectre of extinction will always be present.

7

The Mountain Quail

I remember thinking about Jennifer and her wisdom teeth — two of them impacted — that the oral surgeon had painfully removed the week before. I hadn't seen my daughter since Christmas; now it was late January. Home stretched 2,400 miles away, across a desert, mountain passes that might or might not be plugged shut with snow, endless plains, corn-and-hog country. Seven states in all.

It was time to be thinking of going home.

I don't know how long Macbeth's bell had stopped tinkling but probably only a moment or so. I knew my setter was below me in the brushy creek bottom, and I knew she had stick-pinned a covey of Nevada mountain quail. About a hundred feet below me, streaks of snow lay under the dark-green pinyon and naked gray cottonwoods. More snow spits marked the buckskin-colored canyon walls of this mountain stream. One of those white patches was most certainly my dog.

Excited, I started down the hill, very loudly and very unnecessarily *whoaing* her. One of the quail must have moved, because a snow pile below and to my right shifted just a little. Then I heard the burr of exploding wings and caught the flash of a brown target moving from right to left up the canyon. Too far for a decent shot; besides, I was falling down the hill. Macbeth slammed into a second point, and another bird came goosing out, this time from left to right. I stopped skidding long enough to empty both barrels of the Citori, an act which proved that I know how to waste ammunition.

The reports roared back at me from canyon walls. They also put at least six more, and possibly eight quail, on the wing at once. Most followed the second bird down the creek, but one quail, as big as a small grouse, flew right at me. It passed at such a ridiculously slow speed (or so it seems when the gun is empty) that I could see its brown upper sides and slate-gray back, a bit of chestnut on the upper breast, and that long feather trailing behind its head like the feathered hat plume of a musketeer. I even got a glimpse of light in his eye.

Did you get one? my hunting partner, Paula Del Giudice, hollered from across the canyon.

Of course not, I yelled back. *But now I know what they look like.*

We were hunting in the Smith Valley of western Nevada. The Pine Nut Mountains, foothills that hunch up to the higher Sierra Nevadas, looked like mounds of chocolate and almond ice cream with deep striations from some child's fork and here and there an indentation from a deft stab with the spoon.

Mountain quail country. Only 75 miles from Reno, where my friend, also a bird hunter and full-time writer, lives. Yet Paula had seen her first mountain quail only yesterday. There had been a high wind then. It, and the roaring of Desert Creek as it rushed downhill, spilling its loud way around boulders and hairpin curves, made it impossible for us to pinpoint flushing quail. Even when our four dogs—my two setters and yellow Labrador and Paula's golden retriever, Dolly—had routed them from the mountain sagebrush and willow thickets.

Everything I had read and heard about mountain quail being tough birds to hunt apparently was true. The one quail Paula had seen had given her no opportunity for a shot. Today, there was no wind and the canyon we were working contained a smaller stream that didn't talk so loudly. Now I was determined to put at least one bird from that fine covey in my game pouch.

We started down the canyon, following the sound of Macbeth's bell, our retrievers at respective heel. After maybe 50 yards, the bell stopped and a bird came rocketing out. *Don't they ever hold for the point?* I wondered. Although mountain quail fly high enough for good shots, they are especially adept at keeping a tree, shrub, or whatever

Mountain quail country. The author and Holly head back after a long hunt in Nevada that produced worn boot leather and no birds.

they can find between the hunter and their line of flight. That's why they live along open slopes interspersed with cover and stream bottoms plastered with brush. At any rate, the bird was too far away for a decent shot, and for once, I wished I had trained my dog to be steady to wing. When she ran after the escaping bird, the others flushed wild.

If the bobwhite is a gentleman, the mountain quail ain't. Paula marked some of the birds, about 100 feet up the canyon wall where they zoomed into a pine-covered plateau.

Escape cover is very important to mountain quail, San Stiver, a biologist for the Nevada Department of Wildlife, had told me. *In this country, pinyon pine affords the best escape cover. They'll land right in the tree or in heavy cover nearby.* With those thoughts in mind, I charged up the hill, and, when I reached the plateau, out of breath, surveyed the situation.

Many times when hunting upland birds I ask myself the question, *If I were a bird, where would I go now?* The answer, in this case, seemed obvious enough. Birds would land on the plateau, then run back for the cover of the stream bottom. A staggered growth of pinyon, along with some mountain mahogany, lay between it and the plateau. I started for this cover. Paula, meanwhile, was paralleling my setter, who had remained along the stream and was quite likely working another bird.

Holly, my Lab, had stayed at my side all this time. Suddenly she lunged forward, kicking out a single quail from the other side of a pine. The bird flew right for me, and I could have reached out and grabbed it. Instead, I threw two shells away as it corkscrewed its way through the protective cover. *Why are these birds so impossible to hit?* I don't miss any more than my share of woodcock, for example, that explode like that underfoot, then stitch an invisible seam in heavy cover.

The answer was so obvious: *Then think of them as woodcock, Dummy.*

So, five minutes later I did. Both dogs were casting in front of me when a mountain quail flushed from between my legs. I traced the bird's flight across a pine and when it and my gun barrel reached a window of daylight, I pulled the trigger. The quail went down at once, and when I picked up the handsome bird, it was limp and dead.

The upper chest and upper back of the mountain quail is blue-gray in color. The bird has bar markings of chestnut and white ahead of its wings and on its lower chest. There is a tuft of copper or cinnamon off the back near the leg flanks and ventral area. The throat is a chestnut color, and a single white bar marking to either side of the face begins behind the eye and frames the rufous throat patch. A long, black plume looks like a skinny feather. Actually it is two feathers, one slightly longer than the other, that split apart.

Males and females look alike, except that females sport more olive to the nape whereas males appear more gray. Cockbirds have slightly longer plumes—at least 2.8 inches in late fall and winter. Size of both sexes is about the same, nearly a foot long, and weight is eight to 10 ounces each, compared to six or seven ounces for bobwhites. The mountain quail I held was as large as my hand. No wonder they look like small grouse on the wing.

Mountain quail are, for the most part, an underutilized resource. Hunters rarely impact their numbers to any degree and have little, if any, bearing on the mysterious population swings to which this game-bird is accustomed. Most researchers believe that severe winters and excessive periods of drought contribute heavily to the birds' ups and downs. Man-made changes in their habitat could be other reasons. Lumbering, fires and overgrazing, for example, are chief threats to mountain quail welfare. At any rate, reduced numbers in recent years in portions of their primary range—the Western United States—have resulted in fewer hunters seeking them. Hunters also stay home be-

The author was lucky to bag two mountain quail for four days of hunting. He found the birds above 6,000 feet altitude on the Nevada/California border.

cause, at times, mountain quail may appear unpredictable, be difficult to find, and are equally hard to hit on the wing.

Like I said, they are not very accommodating birds. To hunt them effectively, you better be in shape and have a good shooting eye.

Those who go after mountain quail, though, may be well rewarded, for here is a true wilderness gamebird. Whereas the other quail species often thrive in habitat cultivated by man, mountain quail are nearly always affected negatively by human progress. Because blue grouse, ruffed grouse, and chukars sometimes live side by side with them, mixed-bag hunting is possible. And, like all quail, the mountain species is exceptional as table fare.

Mountain quail are sometimes called mountain partridge or painted quail. In prehistoric times, the birds probably occupied a range much larger than today. For example, according to remains found in caves in the 1930s, they evidently lived in portions of what is now southern New Mexico during the Pleistocene Epoch. Today, however, mountain quail are native throughout much of California and western Oregon. They were released in Washington in the 1800s and currently are thriving in the state's southeastern and South Puget Sound areas. A small population on Vancouver Island can be traced from stockings there and on the mainland 100 years ago. It is quite likely that mountain quail presently in western Nevada, western Idaho, and eastern Washington and Oregon are from transplanted birds, but no one knows for sure.

Releases elsewhere have met with mixed success. Some mountain quail still live in the Hualapai Mountains near Kingman, Arizona. On the other hand, a release of 150 birds in the Sacramento Mountains near La Luz in New Mexico in 1958 apparently failed. So did attempts to establish the bird in Utah and Colorado.

Mountain quail are currently legal targets in California, Washington, Oregon, Nevada, and Baja, Mexico. The best hunting occurs in California where hunters shoot from 50,000 to 90,000 each year. In a

A bird in the hand. Mountain quail are the largest, and according to many hunters, the most difficult to bag of six species of quail that may be hunted in the U.S. The author agreed with that assessment of this unusual gamebird.

good year, Oregon hunters will kill 50,000 or more. As mentioned, the birds are mostly underharvested. Many years ago on a study area in southern California, hunters shot less than five percent of the estimated 2,000 mountain quail living there. That may be partly due to the fact that only one of five hunters used a dog.

I can't imagine hunting for any species of quail without a dog, and for mountain quail, both flushing and pointing breeds can be helpful. That is why I always took both my Lab and at least one of the setters up the slopes with me. Of course, if your partner is some wild fool that lines out for Canada and your license is only valid for Washington, then you may as well hunt without him. With or without a dog, a good hunting technique is to walk the higher ground above stream bottoms with heavy cover. I'm told it is not uncommon to see mountain quail running, their plumed heads bobbing like pigeons on a city sidewalk, ahead of dogs and hunters. Two hunters—one posting farther up the canyon, the other moving toward him—could rattle running birds into flight. Either way they flew, they would furnish targets for at least one hunter, provided he knew where his partner was.

If you really want to give mountain quail more than a sporting chance—and I don't know why you would want to do that when the bird already has the odds in his favor—approach them from below. There is a good possibility you will not have to clean your gun that evening. Typical flushes occur 40 yards ahead of you or your dog, with the birds generally flying to uphill escape cover.

If you are lucky, they will stay along the sheltered watershed, and although you may have to strain your shot through willow thickets, you may be spared a hard climb up canyon walls. Shotguns choked modified are a good compromise, but some hunters rely solely on full choke. Others pick their shots while sticking with improved cylinder choke.

One researcher I came across in my reading believes that mountain quail may be vulnerable to hunting pressure when they fly up and down these stream bottoms. The man is possibly a nonhunter; at least he has never seen me shoot. Further, according to Charley Waterman, who wrote *Hunting Upland Birds*, mountain quail will leave a brushy draw when hunting pressure heats up. Hopefully, for the hunter's sake, they will head for more open sage flats rather than high-country pines.

On the other hand, if you can break up the covey, which usually numbers from six to nine birds (a huge, and somewhat rare covey would contain 15 to 30 quail), the singles will often hold until you practically step on them.

Both pointing and flushing breeds are useful for hunting mountain quail. Paula Del Giudice, a freelance writer and hunter from Reno, is shown with Dolly, her golden retriever.

Mountain quail are migratory, moving—more or less—up and down their habitat according to weather and food variables. A California study showed maximum elevation in summer to be 8,339 feet on the English Mountains. In winter, birds were found as low as 2,000 feet elevation at Hoyt's Crossing. The migration to wintering cover begins in September and peaks in October. In spring, the peak period of movement is mid-April. Mountain quail can fly only about a thousand feet at a time. The migration is on foot.

John Calkins, a friend and fellow writer from East Lansing, Michigan, trapped the Walker River Valley many years ago as a young man. He remembers seeing mountain quail trooping, single-file, through his campsite enroute to lower altitudes. The birds may move no more than a mile in their lifetimes, but some have been found as far as 25 air miles from a tagging location.

Where do you find mountain quail during the hunting season? Slopes to 60 degree angles are commonly inhabited. The exact altitude depends on snow conditions and resulting food availability. In California, habitat is tied closely to dry, mixed chapparal plant species, including grasses, scrub, and low evergreen, and other trees with small leathery leaves. According to a California study, the birds liked moderately open brush and tree cover on slopes of at least 20 degrees.

Summer highland habitat included mixed associations of manzanita, juniper, ponderosa pine, incense cedar, and canyon live-oak. Winter cover included herbs and brush such as chemise, Fremont silktassel, manzanita and scrub oak. In fall, it makes sense to look for birds in either place or between the two habitats. Use 5,000 feet as a start; then move up or down according to local snow conditions. The mountain quail I found in Nevada in late January, for example, were at 6,000 to 7,000 feet.

Prime habitat includes many species, sizes, shapes, and densities of plants. It is impossible to list every type. Coastal region habitat differs from that of the Sierra Nevadas, which, in turn, differs from desert conditions. Low-bush densities may be acceptable in desert areas devoid of snow, but in higher altitudes a high-bush density is important for withstanding snow. When scouting for promising habitat, look for slopes that are 20 to 50 percent covered with trees, shrubs, and grasses and that have a southern exposure and are out of the wind.

In winter, look for birds just below the snowline, especially at the mouths of canyons. In the Pine Nut Range where I hunted, pinyon and juniper speckled the high ground to each side of the canyons. Besides cottonwood, willow and wild rose in subtle shades of pink and orange grew along the stream beds in those canyons where I found quail. I identified rabbit brush, bunchgrass and mountain sage—a greenish plant that grows belt-high and that has a brownish-yellow head to it. When you rub your hands on it, they will smell pungently of sage for hours.

This mountain sage, incidentally, is quite different from what local hunters call antelope sage, a low-growing white sage of the flat valley floor. When snow is deep in the canyons, mountain quail sometimes move out into these sagebrush flats to search for food. Shooting scores, then, I'm told, can soar dramatically. But even when mountain quail are caught in the open, they are rarely more than a single flight from protective cover of the slopes.

Hunters able to identify food types can often use that information to put birds in the bag. Like the other quail species, though, mountain

Mountain quail habitat nearly always contains slopes and mixed associations of brush, trees, and open country. California and Oregon host the best hunting opportunities. Birds may also be hunted in Nevada and Washington.

quail eat a variety of foods. In fall, seeds, fruits, acorns, and pine nuts are important; in winter and spring, green leafage and buds. Key forb species are filaree and legumes, including lotus, lupine, loco weed, and clover. Important grasses are bromegrass, fescue, needlegrass, and ryegrass. Mountain quail also eat grain crops when they are available.

Birds begin to pair up in February or March, and nesting success, according to one California study, is apparently keyed to rainfall. It begins in April after an inch or so of rain has fallen, and, at least in that study, peaked after nine inches of rain. Mountain quail raise a single brood from nests made at the base of trees, rocks, and shrubs often just off paths and roads. Water is nearly always nearby. The average clutch contains 10 eggs, and hatching occurs in May, June, and July.

Ground squirrels, chipmunks, skunks, and California jays are opportunistic egg predators. Foxes, coyotes, bobcats, hawks, and owls likely prey on juvenile and adult birds, but to what extent, no one really knows. In the Joshua Tree National Monument in California, for example, where predators are protected, an excellent adult-to-young quail ratio of 1-to-6 was evident six weeks after hatching. Apparently predators had little impact there.

According to one researcher, drowning is the most common fate that befalls mountain quail. It most often occurs when birds attempt to fly long distances over water.

Hunting seasons begin as early as late August in western Oregon and run through January in Nevada. Because the fall migration period coincides with hunting seasons, mountain quail can be tough to pin down. A good scouting tip is to ask local people whose work takes them outdoors if they have seen any mountain quail. A trapper was responsible for that first covey that Paula and I put up. Other likely scouting candidates are other hunters, game wardens, wildlife biologists, ranchers, lumbermen, rural mail carriers, and delivery workers.

A good time to begin hunting is mid or late morning after foraging

Rest break to look over a prime mountain quail. The cocks and hens are nearly identical. Paula's dog Dolly is trying to help me decide which sex this one is.

quail have had a chance to leave the roost and put out scent for the dogs. The birds typically roost off the ground in the center of a tree or shrub from six to 10 feet tall, the same type of cover they use for a getaway. After the morning feeding, mountain quail will loaf through the middle of the day, usually in the same general area where they eat and sleep. Tracks and dusting bowls in the sand along logging trails and roads are clues to their whereabouts.

Some hunters report success by listening for the rallying call of birds separated from the covey. After breaking up a covey is one good time to listen for it. In late afternoon, as the quail are preparing to roost, is another. It sounds like *cle-cle-cle* or maybe a *kow-kow-kow*. Others have described it as a whistlelike *whew-whew-whew*. I think I heard it on my last evening in Nevada, but I'm not sure.

I was hunting alone, not far from Sweetwater Summit and the California border. It was a Sunday evening, and shadows were sneaking down the mountains while the dogs worked sagebrush flats to either side of a logging road I was hoofing along. The evening thermals were settling in at this 6,500-foot elevation. Feeling chilled, I buttoned my wool buffalo plaid shirt (this red-and-black shirt—along with the absence of a cowboy hat and boots—always marks me as a foreigner whenever I visit the West). I thought I heard a low whistle a few yards ahead. A moment later a mountain quail stepped into the road with my yellow Labrador right behind it. The bird flushed into the shadows before I could shoulder my gun.

I called in the dogs, put Holly at heel, and walked through the sage tangles in the direction the bird had taken. *They always fly to the nearest pinyon tree,* San Stiver had said. And there was a pinyon tree just 40 yards away at the base of a high hill. When I arrived, Macbeth was already *On Point*.

The sagebrush was low enough to shoot over, but I knew if I went in to flush the bird, it would fly uphill, keeping the pine between us. I would have a long shot at best. I broke the Citori, pulled out the No. 8 skeet loads I had used earlier, and replaced them with high-brass No. 6s. I also thumbed the safety to the upper barrel so that I could shoot modified choke instead of improved cylinder. Then, cradling the shotgun in my left arm, I picked up a rock the size of a softball, stepped off to the left of the pine, and tossed the rock with an underhand pitch.

Wings rustled and a quail came boiling out. As it angled up the hill in low flight, I brought the gun up, smoothly it seemed, and broke him. The bird piled into the side of the hill, then rolled down it into the sage. A perfect specimen, he was ideal for mounting, and so I hand-carried him back to the motorhome. Once there, I watered, fed,

Mountain Quail Distribution

and kenneled the dogs, then started the motorhome. My jeans had picked up the sweetly pungent odor of sage, which stayed with me all the way back to Reno.

Now, whenever I smell sage, I think of mountain quail.

8

The Valley Quail

The problem was not in finding the valley quail. The setters had done that job well enough. Chaucer stood frozen, his tail straight up like an exclamation mark minus the dot, his nose six inches from a small tangle of grease brush. Two feet away on the other side of the bush, his sister had this bird nailed, too. Lady Macbeth's tail swept over her lower back like a question mark, her right foot cocked in canine salute.

Bring your thunderstick, Boss, they might have said. *This one's for you.*

That was the problem. The dogs had pinned a valley quail all right, probably a single from the big covey we had busted moments earlier. But the grease brush they were pointing lay 10 yards away on a steep bank across a Nevada irrigation ditch, too deep for me to cross. What to do? A half-mile jog either upstream or downstream would bring me to a bridge. I didn't mind the exercise, nor was I afraid the dogs would break their points during my absence. A second, and much greater problem, was that I would likely miss the bird anyway. Then, it would land on the side of the ditch where Staley Kent and I now stood, and we would have to do it all over again.

Maybe if I throw this stick, the quail will flush, Staley offered. *Then you could shoot it.* She obviously still believed that I could hit these birds.

Staley fired the stick, narrowly missing my setters. They flinched and Macbeth rolled her eyes as if to say, *Why the hell are you throwing things at us? Come over here and do your job.* Back home in Michigan, Dale Jarvis, the trainer who had charged me dearly for staunching these dogs, would have flinched and demanded an explanation, too.

This would never work. Meanwhile, the quail and the two dogs dared each other to move.

There was another option. Holly, my yellow Labrador at heel, was whining. She knew the setters had a bird pinned and she wanted in on the action.

Don't do that either, Dale Jarvis, who had now become my conscience, said.

But it's too far to the bridge, I argued. *And I'll ruin my pants and boots if I cross the ditch.*

You could also ruin months of careful training, but it's up to you. I can use the extra money.

Holly must have sensed my indecision. Suddenly, she broke heel, hit the water with a belly smacker, and charged up the opposite bank. The quail flushed low along the waterway. I missed. The setters didn't suffer from the experience after all except for their loss of faith in me. In fact, Macbeth dashed back to the bush and pointed again. I stuffed two fresh loads into my over-and-under, just as another quail came whirring from the grease brush. Two more misses. Another frantic search in my coat pocket for more shells. Unbelievable, but my dog was still locked on the bush. A third quail bolted out, then two more. Yellow shotshell hulls littered the stream bank where I stood. I think I fired seven rounds altogether while managing to scratch down a single bird.

Valley or California quail, as they are commonly called, are as deceiving a target as any gamebird I have hunted. Have you ever seen a male red-winged blackbird chase a rival? Well, valley quail fly like that, cutting and dodging through the cover. These fleet-winged quail seem faster than bobwhites, but I have no proof to back it up. They flush low and stay low, taking advantage of stream bottoms, trees, and brush to mask their flight. They will zip right through shirt-shredding cover, and if you are using flushing dogs or pointing breeds not steady to shot and wing (like my setters), you will have to check your swing now and then to avoid shooting the dogs.

The more often valley quail are shot at, the more elusive they

Author accepts valley quail from Holly. Action occurred on private ranchland in Nevada. Valley quail are legal targets in eight Western states.

become. Like all Western quail, whole coveys will run ahead of hunters and dogs, then seemingly vanish into the scantiest cover imaginable. There, they might hold as though welded. I have heard that hunters, sorting through the bushes as though they were looking for a lost wallet, sometimes can get these tight-sitting quail into the air.

It was late in January and I was on my way home after a month of hunting quail in Oklahoma, New Mexico, Arizona, and now Nevada. As I stated earlier, my goal was to shoot all six species of quail that may be legally hunted in the United States. The small freezer in my Winnebago motorhome held one or two males each of bobwhite, scaled, Gambel, Mearns, and mountain quail. This was my last hunt of the season, and I was hoping for a prime valley quail cock so that I could pay a taxidermist—assuming I had any money left at all—to mount all six species for me. They would look great on a skeleton of cholla cactus I had picked up in the Arizona desert.

I had stopped near Fallon, Nevada, to hunt on an 1,800-acre cattle ranch belonging to Bruce and Jamie Kent. Bruce, a passionate bird hunter himself, had planned to join me on this late-season hunt, but I lost out to a broken windmill of his that needed immediate attention. So Bruce's 16-year-old daughter, Staley, agreed to go with me. She and her dad like to hunt valley quail. From the number of empty shotshells (not all mine) I saw along that irrigation ditch, theirs had been a swell hunting season.

Some of the largest concentrations of valley quail are on ranches and farms of the Western states, and so the best hunting often occurs on private land. Many landowners, like the Kents, feed the birds in winter when snows grow deep and food is hard to come by. Like the Gambel quail, valley quail are frequent visitors to suburbia. They show up at bird feeders, on the edges of lawns, and in school playgrounds, roosting at night in nearby shrubbery. In the toughest of winters, coveys sometimes come together to number 500 birds or more. Several reputable hunters I talked to have seen coveys that large, and I have read about bands numbering well over 1,000 quail.

I suspect that valley quail know there is safety in numbers. You wonder, too, if they know that sportsmen won't ground swat them. In the morning or late in the afternoon, it is not uncommon to see 50 or a hundred of them loafing along the edges of fields or gobbling grit along the roadside. But, stop the truck, unkennel a dog, or run a couple of shells in your autoloader, and watch how fast they disappear. As my frustrating experience with the grease brush showed, valley quail can stick tighter than burned porridge to a pot. Although they are not the sprinters that scaled and Gambel quail are, they will bob off, their teardrop heads held high, looking like intelligent barnyard fowl. Their behavior makes you think of devious ways to get close, short of starting a backfire, and to force them into the air.

Sometimes, just as you are close to within shooting range, the whole bunch will take wing with a roar certain to throw your adam's apple in your throat. Then one of three things is likely to happen: You will forget to pick a single and miss cleanly; the covey will fly a couple dozen feet and either land in a tree or run into the puckerbrush; they will fly so low that you don't dare risk a shot for fear of shooting your dogs.

Unless you catch them in the open then—which isn't often—shots have to be quick. You'll want a lightweight, fast-swinging scattergun bored skeet or improved cylinder. An ounce of No. 8s in a clay-target load is good firepower.

Valley quail are sometimes confused with their desert-dwelling cousins, the Gambel quail. The males of each species sport black plumes that, to me, look like teardrops or comma marks. But Gambel quail roosters have black patches on their abdomens and scalelike feathering on their bellies. Facial bar markings of the two species are similar, but valley quail have whitish foreheads and chocolate-colored caps, whereas Gambels feature blackish foreheads and rust-colored caps. Other valley quail identifying features include slate-gray chests, black throats, gray-brown sides with light streaks, and speckled feathering on the nape. For topknots the hens sport small brushes that are a dark brown in color. Although the hens have scaling on the belly, too, they lack the facial bars and black throats of the males.

Valley quail begin nesting in April in fairly open cover. Clutches contain an average of 14 eggs, which hatch sometime in May or early June. Family units form summer coveys, and by August begin to grow as broods mix. By the hunting season, coveys often contain 20 to 80 birds. As winter approaches, they may grow substantially larger.

The native range of valley quail extends from southern Oregon through California to southern Baja California, Mexico, but game biologists and conservationists have successfully introduced these birds elsewhere in the West over the past 100 years. Before intensive farming and ranching practices ruined much of the habitat in their native range, valley quail were especially abundant. Excellent to eat, they served as a popular target of market hunters. Records show that thousands were sold in San Francisco each year.

California, where a million or more valley quail may be legally shot each season, offers the best hunting today. Washington and

Oregon may each yield 200,000 birds in a typical year. There are also plenty of legal targets in Nevada, Idaho, British Columbia, and Baja Mexico. Smaller huntable populations live in Utah, Hawaii, and Arizona.

A bird of the Western valleys and foothills, valley quail are associated with brush-choked ravines and riverbottoms. They occupy lower altitudes of most ranges except for heavily forested ones like the Coast and Olympic mountains. In California, they prefer dense, chapparal-covered hillsides. In Nevada, I found them along brush-clogged streams and irrigation ditches stuffed with tule weeds, grease brush, Indiangrass, and tumbleweeds. They also live in lowland sagebrush. In Oregon, valley quail are most often associated with farming in the

Staley Kent of Fallon, Nevada, with a hen valley quail. It was on her dad's ranch that the author finally shot a rooster valley quail to complete his Grand Slam of America's quail.

western part of the state and semi-arid desert lands in the east. In western and south-central Idaho, the birds live along stream bottoms, most notably the Snake River. In the Okanagan Valley of British Columbia, orchards are favored. In western Washington, they frequent cutover areas growing back to brush.

Although valley quail are often seen in open areas, heavy escape cover of brush, thick grass or low trees is usually a short distance away. They like to roost in impenetrable cover, either on the ground or in tall shrubs or low trees. In winter, they prefer evergreens for roosting. Whereas the bobwhite chooses roosting habitat with an escape route in mind, the valley quail picks cover where nothing can get to him.

San Stiver, a biologist with the Nevada Department of Wildlife, is an avid jogger and quail hunter. Both are running sports, especially in Nevada where four species of Western quail live. Stiver explains valley quail habitat and hunting techniques by comparing them to other quail species. *When after Gambel or scaled quail, wear tennis shoes because you're going to have to run flat out. With mountain quail, bring your hiking boots and a short-barreled shotgun for those close-in shots. For valley quail, any good machete will do.*

The birds I shot seemed very small, but that is probably because I had most recently been hunting mountain quail, which are considerably larger. Actually valley quail are about the same size as Gambel, scaled, and bobwhite quail. Their habitat somewhat overlaps that of the desert-dwelling Gambel and the mountain quail of higher elevations. Sometimes hunters get mixed bags. Valley quail hunters also commonly shoot pheasants and Hungarian partridge.

Valley quail are opportunistic feeders that can apparently switch back and forth from cultivated grain crops to wild foods. The availability of water and heavy roosting and escape cover is probably more important than the actual food type. In early fall the birds are apt to feed on filaree, lotus, lupine, clover, and small seeded grasses such as ryegrass, fescue, and bluegrass. Later in the fall, they may rely more heavily on Napa and Russian thistle, deervetch, mullein, and the seeds of sunflower and pigweed, as well as mast from pine and oaks. Buds, grasses, the green leafage of legumes, and leftover field grain, such as milo and wheat, become important food sources in winter.

Although in some areas it may seem as though hunters kill plenty of valley quail, they rarely impact the breeding population. Many years ago wildlife researchers conducted an experiment at San Joaquin Experimental Range in Madera County, California, to see how much of a fall population of valley quail could be safely harvested without

Valley quail roost in dense cover like this. They also seek heavy cover when threatened. Midmorning to midafternoon is a good time to hunt them as they move out from heavy cover then.

damaging the seed stock. Biologists inventoried populations on both an experimental (hunting) and control (nonhunting) area.

Over a four-year period, hunters in the experimental area shot as high as 40 percent of the known population. In March, post-season counts were noticably lower in the experimental area than they were in the control area. Yet each fall, numbers on both areas were about the same.

Successful hunting tactics begin with finding a covey. You can do this by driving roads and watching—even scoping with binoculars—for birds in open fields near edge cover. A band of four dozen or more quail won't go unnoticed for long by ranchers, school bus and delivery truck drivers, or rural postal carriers. So ask around.

Most valley quail live out their lives in an area containing a few hundred yards or less with long-range movements limited to unmated males in spring and translocated birds looking for a home. If quail are spotted by someone, chances are the birds won't be far away. Dusting bowls and tracks are recent calling cards worth checking out. Look for these signs along roadways and at watering spots such as cattle tanks, ponds, streams, and irrigation systems.

As mentioned earlier, private land is often the best place to find valley quail. Ask permission before entering. If you don't know who owns the property, stop at the county courthouse and ask to see a plat book.

Valley quail are talkative, a habit that can work in favor of the hunter. One researcher discovered that the adults make 14 different sounds associated with reproductive, parental, alarm, and social behavior. The contact note of *ut-ut*, usually made while the birds are feeding, is soft and may be difficult to hear. For that matter, to my ears, which are tone-deaf—thanks to a lifetime of shooting firearms and a summer of working at a General Motors pressed metal plant—so is the assembly call. It is a high-pitched whistle that sounds like *cu-ca-cow* and is often written as *chi-ca-go*. Birds that are separated and coveys going to roost often make this assembly call. Hunters can use it to pinpoint the birds' location.

Because valley quail roost in heavy brush, it makes little sense to get up early to hunt them until they have moved from the wall-to-wall cover into a more open feeding area. Mid morning is better yet because the quail will already have fed and will be lounging around in open or semi-open areas. Flushing dogs willing to bust the cover might be more practical than pointing breeds. A dog trained to retrieve is more important than his pedigree.

Early in the hunting season, before fall rains, the birds will concentrate near watering holes. A good hunting tactic, then, is to find water within a few hundred yards of roosting habitat with connecting cover between the two. A brushy ravine or fencerow loaded with vagrant sagebrush is an ideal travel corridor. The farther away from thick, nasty cover you can find valley quail, the better your shooting opportunities will be. Sometimes on a semi-open valley floor quilted with grass or sagebrush, two or three flushes are possible before the quail escape into the junglelike stuff. Although I've never hunted it, I understand that climax chapparal is the worst. The best way to get quail out of mature chaparral is to strafe it with napalm.

Craig Boddington, editor of *Petersen's Hunting* and a California quail gunner by way of Kansas bobwhites, once enjoyed some tremendous shooting on valley quail in the snow. *Bob Robb* [associate editor] *and I were hunting about 60 miles north of Los Angeles in foothills of the Mojave Desert,* Boddington told me. *A freak storm put 18 inches of snow on the ground, and the quail didn't know how to handle it. It shell-shocked them. There was no place for them to fly except into the open. Our shooting averages were great that day.*

Too bad there was no snow when I pulled into the Kents' yard that

Catching valley quail in the open is the best way to score on them. Chaucer retrieves bird the author shot.

January morning about eleven o'clock. Staley said the biggest covey on her parents' ranch held about 60 quail. She knew right where they would be—lounging in an open area between a wheat field and heavy cover along the irrigation ditch.

Sixty quail? I thought to myself. *This could be fun.* I didn't know much about valley quail then. The only other time I had been on a hunt for them was the previous fall when I tagged along with a friend one day. But I was gunless, unwilling to shell out $75 for a nonresident license for only a few hours of hunting.

The quail were right where Staley said they would be—loitering alongside the irrigation ditch. The only other time I had seen that many quail on the ground was at a gamebird farm in Georgia. As we approached, the whole covey began stepping out for brush along the ditch. My setters had seen the birds, too. Now they rushed ahead to cut them off.

A hundred wings in the air at once quickens the pulse of any bird hunter. It can also make him do foolish things, like flock shoot. I missed with both barrels. Most of the quail flew across the ditch, but a few settled down in the thicket a mere 20 yards away. Both dogs stopped in their frenzy to point separate clumps of grease brush a few feet apart. When I gave the first clump a good boot, a quail flushed, and I shot it before it could fly across the ditch. Holly brought that bird back. My first valley quail was a hen.

So were the next six birds, including that one-for-seven shameful shooting exhibition that I described at the beginning of this chapter. Meanwhile, Staley hadn't fired her gun. I asked her why not.

I've shot enough quail this year, she said. Then, as an afterthought. *But you go ahead. You're our guest and I know how bad you want a male to get mounted.*

The daily bag limit in Nevada is 10 quail. If I was going to take home a cockbird, I would have to pick my remaining shots carefully. It isn't easy, though, to spot a topknot on a six-ounce bird that flies as though it is being chased by a hawk with blood in his eye.

When Staley and I reached the end of the Kents' property, we crossed the waterway and started back up the other side. Halfway to the ranchhouse, Chaucer slammed into a rigid point over a low shrub I couldn't identify. I kicked it but nothing came out. Chaucer's eyes bulged. I kicked again, harder, and a little blue-gray target streaked out. The bird folded cleanly on the first shot, and when one of the dogs brought it back, I could see it was a rooster.

Valley and mountain quail sometimes share the same habitat, although generally the valley species are found at lower altitudes.

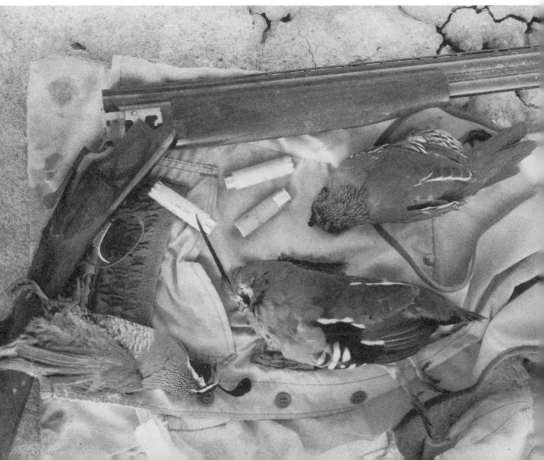

Valley Quail Distribution

Staley was as pleased as I. I turned the bird over and over in my hand, admiring the feather pattern and handsome mix of color. Michigan was more than 2,000 miles away. If the roads were dry, I might get home in time to watch the Super Bowl from my living room couch.

Anyone could see it was time to go home.

9

The Preserves

Yellow sand love dominated the late-autumn earthtones on our watercolorist's field of play. First, she brushed out a wash of the light yellow grass, then stroked in bits of sage gray, sand plum purple, salt cedar green, bone soapweed, russet bluestem. An arc of brown fringed with gray that transected the focal point on her canvas could be a river. Yes, the North Canadian River. And blurring some of the colors gave the appearance that the afternoon wind was up. *A good idea,* you decided. So was her choice of a late-November sky of dull pewter; it enriched the artist's creation with subdued yet concentrated light.

The wind *was* blowing where you stood on a low hill, looking out over the sand-sage prairie near Mutual, Oklahoma. You caught it peeking down your open shirt collar, and it rattled the soapweed heads that nodded across your hunting trousers.

But you weren't cold on this *Opening Day.* Was that because the weight of 10 bobwhites in the game bag tugged at your shoulders? And who could have guessed that the four of you would move 11 coveys and each kill limits today? Especially after that horrible delay this morning at a MacDonald's in Woodward. When the game warden *finally* showed up an hour late, he said he had no $10 nonresident licenses for five days. *Can you use a season permit for a fifty-dollar bill plus change?*

Bad luck turned to good, though, on the 5,000-acre ranch when guide Sam Van Nostrand's pointer, Pete, stood a 20-bird covey while you shucked your gun sleeve and forced three rounds into the 20-gauge pump.

The covey buzzed away like a brown-and-white swarm of over-grown bees. You pulled feathers on one bird, then rolled him cleanly on a second shot. Jerry Hedges, a veterinarian from Vici whom you had met barely an hour before, offered congratulations. You reminded him that he had just smoked a double.

Yeah, but we-all grew up hunting bobwhites, Jerry said. *Folks expect us to hit our birds.*

And so the day went: the dogs buttonhooking through the sage, while you, Jerry, Mike, and Rick followed with Sam, the guide, walking behind and not at all seeming to mind that he was gunless on opening day. Mike was the first to limit, then Jerry, you, and finally Rick. Later, when the light was gone, and you were helping the hired hands clean birds in a back room at the ranchhouse, you smelled barbecued ribs from the kitchen and heard your stomach complain.

I think we got a leg up on that game warden, after all, someone offered.

Such scenes occur across America during the long preserve hunting season, which may be year-round in some states. According to John M. Mullin, owner of Arrowhead Hunting and Conservation Club in Goose Lake, Iowa, and publisher of *Wildlife Harvest*—a magazine put out by the North American Gamebird Association—interest in preserve shooting is increasing after a 10-year decline.

Over five percent of the nation's sportsmen now belong to a shooting preserve or hunting club of some sort, Mullin said, *and many others visit as guests of members. There are several reasons for the surge in interest, but the biggest one is that upland bird hunters are running out of places to hunt.*

Other reasons include amenities for hunters such as meals, transportation, freezing birds, cooking school, conservation lectures, shooting instruction, dog training, and kenneling. Public awareness of the value of shooting preserves has also been heightened by recent articles in such prestigious publications as the *Wall Street Journal* and *Forbes Magazine.*

Bobwhite quail are key targets at many of the nation's private and commercial preserves. According to Mullin, 62 percent of NAGA's 323

Sam Van Nostrand, quail guide and owner of Cross Seven Safaris, from Mutual, Oklahoma, and Lady Macbeth. Author experienced his best day of wild-bird hunting with Sam when their party moved 11 coveys of bobwhites.

preserves open to the public stock quail. So do many of the closed-membership clubs and sportsmen's groups that comprise another 1,150 members. Below the Mason-Dixon Line, quail are king; above it, ring-necked pheasants and mallard ducks are more popular. For a directory of NAGA game clubs offering quail, refer to the Appendix in this book. Your state game department, which usually licenses the preserves, will most likely also have a listing.

Like it or not, preserve hunting for quail is here to stay. Actually, it has been with us for a long time, dating back a century or more and is as much an American hunting tradition as L. C. Smith doubles and L. L. Bean boots. Ironically, in the eyes of some sportsmen and non-sportsmen alike, these same traditions make for alleged elitism and snobbery among some of the established, expensive clubs with controlled membership.

Could be. But because I cannot afford a thousand dollars for a day's shooting or seven grand for a membership initiation fee, I don't know if those charges are true. I do know, however, that unlike wild turkeys or white-tailed deer, which are increasing across America, bobwhites in the wild are not. As quail habitat shrinks and hunting opportunities diminish, controlled shooting preserves—well heeled or not—grow in importance. The goal of most operators is to provide an experience as close to natural wild-bird hunting as possible. Many do an outstanding job, plus offer camaraderie and a host of other benefits. And there are enough clubs around now so that an upland gunner can sift through them to find the one that fits his sporting taste and budget.

What could be more relative, dollar-wise, than the sport of hunting? Hunters have always had, and will continue to have, the range of cost before them (although the bottom line keeps growing more expensive). This is true in clothing, dogs, guns, shells, vehicles, and preserves. The hunt of a lifetime for one man might be keyed to finding others willing to pool gas dollars for the long drive to hunt bobwhites in Tennessee. For another, it might be finding a pilot for his Lear jet so he can go there, too.

You can pay as little as $60 per day for a quality hunt on a quality preserve if you clean your own birds and don't expect any fringes. For

Preserve hunting is growing in popularity among the nation's quail hunters. Long seasons and liberalized bag limits are two of many reasons. *(Nebraska Game Commission photo)*

four figures per day, someone might carry your gun, handing it to you so you can shoot only covey rises. Some states have lowered the minimum size for a controlled shooting area to 100 acres, resulting in an increase of preserves near big cities. On the other hand, in Texas they may sprawl over 20,000 acres each. Some hunting clubs might go through only a few hundred birds in a season. At Riverview Plantation in Camilla, Georgia, they put out 140,000 bobwhites in a recent year. Clubhouse rules can range from a shirt-and-tie dress code at a mansion in upper New York state to jeans and hunting boots at a converted milking parlor in Kentucky.

Besides relative high cost and supposed effrontery, some preserves get knocked for putting out birds that fly no better than barnyard fowl. Bobwhites that are more eager to peck at the ground in front of dogs than to run to cover or freeze. It is tough to raise put-and-take quail that *really act* like wild birds. Overweight bobs that weigh nearly a pound each don't get airborne too quickly. When reared under wire, most don't develop their survival instincts. Indeed, Harry Rutherford, who manages leased ground for the Coleman Company in southeastern Kansas, leg-tagged more than 300 quail one year to see how many were taken by guests of the company and how many might be alive next year. The respective answers were 25 percent and one bird.

Mature, sporting birds that fly fast are available, however, and breeders who have learned how to raise them have found that they cannot provide them fast enough to meet demands. Besides breeding and rearing, though, much depends on how the birds are handled when put out for gunners and what the weather conditions are like. No bobwhite likes to take to the air when it is raining. Some liberated birds never do, especially when handlers deliberately dizzy them at plant out.

John Mullin, who—as a former Soil Conservation Service specialist—learned how to manage land to its maximum potential, has been in the preserve hunting business for more than 30 years. His vision of hunters' increased dependency on the controlled shooting areas is coming true. A former president of NAGA and a widely sought consultant, Mullin pioneered preserve hunting as it is known today. In addition to food plots such as corn, milo, and millet, fields at Arrowhead contain 40 annual grasses and legumes, which Mullin has allowed to spread through natural succession. In addition to his own 225 acres that overlook an ancient bed of the Mississippi River, Mullin leases another 1,173 acres of farmland from his neighbors.

Although I have met Mullin, a living legend among the game club

Many preserves offer sporting bobwhites that fly fast, much like wild birds. Jim Reid swings on a swift target as Greg Koch prepares to back him up.

operators, I have never visited Arrowhead. John Husar, who writes for the *Chicago Tribune*, has. Here is what Husar had to say in a recent column:

> "The Mullins (John and his wife, Gloria) do not exactly plant clutches of dizzy birds to await their doom. They cling to the old ethic that even game-farm hunting should be sport. They, therefore, guarantee that the birds are out there. Now you've got to find them and get off a shot. If you can.
>
> "Mullin rues the day that pay-by-the-bird was born. That economic incentive led in many cases to shooting birds as if they were fish in a barrel. If hunters paid for a certain number of birds, they felt obligated to kill that many. The next step was to make the killing easier, quicker, so there would be more time for more hunters to buy and kill more birds.
>
> "*You go to some of these places, and it's all production line,* Mullin says. *You look out over Field No. 1, or Field No. 2, or Field No. 3. You sit in the clubhouse and watch them dizzy the birds. They put 'em out in little clumps of cover surrounded by clearing. Then you hear your name over the loudspeaker. 'So-and-so party proceed to Field No. 2. Boom, boom, boom.*
>
> "Mullin prefers to charge by the hunt—say a maximum of

three birds, $65, license included. Shoot more and you pay a little more.

"I do believe that people will be willing to pay for a total experience, he says. *The shooting of a bird should be only a small part of the hunt. Out here, we don't sell a bunch of dead birds. We sell hunting. And that means it's going to be a challenge and not a turkey shoot."*

This philosophy, along with specific how-to guidelines, is what Mullin sells working and would-be game club operators—both as a consultant for hire and book author. Mullin's *Game Bird Propagation: The Wildlife Harvest System,* is the 194-page bible for the business.

Because preserves and guided hunting for quail are increasing in importance, I wanted to supplement wild-bird hunting with controlled experiences for pen-reared bobwhites. So I hunted on preserves in four states. I learned that some of the best (and most affordable) pay-for-hire sport occurs on private land in Oklahoma, a state that annually provides a bag of two million or more bobwhites. Ninety-five percent of Sooner real estate is owned privately. More than half of the remaining five percent is military installations and other government holdings where hunting is not allowed. Unless you have an uncle in the Oklahoma oil or cattle-rearing business, your chances of finding a good place to hunt are about as good as convincing the IRS that it should pay interest on the taxes you overpaid.

Sam Van Nostrand, 28, owner of Cross Seven Safaris in Mutual, offers guided hunts for only wild birds on his father's 5,000-acre ranch on sand-sage prairie along the North Canadian River. The fee is $150 per day per gun. Was it worth it? Like I said, we moved 11 coveys that day. It was the best day of bobwhite hunting I experienced while visiting eight states over three months.

Besides guiding for wild birds on private or leased land, some hunt-for-hire operators mix pen-reared quail with wild bobwhites to ensure that clients will get action. One is Grant Irwin, the 23-year-old owner of Black Gold Kennels in Woodward, Oklahoma. Irwin has been guiding for pay since he was 17. In the off-season, he sells cars in Phoenix and trains and raises pointers and setters. Irwin leases the hunting rights on 13,000 acres of cattle range in the sand-sage prairie. A spectrum of fee arrangements averages $185 per day per hunter.

When I hunted with Grant, we found birds along the hillsides and flats in soapweed, little bluestem and sand plum and in the clefts of hills in sumac, coralberry, and blackjack oak. But the bobs, even the pen-reared ones, were unaccountably spooky. For example, upon cresting a high hill, we jumped a covey of 20, then neither we nor our four dogs could find them for a reflush. The quail would run ahead of the dogs, then flush wild when they got too close. I saw 10 sprint soldierlike—in single file—across the road into a patch of little bluestem. The dogs found only two. Later, Grant's fine English pointer, Zeb, nailed a 30-bird covey on the edge of a small pond fringed with cedars. When I moved to within 15 yards, with my leashed setter, in an effort to get her to honor, the birds whirred out the other side and no one got a shot. We did manage to find several singles, however, tallying 15 quail for the morning hunt and several more in the afternoon.

The air had been cemetery still all day while heavy cloud folds low overhead worked in and out of each other as though they were digesting something. A storm was coming and that probably was why the quail had scattered widely to feed. Being thus vulnerable, they were goosey.

I hope it isn't a snowstorm, Irwin said. *Two years ago, we got hit pretty hard with ice and snowstorms. They knocked our birds down pretty bad. Last year we were only 25 percent of normal. This year, though, we're at 75 percent.*

Grant got his wish. That night it rained instead of snowed.

I hunted one other controlled shooting area in Oklahoma, stopping at the Double W Ranch in Beggs, about 25 miles southwest of Tulsa, shortly after Christmas. I was enroute to the Southwest to hunt Western quail but wanted to bag some bobwhites first. The Double W Ranch is owned by Greg and Jeannine Koch, a couple in their late 20s, who also board hunters and kennel and train bird hunting dogs. The

Grant Irwin, quail hunting guide and bird-dog trainer from Woodward, Oklahoma, mixes hunting for pen-reared birds with wild bobwhites on leased land.

Greg Koch of Beggs, Oklahoma, is a quail guide and dog trainer specializing in pointing breeds for pen-reared quail. Koch guides on the Double W, a shooting preserve owned by him and his wife.

Kochs have 11,000 acres at their disposal and actively manage 900 acres for bobwhites, pheasants, and Hungarian partridge. They also supplement with pen-reared birds.

Non-member guided hunts are $215 for a half day and $395 for a full day. Guides, dogs, transportation, cleaning of birds, and refreshments in the field are included.

Koch is a top dog trainer and handler who is getting up to $6,000 each for fully trained pointers and setters. He and a mutual friend, Jim Reid, a former outdoor writer for the *Wichita Eagle-Beacon*, have put together a hot-selling video on Koch's training methods. Reid, who joined us on a morning hunt, helped me shoot bobwhites from food plots of milo next to native bluestem and in draws of blackjack oak with a ground cover of Bermuda grass. The birds Greg had planted out flew well, especially in the covey rise where it all matters.

Quail hunting in America has its roots in the Southeast and Deep South, where the still-popular sport is steeped in tradition. How could I write a book on quail hunting without looking at partridge pea close up, without getting red clay on my boots from walking in Georgia fields? The day after returning from the Southwest, I balanced the checking account, called a couple of creditors to offer imaginative excuses for late payments, then booked a super-saver flight to Atlanta and a two-day hunt at Burnt Pine Plantation in Madison. There, the daily rate for 12 bobwhites is $195 per person.

Steve Smith, a magazine editor and friend from Saginaw, Michigan, joined me in early March as the long preserve season was winding to a close. We rented a car in bustling Atlanta, then witnessed the emergence of spring while driving through the Georgia countryside. Wild daffodils lined the rust-red gravel roads that looked as though someone had covered them with paprika. The wheat was up in greening splendor, and I saw a pod of yellow-and-black swallowtails hovering over a mud puddle when I took a slow curve.

The town of Madison features classical Greek architecture on homes that were here when Sherman marched through. It was late afternoon when we followed the road sign to "Antioch Church, founded in 1809." At the end of a red gravel road with sharecropper cabins to either side stood the white clapboard church. Next to it was a cemetery with weathered tombstones. I read somewhere that in the South you can often find quail around a sawdust pile, a flower garden, or a cemetery. We sat in the car a moment, while rain spattered the windshield. Hard to believe that mere hours earlier we had left a place where spring was a light year away. Here it was bursting all over.

Call me a liar, if you wish, but a covey of quail flew low over the cemetery and disappeared in the gloom of pines on the other side. Smitty and I looked at each other and laughed.

On the slow drive back to the highway in the dusk, we again passed a shack with a rusted antenna atop it. Now, bare bulbs threw shafts of yellow light into the yard, which was surrounded by somber pines. I stopped the car, overwhelmed by a strong sense of *déjà vu*. A mud-colored hound stuck out his head from what looked like a cardboard box that once held a television. As though scenting game, he threw back his head and yelped. Three other mean-looking dogs suddenly lunged from similar kennels to howl at the ends of their chain tethers. I half expected someone from a Faulkner novel to step from the shack.

Smitty inhaled deeply from his ever-present pipe, then blew a plume of smoke out the side window. *Do you realize you're looking at a cliche?* he said.

Yes, I know, like everything else we've seen so far in Georgia.

Burnt Pine Plantation was not a cliche. Instead of a sprawling mansion anchored with Ionian pillars, the clubhouse was a modest

brick home with unraked mortar joints. There was no black dog handler to sing to the pointers. Our guide was Bob "Kit" Carson, 21, who
was earning money to go back to college. We also hunted with Colonel
Gerald Graham, a colorful dog trainer about whom I wrote in the
chapter on dogs.

Burnt Pine is managed by 23-year-old David Blanton, who holds a
degree in business administration. Lawrence Wood, a full-time biologist, manages the 12,000-acre holdings for whitetails and quail. Wood
does a good job. Last year, hunters tagged some 200 deer and shot
more than 30,000 bobwhites, mostly pen-reared birds, but wild quail
are also available. Smitty and I reduced one covey we stumbled across
by only two birds.

**Colonel Gerald Graham, a Georgia bird-dog trainer and quail hunter for more than
60 years, counts bobwhites held by Bob Carson, a guide at Burnt Pine Plantation near
Madison.**

Controlled burning in the South promotes growth of desirable bobwhite foods. Steve Smith takes aim on a single that flushed from broomsedge under the loblolly pines.

Three colors—loblolly green, broomsedge copper, and Piedmont clay red—dominate the rolling landscape in this region of central Georgia. The red clay is mostly subsoil, worn out and exposed over years of growing cotton, which, like corn in the Midwest, is all take and no put.

A fourth color, black, is characteristic in early spring, too. It is caused from burning the property, on a three-year rotation, to remove duff under the pines and to clean up fields. Each of Burnt Pine's 12 quail courses is torched annually. Besides adding potash to the soil, controlled burning eliminates the growth of undesirable plants and stimulates a surge of lespedeza, partridge pea, and beggar lice—all important Southern quail foods. Wood and the others burn mostly at night when conditions of temperature, humidity, and wind are just right, and they are careful to create a slow burn with the correct number of backfires so as not to kill the pines.

Burning of quail habitat is a widespread practice in the South. Some game-club plantations in southern Georgia manicure their property for bobwhites only. They do not release pen-reared quail at all, and guests are allowed to shoot covey rises only. These are the clubs that charge dearly, assuming you can get an invitation to go there in the first place.

The operators at Burnt Pine Plantation allow you to individualize your hunt. In other words, you can expect all your birds in a single covey rise or have them spread out throughout the course. Most of the courses are a half-mile to a mile long and about a quarter-mile wide. They contain broomsedge (also called broomstraw) ringed with loblolly pines and, here and there, a food plot of sorghum or rye grass.

A good handler does not allow the dogs to race through the course to the end. Instead, he ushers them out of the hunt area to loosen up and to take care of personal business, then sends them into the wind or at least across the wind so that they can stitch their way through the cover. The dogs must adapt to the pattern that the trainer, who likely set out the birds earlier that morning, wants. He holds the dogs in the area of the first release until they find the drop, then moves on, thus lengthening the hunt and the client's enjoyment.

Smitty and I went over our budgets a little, potting 75 birds in two days of hunting. It was fine sport, and I was challenged both by the tricky targets of the strong-flying quail and Smith's sharp shooting eye. The only thing missing was my own dogs, but I can appreciate the fine dog handling and bird work by others. Besides, I learn more when my own animals aren't around.

There will always be quail hunting in America, but preserves are going to play an increasingly significant role. I'd like to think we don't need them, but the truth is that we do and they fill an important need with thousands of upland gunners. Besides, how else am I ever going to know what it is like someday to slap down a thousand-dollar bill and challenge someone to show me the bobwhite hunt of a lifetime? I'd like to do it the way some claim it was always meant to be.

Just once, I'd like to bounce on a buckboard wagon pulled by mules while we follow a brace of picture-perfect pointers, Jess and Bob, in the broomstraw. I'd like to see them *On Point*, tails up like fencing swords, a knot of bobwhites pinned somewhere between. I'd like to hear Simon, the black trainer, croon to the entranced dogs in a voice as smooth as Nat King Cole's.

Come on, Bob, stand that bird. Come now, Jess, back that Bob.

I'd like to pick out a scrambling target in the tack-hammer frenzy of wings that marks all covey rises, shoot well—twice—and witness Jess and Bob retrieve two dead birds to hand. Then, I'd like to know the feeling of ignoring the singles, climbing back in the wagon, and watching the dogs fan out in search of yet another covey.

Roger Wells, a field representative for Quail Unlimited, once hunted a half-day for $500 at such a bobwhite paradise.

How was it? I wondered.

Pop break at Burnt Pine Plantation. The hunters are Steve Smith, Colonel Gerald Graham, and Bob Carson. Smith and the author went over their budgets with the excellent shooting they found at this preserve.

Unbelievable, Wells said. *The hunt of a lifetime.*

Yeah, but was it worth it? I mean, how many coveys, for half a grand, did you move?

Thirty-four.

10

The Guns and Loads

I wrote this chapter last because I figured it would be the hardest to do. It would have been, too, had I tried to tell you how to pick the ideal quail hunting shotgun with an eye to comb, heel, and length of pull. Why one model or action is superior to another. Or why you should adopt the Churchill method of shooting as opposed to sustained lead.

Sorry if I disappoint you, but I leave that kind of advice to those who know what they are talking about.

Most of us bird hunters don't really care that much about why one gun shoots better than another. We just know that it does. At the risk of sounding chauvinistic, picking the right shotgun is like picking the right woman. Sometimes your taste may change over the years. Like many of you, my first kiss was with a single-shot .410. I went steady with a 16-gauge bolt-action and married a Wingmaster 870 pump in 12-gauge. When that ended, I flirted with double-barrels for a short time, then had a second go with the pump gun. My current love affair is with 20-gauge over-and-unders—the cheaper field-grade models that I can afford.

Does it really matter what you shoot so long as it feels right and you can hit with it? So your 20-gauge single-shot has a tight hammer and the previous owner's name scratched into the stock with a 10-penny nail? It was only $24 at the garage sale, wasn't it? The cost was a thousand times less than a Lebeau-Courally Boss pattern sidelock in over-and-under, yet you can shoot just as well with it.

During my travels, I got to see the range of quail guns and good shooting by owners tuned to their weapons. In Iowa, Larry Brown trusted his 16-gauge Sauer, which he carried on a sling. In Kansas, 13-year-old Rodney Oursler and his .410 Mossberg looked just right. In Georgia, so did 76-year-old Colonel Gerald Graham with his 20-gauge Franchi automatic with pistol grip. Steve Smith, who went with me to Georgia, shot a straight-grip Ithaca side-by-side in 20 gauge. Smitty says most shooters' misses are due to lifting the head and firing over targets. A straight-grip gun throws the elbow higher, making it unnatural to lift the head, and so he prefers straight-gripped guns. Makes sense to me.

Besides, I don't argue with people who outgun me, which is why I get along with nearly everyone.

Those Kansas farmers swore by their Remington pump guns with shiny triggers and Poly-Chokes. In Missouri, 1100 automatics with Cutts Compensators seemed to be the farmer's scattergun of choice. In Oklahoma, Jerry Hedges was deadly with his 870 pump in 22-inch barrel. In Kansas and Oklahoma, Mike Pearce could have hit fruit flies on the wing with a Ruger Red Label in 12 gauge.

Some of these hunters told me stories about so and so who could kill four, five, six quail on a covey rise. *You have five shots in the auto-loader, see, and you just ignore the lead bird altogether, 'cause if you hit him, then you have to jump around and find another target. No, the way to move through a covey is to start at the back door. You trip the trigger on a rear bird, then keep firing as you pass the others in the string.*

I rarely allow myself to go for doubles, unless the covey rise is staggered, but I suppose that is not a true double anyway. One reason for my reluctance is that it is difficult to mark more than one downed bird, plus keep an eye on the surviving singles for reflushes. Second, sometimes even the best dogs miss shot game, especially air-washed birds that drop to the ground dead and leave little scent. You may have to find those birds yourself. Third, I don't want to compress a day's bag limit into one or two covey rises.

The main reason, though, is that I don't like to see a covey mown down. It smacks of greed. Yes, I can appreciate fine shooting—a couple of birds, sure, but five or six? What does it prove? You can tell how good a wingshooter someone is on one or two birds.

Jerry Hedges of Vici, Oklahoma, relies on this pump gun with 22-inch barrel for hitting fast-flying Sooner State bobwhites.

But I don't mean to get into an ethics argument, nor is it my desire to convince you that my way of thinking is right. After all, each of us lives with our inconsistencies.

The Importance of Attitude

I am sure, though, that good shooting is as much an attitude as it is proper fit, gauge, choke, and load. You have to have confidence in your shotgun and yourself. I used to hunt three-day weekends for pheasants and quail in Iowa. After a layover of several months, I invariably punched holes in the sky five feet behind my targets on the first day. On the second day, by increasing my lead, I at least knocked birds down. On the third, I killed them cleanly. Then, next fall I would have to refind the touch. I envy those wingshooters who never lose it. Steve Grooms, a friend of mine, shot more than 40 cock pheasants one year with less than two boxes of shells. Another time I loaned Mike Cox my pump gun and a handful of shells when it was my turn to drive a weed field in Kansas. Cox killed three ringnecks with three shells *in my gun.* Some guys are just naturally good with any weapon.

I'm not, even with my own gun. And I'm really lousy when I have other things on my mind. In Chariton, Iowa, where I had gone to hunt quail, my friend Willy Suchy agreed to meet me about 12:30 at the state park campground where I was staying. I had the generator running in the motorhome and was just finishing up a long magazine article when Willy pulled up in his truck. In my haste, I hit the wrong keystroke on the word processor. Zap went the entire story—six hours of work down the drain. *Yes, I had failed to make a backup disk.* When things like that happen or when my mind is on the car payment and the overdue dentist bill, I shoot poorly. I get distracted and can't bear down on the business at hand. The same thing happens to my male setter when my female is in heat.

I don't even want to talk about that aborted afternoon with Willy Suchy. If he ever decides to, I know an unemployed extortionist in Des Moines.

The Importance of Positioning

Improper positioning probably accounts for as many missed quail, by good and poor shooters alike, as anything else. If you have a good idea where quail not only will flush but where they are likely to go, you can place yourself in the best possible shooting position. When quail get up, they pretty much head in a straight line, filling the

The author is suffering from a current love affair with over-and-unders. Bottom to top are a Ruger Red Label, Weatherby Orion, Browning Citori, and Winchester 101. *(Randy Carrels photo)*

quickest flushing lane to the heaviest cover around. That will be timber or brush, what I referred to as *escape* or *security cover* in an earlier chapter.

Like a newly hatched turtle knows enough to head for water, quail instinctively know where the security cover is. In nearly every instance, busted birds streak for this escape cover, often flushing low to take advantage of brush and sometimes darting in and out of it. The toughest shots occur when you catch them on the edge of escape cover. Then, there is little you can do except back off 10 yards and fire a rock—hopefully missing your dog—to stir the birds to wing. That is why some hunters train their pointing breeds to charge in on command. Other shooters take turns with their partners—one moves the birds while the other shoots; then they reverse the order. The hunter who triggers the flush will also get occasional shots at errant birds that squirt left and right instead of straight out.

When the cover allows, you can sometimes get between birds and where they want to go. This may force them to change their mind in

There is precious little time whenever quail take to the air. Being ready and in position (note gun up and index finger over trigger guard) are keys to good shooting. *(Nebraska Game Commission photo)*

midair, providing you with another milli-second and a new shooting angle. *There is precious little time* whenever quail take to wing. Close flushes, the ones that occur right under your nose, are the hardest shots of all. That's because they are deceiving—you actually have far less time than you think.

Speaking of in-the-face flushes, Steve Smith walked down to the edge of a swamp one afternoon in Georgia to see if he could find a single he had marked from an earlier covey rise. He found the bird all right. When it flushed underfoot, Smitty stuck out his gun barrel and the bird ran into it and broke its neck. In Missouri, David Denayer told me about how one time his brother Charlie encountered a quail that knocked itself cold after hitting his gun barrel. Feeling pretty smug about not wasting a shell, Charlie reached down to pick up the bird. When it buzzed off, he threw away a handful of shells on misses.

Stay Tuned to Your Dog. Being in tune with your dog through eye contact can help with positioning yourself for the best shots, too. Lady Macbeth in particular flicks glances from me to birds she has nailed. Knowing where they are, then, helps me to determine where they will go. Of course, it doesn't always work out the way I think it should. One time in Iowa, Macbeth told me with her eyes that she had a bobwhite pegged on the other side of a swath of bootjack. The snipe that zinged out surprised me so much that I missed with both barrels.

Another time in Oklahoma, Macbeth insisted that a big covey was in the soapweeds ahead of us. There was a big covey all right, about 30 birds. But they flushed a few feet off to our left a split second after

When hunters take turns forcing the flush, sometimes they both get action. Jim Reid and Greg Koch show how it is done.

the single at our feet decided it could no longer take the heat of my dog staring it in the face. I was swinging through on the single when the roar of wingbeats on my blind side caused me to lift my head. Sure, I missed.

Approaching the Point. A brief, but important, comment about working with your dog. When moving in on a point, always let the dog see you. A 45-degree angle is about right. And because your pointing partner is in a trance, never shoot over his head. (How would you like it if someone fired off a round behind your back?) At best, you will only make him nervous, but you can also destroy all staunchness and might even render the animal gun shy..

Further, hold the gun about a third of the way up and at a 45-degree angle so that you are looking over the muzzle. Any time you are carrying a gun—whether approaching a point or not—place your thumb on the safety and point your index finger on the same plane as the barrel but along or over the trigger guard (never on the trigger itself). That way you will be always ready yet exercising safety at the same time.

Many hunters use the step-and-slide approach to birds being stood by a pointing dog. The method works well, especially when birds are spooky or when poor footing might unbalance the shooter. By simply sliding your left foot forward one step, then drawing the right foot after it, you will never be off balance.

Play the Wind Game. Which is worse, a high wind or no wind? *Both are equally bad,* says Colonel Graham, *because you need some wind for the dogs. But too much wind throws the scent all over and makes the birds nervous.*

When I hunted with him, the colonel was consistently tossing handfuls of broomstraw into the air. He does this for two reasons. One is to help him hunt into or across the wind so that the dogs get full advantage of available scenting conditions. The second is to get himself into shooting position because he knows that quail, when given the chance, nearly always flush into the wind. Of course, in a real blow, they will then catch the jetstream and zoom out of range as though hurled from giant slingshots. Shooting scores suffer on windy days.

Gauge and Choke

Steve Smith believes that the 20 gauge was designed with quail hunting in mind. The size and fragility of the birds demand nothing heavier. A one-ounce load of shot in 20 gauge strings farther than, say,

Twenty-gauge guns with an ounce of shot in a target load are ideal for hunting quail.

a 16 or 12-gauge round. Because most shots at bobwhites are straight-aways, you catch the target with the beginning or end of the string. On the other hand, by using the one-ounce loads in larger gauges with correspondingly shorter shot strings, you are more apt to hit birds with the full impact. Then, you will pouch feathers, not meat.

Twenty-gauge shotguns are generally lighter, easier to carry, and faster handling than the bigger bores. My favorite quail gun is a Browning Citori Superlight that weighs 6 pounds, 11 ounces. With 24-inch barrels (mine are 26-inch), you can scale down this fine gun to only 5 pounds, 12 ounces. There is a 20 gauge that's even lighter—the Model 37 English Ultralite made by Ithaca. The five-pounder I used a few times on my Midwest trip made me think of sparrow hunting in junior high school with a Red Ryder BB gun.

With 20-gauge guns, you have a tendency to get on the bird right away, too, Steve said. *After all, good shooting is a reflex action, and where you get into trouble is when you think about your shots. Time and again, I have seen first-time shooters on the skeet range smoke their doubles—out of pure reflex shooting—then miss the singles because they had too much time to think about hitting them.*

There is nothing wrong with using shotguns other than 20 gauge for quail. On preserves where pen-reared birds are apt to flush close and courses are manicured for open shooting, a 28 gauge is a fine choice. Many Western quail hunters, and, to an increasing degree, Midwest bobwhite gunners, rely on 12-gauge guns. That is because shots are often taken at greater distances and because pheasants,

Gary Sears likes a Poly-Choke on his Remington 1100 for hunting the strip-mine country near his Missouri home. With a twist of the Poly-Choke, Gary can set his pattern to any desired.

Improved cylinder in the bottom tube and full choke in the top was the right over-and-under combination to enable the author to bag these scaled quail in New Mexico.

prairie grouse, chukars, and Hungarian partridge are other targets that require more punch than quail do to put down.

Which leads us to a discussion of choke. Most single-barrel-toting quail hunters choose improved cylinder or modified. Those with twin tubes, like me, usually prefer a barrel of each. Screw-in chokes, available on many of the newer model shotguns, are a quail hunter's boon. When I bought my Citori, screw-in chokes had not yet appeared. Knowing that on my trips I would be hunting on all conditions of terrain and weather, I borrowed a couple of 20-gauge over-and-under scatterguns with removeable chokes to see how they would perform. In Kansas, I added improved cylinder in the under barrel and full choke in the upper tube of a Winchester 101, then stepped out after those running scaled quail I had heard so much about. The full-choke barrel proved ideal for the 30 and 35-yard covey rise shots. The more open barrel was just right for the singles that held for close flushes.

That improved cylinder/full choke combination also did the job on scaled and Gambel quail in New Mexico and Arizona, only I was using a Weatherby Orion, another fine over-and-under. Praying that the airline would not lose it, thus forcing me to fork over $800, I took the borrowed Orion to Georgia for a go at those close-flushing plantation quail. I shot reasonably well for a change, thanks to skeet choke in the lower tube and improved cylinder in the upper.

Loads

Closely allied to choke and gauge is the type of load. Like shotguns, no one shotshell is the hands-down winner for quail. Although I have no statistics to report, No. 8 shot in a target round is probably the most popular load among quail hunters. It is most likely followed by No. 7½ and No. 9. A few hunters use No. 6 shot, too. Years ago when it was widely available, fine No. 10 shot was popular with some bobwhite gunners. But it is difficult, if not impossible, to obtain today. Ballistic Products, Inc. in Minneapolis, a major supplier of components to the nation's shotshell reloaders, has not handled No. 10 shot for several years and, when I called them, knew of no source for inclusion in this book.

Shot Size. Why might one size shot be advantageous over another? Consider the following table, which shows the number of lead pellets in a one-ounce load:

No. 6 shot	223 pellets
No. 7½ shot	350 pellets
No. 8 shot	409 pellets
No. 9 shot	585 pellets
No. 10 shot	868 pellets

No. 8 and No. 9 shot work fine for close-in shooting with open chokes because there are more pellets to make a full pattern fast. As their shots increase in distance, though, most hunters choke down to keep the integrity of their pattern—in other words, they also use heavier shot, which penetrates better at greater distances.

Wind Velocity. There are some other considerations to think about when choosing a quail load. According to the Nilo Shotshell Efficiency Test by the Olin Corporation, wind can greatly affect shotshell patterns. When the wind is blowing at 10 mph, for example, a pattern of No. 4 lead shot will move six inches at 40 yards. Wind does not alter the shape of the pattern; it merely moves the pattern over. The smaller the shot size (and the stronger the wind velocity), the greater the amount of movement.

In Nevada, I knew I would have a tough time bagging mountain quail, and so I wanted to be ready if the chance presented itself. As I related in that respective chapter, I shot only two birds during four days of effort. For the first score, I relied on my old standby Citori with No. 8 shot. (Federal Premium Field Load with 1 ounce of shot and 2½ drams of powder. Equivalent loads include Remington Shur Shot Field Loads and Winchester Upland Field Loads.) The next afternoon when I entered the Smith Valley at about 7,000 feet altitude, the wind was blowing hard. It danced through the pinyon pine, making it appear as though the trees were breathing. I figured I might benefit from a heavier load with larger shot, and I made sure, too, that I had one barrel in full choke for a long poke if needed. I screwed in improved cylinder and full Winchokes in the 101 and grabbed a handful of Federal Premium Hi-Power Loads (1 ounce of shot, 2¾ drams of powder) in No. 6 copper-plated shot.

I only got to fire one shell that afternoon, but it did the job. At 30 yards I killed the only mountain quail I saw as it tried to escape up a hillside.

Altitude. While on the subject of altitude, Western quail hunters should keep in mind that the higher one travels, the less air resistance there is to a shotshell pattern. Tests, for example, have shown that modified patterns at sea level may turn into full-choke patterns at 5,000 feet.

Temperature. Temperature is yet another, though perhaps less important, consideration for quail hunters. The colder that lead shot becomes, the less penetrating power it has. Muzzle velocity of No. 8 shot, for example, is reduced 25 percent at −40 degrees than it is at 70 degrees. If you are hunting in bitter cold conditions, therefore, you might want to slip a couple of shells in an inner pocket to keep them warm.

Cover Type. Heavy brush conditions call for finer shot. In Missouri, for example, I relied on No. 9 shot in improved cylinder or skeet choke tube. Increased number of pellets helped me strain the pattern through dense brush and thickets that covered the abandoned coal strip-pits where we were hunting.

Time of Year. As we saw earlier, when winter comes on, screening cover shrinks, concentrating quail and making them more vulnerable

Good quail loads. Note pellet-size difference of No. 6 shot from No. 7½ and No. 8. *(Randy Carrels photo)*

to predators. Adding hunting pressure turns quail into nervous flushers. Sometimes they won't wait for the dog to pinch them into holding. Also, juvenile birds have grown into strong-flying adults who know how to separate themselves from danger in a hurry. Fully plumaged, they also need more punch to be put down. The late season is when many hunters leave the No. 8 and No. 9 loads in the gun cabinet and reach for No. 7½ or even No. 6 instead.

For the most part, quail hunters probably don't need *buffered shot*, but if you are hunting in an area where there are pheasants or other big birds, it can certainly help. In Iowa, it was frustrating to have to switch back and forth from pheasant to quail loads. Ever since Steve Grooms began touting the merits of copper-plated shot a few years ago for stopping pheasants cold, I have been relying on it in No. 6 shot in a field or magnum round. That is too much firepower for quail, but copper-plated shot is now available in smaller pellets. Winchester Double-X Game Loads in No. 7½ magnum 20 gauge contain 1⅛ ounce of shot and 2¾ drams of powder. Remington Power Pattern and Federal Premium Field Loads now come in No. 7½ and No. 8 copper-plated shot in only a 1 ounce load with 2½ drams of powder.

You can cleanly dust quail with copper-plated shot in No. 7½ or No. 8. And you can stop a pheasant's cackle with it if you hit him in the head.

What about *steel shot*? Is there a place for it among quail hunters? I think so. Because steel is lighter than lead, there are more pellets to the ounce. One ounce of No. 6 shot contains only 223 lead pellets but 315 steel pellets, an increase of about 35 percent. And the standard 20-gauge steel load is one ounce. True, you don't gain more shot in a shell designed to hold only so many pellets. What you do gain, however, is less weight. And because steel is lighter than lead, it shoots faster and patterns more tightly than lead. Of course, that also means that it slows down faster, too, usually after about 30 yards. Steel shot may have merit, then, as a lightning-quick load at short range.

The last time I hunted pheasants after a break of several months, I turned to steel shot when I just couldn't seem to lead far enough and fast enough on those long-tailed speedsters. It paid off with improved scores and confidence. Soon I had my shooting eye back and turned

Which shells to use—quail loads or pheasant loads? It is not an easy choice if you are hunting where both gamebirds live. Copper-plated shot is one answer.

again to lead loads. I have not used steel shot on quail but see no reason why it wouldn't work, too. Both Federal and Winchester now offer manufactured loads in No. 6 steel shot. As to the number of pellets per ounce, No. 6 steel approximates No. 7½ lead.

All the ballistics and statistics notwithstanding, some of America's best quail shots are men and women who grew up with shotguns in their hands. Natural wingshooters, they know nothing about the finer points of lead and follow through. They simply go out and shoot well—with their own or borrowed guns—day after day, season after season.

The best way to become a good shooter of quail is to step out and do it. A big dose of humility helps now and then, too. I get to experience plenty of that, thanks to the people with whom I hunt.

11

The Quail Dogs

Hills in the sand-sage prairie of Oklahoma were the hardest on old Sam. Every time the 13-year-old lemon-and-white pointer topped one, his sides heaved and his unsteady legs wobbled like bowling pins about to tip over. Sam's jowls hung and his knees were swollen with arthritis, too. But a snootful of bobwhite scent gave the old dog dignity and new life. You could see it when he went *On Point*. Nose as low as the sand burs, buggy-whip tail straight up. Then, only the deep bow in Sam's back gave his age away.

Sam had heart, too, He kept up with us hunters, every now and then lunging forward after the younger dogs whenever he got his second wind. He honored at every opportunity, sometimes as far as 100 yards away. Instant honoring was a good way to catch his breath. He knew, too, that if timed just right, he could sneak in a false point every so often without blowing his cover. *The older he gets, the more he does that,* said Grant Irwin, Sam's owner.

I was hunting with Grant, who trains dogs and leases land for guided hunts near his home in Woodward, Oklahoma. Later in the day old Sam retrieved a bobwhite I had shot from a stream bottom.

Grant let him gum the bird awhile before giving it up. I didn't mind; after all, it was Sam's first quail of the season.

Quail dogs, young and old alike, make the sport, sport. I don't think I would hunt quail without a dog although I recognize there are those who do and who seem to enjoy the game as much as I or anyone else. But *The Bird*, *The Dog* and *The Hunter* are like key players in a grand drama. *The Bird* is the whole purpose of the play and provides the hoped-for promise—a covey rise. Remove *The Dog* and what do you have? An epilogue with no prologue, for *The Dog*—whether he is a flushing or a pointing breed—gives the first clue to the unfolding drama. Take away *The Hunter* and there is no chorus or critic. No chronicler to record the event in memory, over a campfire beer that night, in a slide talk months later, on the printed page.

Colonel Gerald Graham, a Georgia quail hunter and dog trainer for most of his 76 years, explains the importance of dogs to hunting quail much better than I: *I wouldn't give you a dime to shoot all the quail in Georgia without a dog, but I'd walk to Atlanta to see a pretty point.*

Old Sam with his first retrieve of the hunting season. Grant Irwin, his owner, let him gum the author's bobwhite awhile before giving it up.

What Makes a Quail Dog?

Nearly any bird dog that has a good nose, a tractable disposition, and a reasonable amount of intelligence can be taught to hunt quail. Because bobwhites in particular hold so well (at least the farm-bred bobs do; wild birds can be something else entirely), most serious quail hunters prefer pointing breeds, but there are plenty of good flushing dogs in service, too. English pointers remain a favorite in the Deep

Pointing breeds like the author's setter, Lady Macbeth, in photo are most popular among quail hunters. But flushing breeds like Mysti, a golden retriever owned by Mike Pearce of Kansas, perform equally well, too.

South and in Oklahoma and Texas. New Mexican hunters prefer Brittanies. Arizonans like Brits, too, along with German shorthairs. Midwest bobwhite hunters lean toward setters and Labrador retrievers. In Nevada, setters are most popular. Springer and French Brittany spaniels, Gordon setters, German wirehaired pointers, viszlas, griffons, weimaraners, and pudelpointers are lesser-known dogs that can all shine when sent out to hunt quail.

People are like religion when it comes to dogs, Colonel Graham, who was the key aide to General McArthur during World War II, told me. *They get attached to one breed, and then they become blind to the good points of others.* When I hunted with the colonel at Burnt Pine Plantation near Madison where he guides part time, he owned 31 dogs at the time. They included pointers, setters, Brittanies, Labradors and a Chesapeake Bay retriever. During a rest break one afternoon (at my request, not his), we talked about the merits of different breeds.

What do you look for then, I asked, *in a quail hunting dog?*

The colonel picked a couple of beggar lice from his hunting pants. *He has to like feathers,* he said.

The breed, then, is much less important than the dog himself. Is he spirited and does he look for birds in the likely places? Does he have guts enough to hunt all day, and will he hunt under all conditions—bone-dry days with stifling heat, freezing ones when ice balls form between his toes? Does he circle the tough cover—blowdowns so tangled they could stop a bulldozer, fencerows so thorny they could turn back a machete—or dive into it? Does he *Hunt Dead* and will he retrieve to hand? If he is a flushing dog, does he range within shooting distance? If he points, is he staunch and will he back the other pointers? Does he kennel on command and obey other important orders?

Most importantly, perhaps, does he enjoy hunting with you and for you, and do you appreciate what he is all about?

There is nothing more grand than seeing a quail dog do what it was bred to do and do it very well. Even if the owner did not train the animal, he can take a tremendous amount of pleasure and pride for seeing that someone did. The truth is, few hunters have the patience, fortitude, and knowledge to train their own hunting dogs to completion.

Training the Quail Dog

There is nothing wrong with trying to teach your dog everything you can. And there are several good books available today on how to do it. Good ones I have read and borrowed from include *Hunt Close* by Jerome Robinson, *Gun Dog* by Richard Wolters, and *Gun Dog Training Spaniels and Retrievers* by Ken Roebuck.

The problem with any book on dog training is that every dog is different, and no one book can explain what to do in every instance. The best trainers tell me they are constantly learning from the dogs left in their care. The honest ones admit that there are dogs even they can't train.

Also, the training methods change. Fifty years ago, writer Ozark Ripley advised hunters whose quail dogs chased rabbits to kill every

Rodney Oursler of Kansas plays keepaway with Chaucer. All hunting is a learning experience, but bobwhites are the perfect gamebird for young shooters and young dogs.

rabbit they saw, then tie as many as possible around the errant dog's neck. After a few days, the dog will grow to hate rabbits. The same treatment will cure chicken killers, especially if you soak a dead hen in coal tar or add coal oil disinfectant before making the dog bear his cross.

And just recently, I heard about stopping a dog from creeping by squirting him in the face with a water pistol.

The tactics, old and new, may or may not work. Few hunters have enough experience to understand the nuances of bird dog behavior. Nor do they know when to apply specialized training tactics. Consider the electric shock collar. Put into the hands of a neophyte, it can do more damage than a zoo monkey with an arc welding torch. I once had a hard-headed setter named Brinka that liked to separate herself from me by a minimum of three hills. One day I put a borrowed shock collar around her neck and told her to go have fun. When she got out about a half-mile, I zapped her, and she went straight into the air like a small white missile. Brinka came back all right and wrapped herself around my legs for the rest of the afternoon. Shocking her was a stupid, cruel mistake on my part. On her own, she was at least hunting and having fun.

I heard a story about a man who reached out and touched his pointer to teach him a similar lesson, but the shock button stuck on his lightning stick. He never saw his dog again. There is a time and place for using the shock collar. Most hunters, including me, know neither.

If this sounds like advice to let a professional do a professional's job, that's because it is. There is nothing wrong with teaching your dog all that it, and you, can absorb. But consider letting a veteran finish the job. Besides experience and expertise, the professional dog trainer sells you time. Most quail hunters with dogs don't have enough time to devote to their dogs. I know I barely do with my three.

Not counting initial costs to breed and build a kennel, those dogs cost me an average of $300 each per year to board. Buying and raising a hunting dog is an investment, one that can pay tremendous dividends of enjoyment over many years. Spending whatever you can afford for professional training is one good way to realize the full worth of your dog.

Hunting the hell out of him is another. If you get into quail often enough, the dog will learn that to hunt near you is fun because it means action for him. Hunting forms a strong bond between hunter and dog, plus it helps to correct problems from dogs left too long in the kennel.

A brief comment on pedigreed animals. Many hunters mistakenly believe that dogs with pedigrees as long as land abstracts make the best hunters. That they somehow train themselves because, well, it's in their *genes*. It usually doesn't work that way. The only thing a pedigree guarantees is that you will know the name of your dog's ancestry. It does not assure that you will have a good hunting partner. Consider the following tale of woe.

Brinka

Brinka was the first dog for which I paid legal tender. Until I broke the budget and laid out $150 for her, I had traded things like a busted shotshell reloader and a deer rifle with cracked scope for my bird dogs. In return, I got other people's problems. But Brinka held all the promise in the world or so her parentage – champion field trial stock – said.

You can stop smiling, you readers who know all about hard-running, knuckle-headed setters from pure field trial stock. Brinka was so impressive in her first year that my Iowa hunting friends encouraged me to have her bred right away so they could have puppies ready for next year. When next year came, I couldn't have sold Brinka for six cents a week. You don't lose control of a dog when you never had it in the first place. Brinka grew bolder and began hunting on her own, lengthening the distance between us. You can't expect a dog to hold a point forever, especially when you can't find the dog. So, after waiting and waiting for me to find her, Brinka began bumping birds. In time she stopped pointing altogether.

This went on through her third hunting season while I tried everything (including that shock treatment fiasco), *short of professional training,* which I couldn't afford. I was right, too. When I finally took Brinka to a trainer, he said he might be able to straighten her out, but it would take a long time and cost a lot of money. Instead, I decided to breed her to a close-working gun dog with a reputation for siring puppies that were mild-mannered, easy to handle, and usually grew into good bird dogs. I would start over with a pup. The breeding with Bandit went so well and produced so many fine-looking puppies that I arranged another.

I still hunted Brinka, but I was tired of coming home from woods and fields with a bad case of heartburn. So when Brinka was five, I gave her to a tough-looking Sicilian from Detroit.

Nick said he worked part time as a bodyguard for middleweight

Consider letting an expert train your quail hunting dog. Most professionals, like the trainer at left, eventually transfer the loyalty and commands to the dog's owner (center). *(Laura Albrecht photo)*

fighter Thomas Hearns. Because I believed Nick, I told him everything about Brinka's faults. We talked for several hours. I learned that underneath that bar-bouncer exterior was a man who also had a soft heart for setters and loved to hunt behind them. He fully understood that, with Brinka, that might be a long, long way. Actually Nick didn't expect to go home with a dog at all. Having read my ad for puppies in the *Detroit Free Press*, he drove a hundred miles on bad roads in an old Chevy with a loud muffler, just to *see* the pups. He knew he couldn't afford the $200–$300 I was asking to buy one.

I can still see my girl sitting up high in the front seat of the old Chevy as Nick rumbled out of the farmyard. He called a couple of times to update me about Brinka and to tell me things about her that I already knew, but I never saw him or the dog again. She lives on through her pups, though—Lady Macbeth and Chaucer—the dogs I kept from each of Brinka's litters.

Dogs That Train Themselves

A man may have to go through a lot of animals to find the one dog he really wants. There is an old saying among bird-dog people that each hunter is allowed to own one outstanding dog in his lifetime. Colonel Graham, for one, doesn't believe it. He said that he has had four great ones in the past three years alone. *And I didn't do a thing to train one of my best dogs*, the Colonel modestly admitted. *God sent him down to me fully trained.*

Can a quail dog train itself? Probably not, but the owner can set the stage for the dog to learn all that it can. If the dog is intelligent, loves his play, and wants to please his master, he will transfer what he learns to the hunting partnership. You can help assure that this happens by seeing to it that early in life the dog bonds to you and develops good habits. Again, a good training book will show the way.

At age five now, Macbeth is turning into a good quail dog, and Chaucer is beginning to come around after a slow start. Neither will ever get into the Bird Dog Hall of Fame, but they make quail hunting fun for me (and for themselves). Macbeth, in particular, is a joy. As a puppy, she spent a lot of time under my feet while I sat at the typewriter. In evenings, she chased a wing tied to a fly rod back and forth across the lawn. When she was six months old, I enrolled her in an evening obedience school, and after her first year in the field, she spent six weeks with a professional trainer who worked to staunch her and to cut her range.

Macbeth taught herself to retrieve in Kansas when she was two. Along with the other dogs, she would charge to a fallen quail, then when they tried to take it away from her, she brought it to me for safekeeping. That fall my game bag carried several bobwhites that I had not shot. Macbeth has a good nose and solid bird sense, but most of all she loves to hunt with me.

Like most setters that are good—or at least on the edge of being good—Macbeth can be stubborn, too. Occasionally she doesn't like forking over a bird. I have to carry a leash for those times when she would rather find a live target than *Hunt Dead*. She is a "me firster," too, who now and then needs a check cord to keep her from breaking in on other dogs' points.

At age five, my girl still has a lot to learn about quail. Then, again, at age 40, so do I.

The Education of Chaucer

I had a serious problem with Chaucer, my male, who is a year younger than Macbeth. Chaucer missed his entire first year of hunting when he contracted parvo a week before bird season. Because I spent much of the following fall in Alaska, he only got to hunt a few times, mostly on short trips near home, although he, too, spent six weeks with the trainer. Chaucer was three when I took him across the coun-

Working a puppy on a fly rod helps bond dog to owner. Besides, it's fun for both of you. Author plays with a young setter from one of the litters he has raised.

try to hunt quail. Little did I know the extent of his problems or what the outcome would be.

I keep a journal whenever and wherever I go. The best way to tell Chaucer's story is to share with you some of the entries from the Midwest portion.

November 7. I'm afraid I will have to get rid of my dog. The main problem is Chaucer's disposition. When he doesn't want to do something, he growls at me and shows his teeth. These menacing threats occurred several times today, mostly when I tried to kennel him in back of Larry Brown's truck with Jake, Brown's male pointer. I can't see spending the afternoon in some Iowa doctor's office waiting for a tetanus shot. I'll hunt Chaucer on the rest of this trip, but this Jekyll-and-Hyde personality will have to go. Or he will.

Incidentally, Brown, of Brooklyn, Iowa, is the perfect hunting partner. He never criticizes another man's dog. Not even when the dog lifts a leg and pees on his hunting trousers, as Chaucer had done to Brown a month earlier when we hunted woodcock in Michigan's Upper Peninsula.

November 15. Raising dogs is like raising kids. When they misbehave, you don't know whether to beat them or ignore them. And when they're bad all day long, you could kill them. I am still having problems with Chaucer. This morning in Kansas, he refused to kennel with the other dogs after I let them all out for a brief run. He was probably upset because Macbeth got to spend the night in the Winnebago with me. How could he know that yesterday, thanks to a field of miserable cockleburs, she badly ripped the skin on the pits of her front legs? Anyway, I had to road Chaucer alongside the motorhome for a couple miles. That made him too tired to argue, and he kenneled the minute I opened the trailer door.

Later this morning, while we hunted a huge field of cut milo, Chaucer was off scouting a shelter belt a half-mile away. He and the deer that ran out the other end were little specks on the horizon. Then, this afternoon while we stood around comparing our pheasants and quail and making excuses for the ones we missed, Chaucer began chewing on one of the birds. When one of the hunters tried to take the pheasant from him, he was greeted by a throaty growl. There is nothing more embarrassing than a delinquent dog. Finally Chaucer backed off and dropped the bird.

I've taken to calling my dog *Lunchmeat.* And I'm ready to give him away to the first farm family that wants him and would furnish a good home.

November 18. Lunchmeat's problem, of course, is that he is socially ignorant. Dale Jarvis of Metamora, Michigan, who had trained him, told me the jury was out on whether or not he would amount to anything. *I don't think he'll ever be as good as your female* (whom Dale had also trained), *but it's largely up to you.*

I can't allow three dogs the run of my house. And Chaucer has had to take his turn with the others, riding to the office with me, walking up town to get the mail, and so on. When you have more than one bird dog, you tend to hunt the better one, and the reserve player stays on the bench.

I'm not making excuses. The truth is, my dog's poor behavior is my own fault. The best I can do now is to make no expectations of him. Let him have fun and try to socialize him more. Who knows? Maybe Lunchmeat will come around.

November 20. Today, Mike Pearce—my Kansas hunting partner—and I stopped at Golden Prairie Hunting Service in Sublette, after three days of tramping for quail in the Cimmaron National Grassland. Golden Prairie owner Jeff White, a good friend of Mike's, had booked a pheasant hunt for some out-of-state clients. He wanted Mike and his fine golden retriever, Mysti, to handle guiding chores. I could accompany the group as a photographer. While Holly and Macbeth got a bonus day's sleep in the kennel, I put Chaucer at heel on a leash. The birds flew well, and we were treated to fine dog work and good wingshooting. Chaucer and I both had fun. Maybe he is getting the message that where there is gunfire, there are birds.

November 24. I've been hunting Chaucer on a 20-foot check cord every day, and he seems to be responding. He is warming up to people, even allowing them to pet him. Everyone calls him Lunchmeat now, but it is all in fun. When I let him off the leash for a few minutes at a time, he stays fairly close. Today, we were hunting osage orange hedgerows between cornfields near Newton, Kansas. One time Lunchmeat ran off a bit too far, to check on some cattle in an adjacent field. The electric fence was on, giving him a jolt strong enough to send him back to me with his tail between his legs.

The bobwhites sat tightly today because the ground was wet and

The author's male setter began to come around after a couple weeks of daily hunting. Soon the author stopped calling him Lunchmeat and started referring to him by his real name, Chaucer.

the sky was sleeting off and on. Macbeth made several fine points, her nose inches from the ground, left foreleg cocked, that brown eye rimmed in pink darting from me to the birds and back again. With the help of the check cord, I forced Chaucer to honor his sister's points, softly *whoaing* and encouraging him all the while. He is definitely coming around.

November 26. I didn't get to see the sun shine in Missouri during three days of hunting there off and on in the rain. The sky was like a wet, gray rag today on this, my last hunt of the Midwest trip. The birds were not foraging much and leaving little scent when they did. I was hunting near Hume in west-central Missouri. David Denayer, whom I had met in a turkey hunting camp in northern Missouri the previous spring, had invited me here to hunt bobwhites in the strip-mine country near his home.

Today was a five-setter day. Gary Sears, David's brother-in-law, brought along his three-year-old Llewellin named Lou. David used his veteran male, Duke, and a four-month-old pup named Pretty Girl. I hunted my two setters, purposely leaving Chaucer's check cord in the motorhome. We walked for two hours without flushing a quail. As we cut across a five-acre patch of milo, I suggested that we slow up and let the dogs work the other end. I had a hunch that heavy cover next to the grain field might hold a covey, which could then easily duck back and forth from shelter to food.

Macbeth's flag went up first. By the time we got to her, Chaucer also had the birds trapped. My two dogs faced each other at 10 feet, and for the first time, I realized how their tails looked like punctuation marks. Chaucer's was an exclamation; Macbeth's a question mark. *Easy, easy,* I told the dogs as I snapped a quick picture with the little pocket camera I usually carry in the field. But my voice quavered a little and my hand shook with excitement. For 30 years I've been hunting birds, mostly without good dogs. Now, maybe I had found the one-two punch that all bird hunters dream of.

Duke sneaked to within 20 feet, then stretched into a fine, low-slung honor that reminded me of an elastic strap pulled to the breaking point. A little farther behind, Lou backed, too. Even Pretty Girl stopped for a moment. After David and Gary had sidled into shooting position, I stepped in to flush the birds. Twenty of them came out in a roar and headed for the thick brush 20 feet away. I couldn't get a shot, but my partners each scratched down a bird.

On the long walk back to the car, we felt wet slaps of rain in our faces and heard tree limbs groan overhead in the wind. I was thinking about my new-found luck, when David interrupted my thoughts.

Chaucer and Lady Macbeth with their first double-teamed point. A covey of 20 bobwhites flushed seconds after this photo was taken. Note water the dogs are standing in. Hunting (and shooting) conditions were miserable in Missouri that rainy November day.

How much did you say you wanted for Lunchmeat? he asked.
He isn't for sale, I said. *And that isn't his name anymore.*

What Trainers Look for in a Quail Dog

Although bobwhites in the wild are more elusive today than ever, they still tend to hold better than most other gamebirds for a pointing dog. And because most quail dog trainers work with pointing breeds, they are the subject here.

Colonel Graham believes a good dog is one who realizes that the handler knows where the quail are. The logic of this theory is that the dog will always hunt near the handler. One day the colonel proved this to my hunting partner, Steve Smith, and me when he put down seven of his dogs—five setters and two pointers—at the same time. We were hunting one of Burnt Pine's 12 courses, a big field of broomsedge ringed by loblolly pines. Although the field went on for a half-mile or more, none of the colonel's dogs ranged farther than 100 yards. Jackson Five, his prize setter, found most of the quail that day. When Jackson Five or one of the others locked up, the colonel would not flush the bird until all the dogs had stopped hunting and honored the point. Believe me, a seven-dog train is something to see!

Most of Colonel Graham's hunting is done on preserves. Hunting birds in the wild, of course, may result in long days without a flush, and that can be frustrating for dogs, who then might have a tendency to increase their range. But that is not necessarily bad.

Greg Koch from Beggs, Oklahoma, has trained some of the country's finest quail dogs. Koch, who also owns an 11,000-acre shooting preserve, the Double W Ranch, classifies pointing dogs into three types: *wide rangers, medium rangers,* and *pure lacers.* The merit of each depends upon the type of habitat you are hunting.

The *wide ranger* is a straight-line dog who takes on a linear subject, such as a fence line or creek, and runs it to its end. He does not cast but rather hunts according to objectives—a thicket here, a weed patch there—along the line of travel. A good *wide ranger* gets on the down-wind side of cover and may go out as far as 400 yards. He does the work while you survey his progress like some field marshal. When he slams into a point, you slide on down there and shoot the bird. Wide-open country such as that found in western Oklahoma and Texas, eastern Colorado, and portions of Kansas and Nebraska are custom-made for the *wide ranger.*

The *medium ranger* works cover out 100 to 200 yards from the hunter. This dog, too, hunts objectives, but he does it through purely casting or through a combination of quartering and running a straight line. This is a dog that knows enough to hunt the edges of cover and laces back and forth between the cover. His hunting habits resemble a windshield wiper, and he is valuable in mixed covers of fields and timber.

According to Greg Koch, the *pure lacer* is one who stitches the seam—that is, makes tight casts and hunts close enough to wipe your boots. He is unreplaceable in heavy cover such as brushy fence rows and creek bottoms.

Another veteran dog trainer with whom I hunted is Harry Ruther-ford of Andover, Kansas. Harry's father trained bird dogs for 50 years, and Harry himself has been at it for 36 years, the last 16 in a full-time capacity. Rutherford feels the complete dog is one that hunts the available cover, ranging out as far as a half-mile if necessary, when cover is scant, and staying reasonably close—within a couple of hundred yards—when cover is heavy. He believes that each dog has a range at which it feels comfortable, but that he should hunt from objective to objective. The dog should be spirited, too, keeping his tail moving at all times, and hunting hard.

Rutherford believes that the wise hunter will arrange his hunting plan so that the dog can take full advantage of any wind, heading either into it or across it. On the other hand, the smartest dogs tack with the wind anyway, even when you are walking with it at your back. Such dogs actually hunt closer then because they sweep back and forth seeking scent.

How far should your dog range? Harry believes in letting his go as far as they want. *Ninety-nine percent of them will cut their range in half when you begin shooting birds,* he told me. The biggest problem is not that the dog ranges so far but that the hunter doesn't trust him. *You have to trust your dog if the partnership will ever amount to anything.*

A week later, Harry's words rang true for me in southwestern Kansas where Mike Pearce and I had gone to hunt mixed-bag bob-whites and scaled quail. While hunting in a high wind with Lawrence Smith of Elkhart, Mike and I took turns losing our dogs. First Macbeth disappeared in a field of still-standing milo. Then Mysti, Mike's golden retriever, vanished for a half-hour. We finally got the dogs back and resumed hunting—Mike keeping Mysti at heel so that she wouldn't bust my girl's points. Before long, Macbeth stabbed a big covey of bobs at the end of a fencerow. On the flush, some of the birds caught the wind and sailed far out into a big field of harvested milo.

Macbeth chased them over a hill a quarter-mile away. I wasn't too

Medium-ranging dogs found this covey of bobwhites in the sand-sage prairie of Oklahoma.

concerned because I allow her this little pleasure after every flush. It breaks the tension for her; besides, she always comes right back to resume hunting. Only this time she didn't come back. Mindful of the fact that I had already lost her once, I waited about five minutes, growing more and more alarmed as the minutes ticked by. I blew my whistle but the signals were down between us in the high wind.

Excuse me, I finally said to Lawrence and Mike, *but I have a dog to punish.*

When I reached the top of the hill, I could see Macbeth was on point another quarter-mile away. I waved for my partners but they motioned me on. *Trust your dog.* Harry Rutherford's words kept popping into my mind. When I reached Macbeth, she gave me a look like *What took you so long?* I couldn't believe that a quail could hide in milo cut only three inches from the ground. I stepped in and when a little rooster buzzed out, I killed him cleanly.

I don't think my dog would have forgiven me had I missed.

Dogs Have Their Days, Too

The more you hunt quail with your dog, the more realistic your expectations of him will become. Like their owners, dogs have days, too, when they are not up to par. Overworking the animal is one reason. Someone once figured that for every mile a bird hunter walks, his dog probably travels three miles. During the Midwest portion of my trip, I hunted bobwhites for 23 of 25 November days in four states. This rigorous hunting schedule soon exhausted Macbeth, whom I was hunting more than the others, and so I learned to rest her at half-day intervals with a full day off every four or five days. This timetable of periodic R and R became easier to follow as Chaucer improved in the field.

Besides fatigue, illness or injury, there are other reasons—some of which defy an explanation—that bird dogs don't perform consistently day after day. Some one-man dogs, in particular, can't handle the pressure of a large group of hunters who have their own dogs along. Too much confusion from too many whistles, hunters moving in over points on the standing dog's blind side, untrained animals that won't back, and one or two that bust points can unnerve your dog and contribute to a shoddy performance.

Just as parents hope their children perform to perfection in the school Christmas play, everyone who owns a quail hunting dog wants his charge to shine in the company of others. Like parents, though, sometimes we push too hard. I didn't realize, for example—until

Harry Rutherford gracefully pointed it out to me—that I was a bit whistle-happy in my commands to Macbeth.

She knows where you are, Harry cautioned, *and every time you blow that whistle, you are telling her she doesn't need to check in with you. Besides, it confuses my own dogs.*

In this book, I have tried to refrain from lecturing. But I'm going to make an exception here. *Never tell another man's dog what to do.* Your

Mysti, Mike Pearce's golden retriever, proudly displays a fetched bobwhite for the camera. Good retrievers cut crippling losses by 50 percent or more.

commands confuse the animal, anger the owner, and have all the possibility of ruining the hunt. Maybe even a friendship. Let's go for broke on this subject: *Never criticize another man's dog. Even if he asks for your comments, temper them with discretion.* Would you tell your wife she looks like a whale bobber when she asked your opinion about a new dress that accentuated a bulge or two? Probably not, unless you are looking for a frying pan alongside the head. Enough said.

Incidents like rolling in fresh steer manure (a disgusting practice that setters are prone to do) can prejudice a hunter toward his dog so that he loses all sight of good behavior. Macbeth upset me pretty badly one day in Kansas when we were hunting cropfield hedgerows near some oil wells. The rigs that were pumping looked like giant prehistoric birds feeding on something. Macbeth ran over to investigate a silent one, then lay down in a nearby pool of black crude. For the next three days, she looked like she was wearing exotic panty hose. For at least a week, the inside of the trailer reeked of oil. And so I forgot to reward her for the quail (which had oil all over their feathers) she retrieved that day.

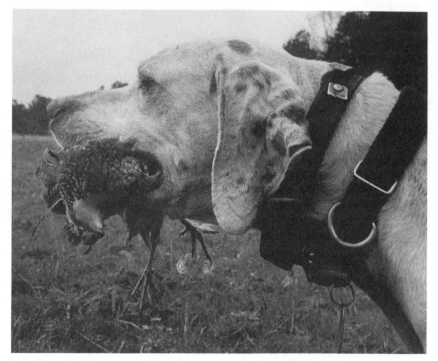

Dogs have their days, too. This pointer apparently is having a good one. Pointers are the hands-down favorite among bobwhite gunners in the South and East.

High winds make it hard for your dog to both hear and see you and weaken communications, sometimes resulting in sloppy bird work. That is also because strong winds tend to make quail jumpy. Further, poor scenting conditions can make it hard for your dog to do his job right. Harry Rutherford looks at all hunting days in terms of whether the earth is inhaling, exhaling or being stagnant. When the ground is inhaling, it is sucking in moisture and scents. Inhaling days are those of low atmospheric pressure, low-lying clouds and precipitation. On the other hand, high-pressure systems, drying conditions, and rising thermals result in the earth releasing, or exhaling, moisture and scents. Stagnation occurs when a weather change is imminent. The best scenting conditions for dogs are exhaling-earth days; the worst are inhaling days.

Your dog doesn't understand the difference. Because you do, it may help you to adjust your expectations of him.

The Case for the Two-Dog System

Dogs hunting in tandem doesn't mean that two will find twice the number of quail that one would. In fact, two dogs might not find any more birds at all. Whether or not they do depends on the cover, the scarcity or abundance of birds, and the way the dogs hunt. Teams that have varied ranges or that hunt objectives differently can complement each other, though, especially if they honor each other's points. Another advantage of the two-dog system is that a backing dog may lead the hunter to the one frozen over the bird. While hunting in Georgia, for example, we lost a small setter in heavy broomsedge for a half-hour. A second setter found the missing dog on point, and, by honoring, helped us to locate her.

On the one hand, Macbeth hunts fast with her head up much of the time. When she scents game, she grows even more frantic to find it. Her methods cause her to bump birds occasionally, and, no doubt, to miss others. On the other hand, Chaucer hunts more slowly, with his head down. Upon scenting quail, he slinks low like a lion stalking a kill.

When I knew I could trust Chaucer, I began to hunt the two together, especially on days when we expected to spend only a few hours in the field. Because my dogs range and cast differently, in harness they do a fairly good job of covering a habitat. Otherwise, I hunted them separately, putting down the fresh dog when the other grew tired. Having a spare dog proves helpful, too, on days when his partner is off the beam or perhaps injured.

Few dogs can hunt all species of birds consistently well, and that is yet another reason for owning a pair. Some hunters' team may be a pointer/flusher combination. When seeking quail or ruffed grouse and woodcock, they kennel the flusher and let the pointer do the field work, then reverse the order when the target is running pheasants. If the flushing dog is a Labrador or golden retriever, some hunters like to heel the dog on quail, then send it in to fetch downed game.

A few bird dog trainers, including Harry Rutherford, refuse to hunt pointing breeds on pheasants under any circumstances. Because today's roosters run so hard, pointers may force the flush, then carry this bad habit over to coveys of quail. In regard to the Western species of quail that run, forcing the covey rise can be advantageous because the separated singles will then hold for pointers. It takes an exceptionally smart one to know the difference, though, and that is why some Western hunters rely strictly on flushing breeds for quail hunting. Others with pointers make their dogs hunt close.

Pointing breeds should honor each other's points. In the photo, two setters back a classic point by an English pointer.

The two-dog system can consist of one flushing/retriever at heel and a pointer or setter to work the birds. The hunter is Roger Wells of Americus, Kansas.

Although as a rule, Rutherford doesn't train pointers and setters to be steady to wing or shot, one time he staunched a man's dog—at the owner's request—to the covey rise. Shortly afterward, the owner complained that his dog was busting points, and so Harry spent five more months retraining the animal. When he returned him to his owner, the man admitted that he had been hunting pheasants with him.

To Bell or Not to Bell

I like to hear a bell on a quail dog. Beepers that monitor Dog's whereabouts, then increase in tempo when he is on point, are probably more practical. But they are not for me. Besides, I can learn some things from the sounds that a bell makes. I can tell, for example, if my dog is drinking in the stream because the clapper will make a clunking sound when it touches the water and a loud, invigorated clang when she shakes her coat dry. If Macbeth or Chaucer is creeping after a bird, the bell will tinkle, and, of course, when it goes dead, my dog will be standing at attention.

A small copper bell used to collar sheep sounds about right to me, but different bells have different sounds. Brass ones that deliver a steady cadence make me think of harness bells on a sleigh horse. Copper, nickel, and bronze all have different tones, too. Some Swiss cattle bells impart a musical quality, not unlike a songbird pouring forth liquid notes.

To me, a special magic exists whenever I hear belled pointers or setters working a brushy stream bottom on a still morning in late fall. Sometimes there is fog, which adds to the surrealism surrounding such a hunting scene. The tinkling of the bells floats through the heavy air. Far ahead of the dogs, you may hear—but not see—a deer or two crash into the woods. Closer to the dogs are songbirds whose fluttering wings signify a last-second getaway. A drop of blood in their midst is the resident cardinal. The bell stops! And now you know that somewhere in that stream-bottom tangle a dog has turned to stone.

Bells on bird dogs help to make quail hunting the wonderful sport it is.

Care of Your Dog in the Field

Boarding and training your dog can be expensive and time-consuming. But, for a little more time and money, you can ensure that he will hunt to his full potential. Good dog care in the field is mostly common sense, yet it is surprising how many hunters neglect it.

The Home Away from Home. Dog cages in the backs of pickups and station wagons may work well for you, but they mean cramped quarters for your dog. Make the animal comfortable on those long trips by letting him out often to stretch and relieve himself and to get water. Add a soft bedding of straw, throw rugs or a burlap bag of cedar chips. In cold weather, cover the cage with a sleeping bag or heavy blanket. A short-haired dog, or one that is wet, will then stay warm and dry during the night.

Because I planned to haul my dogs thousands of miles, I made special arrangements for their comfort (and mine). Except to keep an eye on an injury or to give them a special dose of TLC, I did not want them traveling or sleeping in the motorhome with me. I had no extra space, and it was hard enough keeping down the bird feathers, shotshell husks, and boot mud without having to pluck setter hairs from my coffee mug each morning, too.

So I bought a used trailer for $450. A good trailer, too, with 16-inch wheels, steel frame, and wooden sides. The previous owner must have loved his dogs because it contained two compartments—both high enough for the dogs to stand—a fiberglass roof that was waterproof and acted like a skylight, and sliding windows for ventilation. I added straw and a bag of cedar chips. While on a short test trip, I checked it for carbon monoxide fumes from the motorhome exhaust. This over-the-road kennel was a warm, safe, dry haven for my dogs, and they loved their second home.

The few times I rented a motel room, I let the dogs in for the night when it was allowed, and a time or two when it may not have been but I didn't ask to find out. After all, they have vacuum cleaners to sweep up hairs in those $30-a-night motel rooms. The dogs loved the extra attention, and the only problem I experienced was in Laramie, Wyoming, after I let them out the next morning. When I answered a knock on the door, there stood the owner with a snow shovel in his hand. He pointed to the sidewalk and asked me *to do right by my dogs.*

Food and Water. During the off-season, I feed my dogs a dry food containing 21 percent protein and eight percent fat. I increase this during the hunting season to 30 and 12 percent respectively. A soldier, a hunter, or a dog doesn't function very well on an empty stomach. During hunting season, I add table scraps and the contents of restaurant doggie bags when they are available. I stopped giving my dogs bones, though, when a setter I once owned suffered a splinter that somehow traveled through the roof of her mouth and abscessed behind the right eye. It cost me an *Opening Day* and $72 for emergency surgery, but it would have been worse had she lost the eye.

This large kennel on wheels was comfortable and warm for the author's three traveling companions.

Feed your dogs at night, but because they might be too tired to eat, keep food available until a half-hour after their morning stretch. Don't hunt a dog, though, for at least a couple of hours after he eats heavily. A dog with a twisted stomach can die in the field. You can keep the energy level up on a hard-working dog by giving him a snack a couple of times each day. Dr. Ted Schaub, my veterinarian, recommends a piece of candy, a burger patty, or a small dose of honey or molasses. Chocolate is out, however, because it contains a product related to bromide and can cause seizures. Some hunters carry a tube of Nutri-Cal, a high calorie, palatable dietary supplement.

There are dogs, of course, that get protein during the day by eating the birds they are supposed to deliver to hand. And many years ago, a practice in vogue with quail dog trainers was to pop the heads on birds and feed them to the animals. The logic of that primitive practice was to feed a dog meat if you wanted him to hunt hungry and be a meat dog. When I hunted in Missouri, I noticed that one of the fellows tosses bobwhite heads to his three-year-old Brittany, Buster. Long ago, I learned that when you are in someone else's stable, you eat his hay without commenting about it. But I wondered why the dog kept hanging around after I pocketed a bird, head still intact, that he had retrieved for me. And I didn't say anything when he lay down and ate the next quail I shot.

If water availability is a problem, such as in the desert, carry a five-gallon bucket with a lid on it in your vehicle. Splashing water from a canteen on a handkerchief, then moistening a dog's mouth and nose will give him at least a little relief, plus it will temporarily sharpen his ability to smell.

Cardiac Arrest. Dogs don't suffer heat strokes or heart attacks like people do, but they can die from cardiac arrest resulting from shock or seizures. Getting shot, hit by a vehicle, bitten by a rattlesnake, shocked electrically, or stung by insects are the most common causes of shock and seizure. Symptoms vary with the individual dog, but they include disorientation, hyperventilation, increased drooling, twitching, loss of bodily functions, and running in place. If faced with this condition, follow the same procedures as you would for a person: Keep the victim warm and calm, try to stop the bleeding, check for broken bones before moving, and try to get to a doctor as soon as possible.

Hypoglycemia. This condition occurs when there is a sudden drop in the body's blood sugar level. Symptoms are similar to the above but also include comas. In dogs, hypoglycemia can result from poor nutrition, stress, overexertion, or too much heat or cold. Giving the animal a high-energy food along with rest and shade or a blanket should restore it to normalcy.

Vaccinations. Before taking your dog in the field, make sure he has been vaccinated for rabies, parvo, and distemper. Because heartworm disease is now widespread throughout much of the United States, you should be pilling your dog throughout the mosquito-breeding season. Even as far north as Michigan, veterinarians recommend daily heartworm pills from May 1 to December 1.

Local Hazards. Consider local hazards where you plan to hunt. Chiggers, ticks, and fleas can make life miserable for your dog, and you should check him periodically for these insect nuisances. In the Southwest, gila monsters, certain toads, and some snakes can poison your dog. In Arizona, javelinas have been known to kill dogs; in Oklahoma, coyotes have earned that outlaw honor. In Nevada, both Macbeth and Holly blundered into bobcat traps while we were hunting mountain quail along a canyon with a live stream. Luckily they didn't break any bones. Pickers, thorns, burs, foxtail awns, and cacti needles are other local pitfalls that, if you are aware of them, can be expected or avoided.

Snakes and Snakeproofing. Because I hunted the desert in the dead of winter, I had no problems with snakes. In October and November, however, snakes can be hazardous to both dogs and hunters. Western diamondbacks, I'm told, are the worst because of their relative abundance and great size, sometimes reaching six or more feet in length. But sidewinders and blacktail, banded rock and prairie rattlers are others that can make your dogs deathly ill if not outright kill them. Some hunters do not venture into snake country until a succession of cold nights puts snakes in the ground and keeps them there. One Arizona hunter told me that his friend, a biologist for the game and fish department, gave up hunting desert quail altogether when snakes killed his Brittany and shorthair in a single season.

One October, Eddie Munoz, with whom I hunted in New Mexico, lost a Brittany-in-training, a two-year-old named Governor, to a big coontail—another name for the Western diamondback. From the distance of six feet, another hunter saw the snake poised to strike Governor who had gotten too close. Eddie's friend shot the snake in mid-strike and actually cut the killer in half. Even so, it managed to strike the dog on the left shoulder, leaving punctures the size of .22 caliber bullet holes. Although the men got Eddie's dog to the veterinarian within 45 minutes of the attack, Governor was dead.

Some trainers will snakeproof dogs by equipping them with a shock collar, then leading them to a rattlesnake. As the dog ap-

Eddie Munoz of Gallup, New Mexico, puts homemade boots on his Brittany, Fred's, feet. Bicycle or motorcycle inner tubes and adhesive tape work well to protect a dog's paws against cacti and sand burs.

proaches, the snake will curl into striking position, its rattles buzzing loudly. When the dog moves in to investigate, the handler gives him a shot of juice. A single shock is usually enough to produce one of two future reactions. The next time Dog sees a rattler, he will either bark violently while circling it without coming too close, or he will pretend that he doesn't see it at all, even averting his eyes from looking that way.

Booting Your Dogs. In Oklahoma, we booted dogs for sand burs; in New Mexico, for goatshead pickers and prickly pear. In some parts of the country, foxtail awns, I'm told, are a problem because they tend to break off and work into a dog's toes under the nails. I guess my dogs were lucky in that respect. But they were not lucky with cockleburs in Kansas and Iowa nor in Arizona's Sonoran Desert where the culprits are mesquite and dozens of cacti species, as well as other plants that stab, rip, slice, and puncture. The worst is a medieval torture-chamber candidate named teddy bear cholla, a striking (in more ways than one) pale-lemon cactus that appears fuzzy and even seems to glow in the light of late afternoon.

Teddy bear cholla contains hundreds of stinging spines that, when touched, appear to slap back as though they are traps set on hair triggers. When you pull the quills from the skin, blood follows. Dogs either learn to avoid this desert nightmare altogether, or they foolishly blunder into it again and again. Macbeth stayed away after getting zapped a few times. On the other hand, Chaucer seemed to go out of his way to find the horror. He didn't have to look far where we were hunting, near the San Pedros River southeast of Tuscon. When Chaucer came limping back to me, howling, he looked like he had taken on a patrol of porcupines. And lost. Spines stuck out all over him, and a foot-long chunk of cactus pinned his hind legs together. Because Chaucer had foolishly bitten at his assailant, my dog's nose, gums and palate were so full of spines that he couldn't close his mouth.

It was no fun for either of us. I learned that you can't remove cholla cactus barbs with your bare hands. An afro comb will get rid of some of them, but you will need a pair of needle-nose pliers or a long tweezers to pull out the rest.

Booting dogs in the desert and grasslands where there are pickers is a good idea. Some hunters cut up old bicycle or motorcycle inner tubes, pulling them over their dogs' feet like stockings, then folding over the ends and securing with adhesive or electrician's tape. You can also buy leather or rubber boots ready-made from any of the dog supply houses. The best ones I have found are made by the Lewis Dog Boot Company, 3330 West Randolph, Emo, Oklahoma 73701. A set of four rubber ones costs about $20.

Checking Your Dog for Problems. Inspect your dog each night for burs, pickers, thorns, and needles as well as cuts and abrasions. Apply a little first-aid antiseptic, such as Neosporin, to open wounds. Some hunters toughen their dogs' footpads by coating them each night with special products that harden them.

Memorable Moments with Dogs

There is nothing more rewarding than watching a springer spaniel speed lacing the cover, than a pointer standing tall, than a retriever with the taste of Bird in his mouth. I am fortunate to have hunted with quail dogs of many different breeds in many different places. I told you about old Sam at the beginning of this chapter. I'd like to end it with the story of Pretty Girl, David Denayer's black-and-white setter who was four months old at the time I hunted with the two of them.

Denayer had had to put to sleep his 13-year-old setter, Jake, the previous fall. (*Death had him by the pantleg anyway,* David said, *but that didn't make it any easier.*) David knows that Duke, his six-year-old male,

Making your dog comfortable increases his pleasure and ultimately yours. Marilyn Underwood gives some TLC to Tray, a Brittany male owned by Hoyd Patty of Patagonia, Arizona.

is a capable quail dog but will never replace Jake. Pretty Girl is his best hope.

We were hunting in the rain on a two-bandana day — one handkerchief for the nose, one for the eyeglasses. For three days, Pretty Girl kept up with us, mile after mile, as we slogged up and down abandoned strip-mine pits, called *dumps* by the local people. Farm fields of winter wheat, soybeans, and milo flank the dumps. In between is a mosaic of quail cover — osage orange, sumac, hawthorn, coralberry, black locust, foxtail, wild sunflower, ragweed, and native prairie grasses. Because of the turn-down day, the bobwhites were hanging out in this heavy cover.

I was sucking on a persimmon fruit while ambling along, my thoughts on Thanksgiving and the fact that tomorrow I would be turning the motorhome north and heading home. Pretty Girl was snooping in the grass a few feet in front of me. Suddenly, her nose thrust forward, lips curled back, and she tightened into *First Point*.

Just once, I would like to get down on all fours and be able to inhale the odor of Bobwhite. I want to know what it is like to have eyes water, body tremble, chest tighten from shallow breathing, throat ache from a wild heart fighting to get past. Maybe somewhere in another time another Hunter did just that, and maybe the scent from a crude blueprint of today's bird flooded him with sensation.

How lucky that we modern hunters at least have partners to experience it for us.

12

The Comfortable Hunter

Many things can go wrong on a quail hunt. Cars, dogs, weather, even your hunting partner that you thought you knew so well can turn on you without warning. Surely you know about those days when you can't hit your fanny with a bass fiddle. How about the guy at the Mobil station who gives you bum directions to his uncle's farm? Instead of finding *bobwhites thick as blackbirds,* you find yourself looking for a tow chain and tractor to get out of the ditch. Rosie's Truck Stop breakfast (recommended by Rosie's sister, Ruby, who owns the motel next door where the shower water is colder than Great Slave Lake in the Northwest Territories) gives you heartburn so bad your eyes water. Rosie's specialty is hash-blacked potatoes.

Even the Rolaids you buy at the pay counter are stale.

Sound familiar? On an upland gamebird hunt in South Dakota one time, I lost my dog for hours and my new $90 Bean coat forever: It blew off the top of our rental car somewhere on I-90. We're talking about the Domino Syndrome here. That same day I left my shotgun in the motel room and missed an hour of prime hunting time. At day's

Being dry and comfortable makes a successful hunt all that much more worthwhile. The young hunters are Rodney Oursler (right) and his friend, Kelly, who hunted with the author near Newton, Kansas.

end the blisters on my ankles from a new pair of boots were the size of quarters.

Days like that. Hunt birds often enough and you will experience them, too. That's the bad news. The good news is there are things you can do to avoid, and maybe alleviate, some of these problems. Knowing how to hunt comfortably is a start.

Quail hunters that are wet, exhausted, too cold or too warm, hungry enough to eat their dogs, so thirsty their tongues hang to the whistles around their necks can't concentrate on the sport. So they miss their shots, find fault with the dogs. In general, they make the day miserable for themselves. And they ruin it for everyone else.

Hunting Light

What is "comfortable" anyway? To me, it means staying dry and warm while hunting as lightly as possible. When you're trekking up to 10 miles a day—not an unreasonable distance if you are chasing Western quail or Midwestern bobwhites—these requirements are not a luxury. They are a must. But clothing that makes one person sweat may provide scant protection for another. Therefore, when trying to decide what to wear, you should think about more than the weather forecast. Consider your own body metabolism, for example. Take a hard look, too, at how far you plan to walk, what altitude you will experience, and what type of terrain and habitat you will cover. Then consider the total amount of weight you will move.

Here is some simple arithmetic. Assume your hunting pace is one-yard strides. Because there are 1,760 yards to a mile, for every mile you walk, you will take 1,760 steps. Five miles equals 8,800 steps. For every extra pound of weight, any kind of weight—gun, shells, clothing, lunch, body fat, whatever—you will be moving *about 4½ tons.* I confess that math was never my strong point, and I imagine some physics ace could blow this theory apart. Still, it makes enough sense to me that I now question those temptations to tote extra gear.

Like shells. One Federal 20-gauge Premium shotshell containing 2½ drams of powder and one ounce of No. 8 shot weights 1.25 ounces on my postage scale. Twelve shells, then, weigh one pound. Depending on how far I plan to be from my vehicle, I usually carry between 10 and 16 shells. Most of the time, you don't need that many. On the other hand, there have been times when I wish I had more. Every hunter must live with such personal decisions.

There are other ways to lighten up, too. Get rid of the car keys, loose change, wallet, and two-inch belt with two-pound buckle. Suspenders are not only lighter, they are more comfortable anyway. Substitute a small pocket knife for the belt model. Instead of a Thermos, carry an apple, and a couple pieces of hard candy. A chunk of beef jerky provides all the protein that a bologna-and-cheese sandwich does and it is much lighter. A granola bar or candy bar gives quick energy for some. As a full-time freelance writer and photographer, I found a new way to go light last fall. Whenever I can afford to do it, I now substitute my heavy 35mm cameras with motordrives for a compact point-and-shoot model.

Here is an easy way to find out how much gear and clothing you are lugging into the field. Separately weigh everything on a baby scale or postage meter. Then add the totals. When I did this several years ago, here is what I came up with:

Nylon-faced shooting pants and
suspenders .... 2 lb.
Shooting jacket with game pouch ...... 2 lb.

Flannel shirt, underwear, 2 pair of socks (one lightweight, one medium weight)	1 lb.
12 20-gauge shells	1 lb.
20 gauge over/under	6 lb., 11 oz.
Boots (leather uppers/rubber bottoms) ..	2 lb., 14 oz.
Hats, cotton gloves, handkerchief	6 oz.
Total Weight	15 lb., 15 oz.

The lack of weight, then, goes a long way toward being comfortable, and it is an important consideration when choosing clothing for your hunt. Because there is no way to measure an individual's body metabolism, only trial and error will teach you what to wear. Some hunters, following the you-can-always-take-it-off-if-you-have-it-with-you theory, wear everything. Considering the following general guidelines might help them hit the mark more often.

Warm-Weather Hunting

When the temperature is 60 degrees, or warmer, most quail hunters can get by with a pair of jeans or lightweight trousers with nylon facing, polo shirt and/or flannel shirt, and shell vest with game pocket. A mesh-type shooting cap is comfortable, and you can buy them with green underbrim to cut glare and help your shooting score, too. Cotton underwear is fine although you might want to consider a thin layer of polypropylene next to the skin.

When I hunted in the desert, for example, cool mornings called for polypropylene. When the day grew warm enough to make me sweat, the polypropylene wicked enough moisture away to keep me comfortable. Another nice feature about this amazing synthetic fabric is that you can hand wash it, and it will dry in a half-hour, even less in the low humidity of the desert.

Vests with meshed-fabric game bags are comfortable and practical for the warm-weather hunter. I used two types of vests. One has all-gauge elastic shell loops across the breast. A good tip to keep shells from falling out, when they are thus exposed or the elastic is not strong, is to store them with the brass side down. The other vest features roomy side pockets with shell loops and protective flaps. Adjustable shoulder straps and belt with Velcro fastener allowed me to wear the vest over other clothing on colder days. And because it is sleeveless, it doesn't bind my shooting. Those spacious cargo pockets hold shotshell hulls, too, when I remember to pick them up.

Warm, dry feet are crucial to comfort. I expected to hunt under all conditions during my cross-country trips. The five pairs of different boots I carried in the motorhome included 10-inch uninsulated, leather uppers/rubber bottoms; the same type of boot with felt pacs for insulation; 10-inch uninsulated, all-Gore-Tex leather; 6-inch Gore-Tex canvas with leather; and all-rubber dairy (Wellingtons) boots. I wore them all at one time or another.

Boots with rubber bottoms and leather tops are probably the favorite among most fair-weather quail hunters. They are light in

Marilyn Underwood was comfortable in a lightweight shooter's cap, long-sleeved flannel shirt, and lightweight trousers while hunting Gambel quail in Arizona.

weight (the original Bean's Maine Hunting Shoe weighs 2 pounds, 14 ounces in the 10-inch-high model) and are ideal for hunting in creek bottoms and otherwise wet terrain. However, in warm weather my feet sweat too easily in them. A better pair of boots for me was the low-cut hiking shoe made of Gore-Tex and leather. Gore-Tex material has the remarkable ability to both breathe and be waterproof at the same time. It is also light. The pair I wore weighed only three pounds and was surprisingly warm, even when I wore only a single pair of tube cotton socks.

Some warm-weather hunters wear tennis shoes, a good idea perhaps if you are chasing scaled quail. A bad idea, though, if there are snakes above ground.

Moderate-Weather Hunting

Moderate weather, for the sake of definition, is 30 to 60 degrees. On the upper end of this range, a flannel shirt, bird-shooter's vest, nylon-faced pants, lightweight boots, and Jones or shooter's cap are ideal, for me. As the temperature approaches freezing, though, I switch to leather/rubber footwear or to the all Gore-Tex leather boot with a pair of medium-weight wool socks over cotton tube socks. I might add a turtleneck shirt under a flannel one and substitute a hunting jacket for a vest. When gun barrels grow cold to the touch, it is time for a thin pair of leather gloves, cotton jerseys, or lightweight wool gloves with nonslip fingertips. I don't like to shoot with gloves on, though. And because I'm right-handed, I wear the glove only on my left hand, as long as I can stand it.

Harry Rutherford, a dog trainer and shooting preserve operator with whom I hunted in Kansas, dresses differently from any other quail hunter I know. He *always* wears gloves and a hunting jacket, even when the weather is warm. When Harry hunted doves in Mexico in August, he wore his jacket and gloves. His logic is that if he is used to the extra clothing in warm weather, it will not affect his shooting in cold weather. Does it work? Well, you don't question a man's reasoning when he shoots more quail, between 1,000 and 1,500 birds each year, than anyone else in Kansas.

Cold-Weather Hunting

When I think of cold weather, I remember that late November morning in southwestern Kansas when the temperature seemed stuck

Moderate-weather hunting, such as late November in Iowa, calls for slightly heavier clothing. This is Larry Brown of Brooklyn, Iowa, with his pointer, Jake.

at 23 degrees on an Elkhart bank. Weather forecasters predicted that the wind, out of the north now at 10 mph, would triple by noon. For once, they were right. The ball bearings that froze in our dog whistles made a high-pitched scream when we blew them. Little ice particles on my beard threatened to muzzle me. To prepare for this bitter day, I slipped on a two-piece suit of medium-weight polypropylene underwear under a pair of 18-ounce woolen pants and a chamois shirt. Then I added a downhill ski vest and my regular hunting jacket. Woolen shooting gloves, ski cap, and the all-Gore-Tex boot with two pairs of socks completed my defense against the cold.

Wool is a wonderful fabric for cold-weather bird hunting. My friend Ron Spomer put me on to it when we chased pheasants and bobwhites in Kansas a few years ago. One frigid day in December, we hunted near Concordia in a foot of snow topped by an inch of ice. The temperature was four degrees and the wind was up. Ken Lowe, another friend of mine, and I had driven out from Michigan, expecting to get a respite from winter.

It was interesting to see how differently the three of us dressed for that bitter day in Kansas. Ken wore a heavyweight Gore-Tex coat, parka and pants, but was too bundled up to shoot well. I donned downhill ski bibs over insulated underwear, plus the other clothing I have already mentioned. I was warm enough, all right, and had freedom of movement for fast shooting, but I tore the bibs in several places on barbed wire. Ron wore woolen pants and woolen shirt over polypropylene, then slipped on his shooting jacket. He was dressed just right.

Wool is warm and doesn't scratch if worn over long underwear. When tightly woven, it turns back briars and even barbed wire. I have since learned to rely on it for cold-weather hunting.

Although I've never worn silk, I'm told that long underwear made of silk is exceptionally lightweight, warm, and comfortable. It is ex-

An all-Gore-Tex leather boot, flannel shirt with jacket, and woolen pants over polypropylene underwear are ideal for cold-weather hunting. This is the clothing the author wore while hunting during a frigid snap in southwestern Kansas.

pensive, though, and not as easy to care for as polypropylene. Cotton long underwear or flannel longjohns are fine, too, except they become clammy and lose their insulating value when wet. Cotton is a poor fabric to have next to the skin whenever hypothermia could be a threat.

Fishnet underwear is OK, I suppose, but it leaves waffle marks on my behind and is uncomfortable to wear anywhere except when you are walking.

Special Conditions

As a kid, remember how your forehead wrinkled in pain whenever you ate ice cream too fast? A high wind, edged with polar cold, has the same effect on a bird hunter walking into it. Wearing a face mask or warm parka is the best way to avoid this painful condition. Plus the extra garments give you a handy excuse for explaining why you missed those crossing shots. (*My parka got in the way, My face mask slipped,* and so on.) You'll appreciate that tube of chap stick you carried in the shirt pocket, too, as nothing makes lips crack like a cold, dry wind.

A good tip for hunting in deep snow is to wear gaiters. Secured with elastic or Velcro, gaiters come in different lengths to fit over hunting boots and pant cuffs to keep snow out. They also help to keep boot laces tied although you can correct that problem easily enough by tying a double bow to your knots.

Footwear

A word on footwear. Select a nonslip sole. Although I rate my Bean boots right up there with apple pie and hot dogs (one pair I've owned for 22 years has been resoled four times. A puppy that chewed on the leather uppers grew up, lived a full life, and died during that period), the chain pattern in a gummed rubber sole can be slippery on wet hillsides and ice. A waffle pattern in a Vibram sole is better. When hunting in mountain country, consider a heavier hiking shoe to give you good footing in scree. You'll want a high-cut-style leather boot when hunting snake country in warm weather.

Although low-cut hunting/hiking shoes are lightweight and comfortable, I wouldn't buy them without ankle protection. Other than bramble scratches and sore muscles, turned ankles probably cause quail hunters the most grief. Because your pantlegs will barely cover

Rubber Wellingtons are comfortable and practical when field conditions are wet, such as they were in Georgia. Steve Smith tucks in pants cuffs while Bob Carson looks on.

ankle-high boots, consider, too, only models that contain a layer of foam or other protective material to keep out trash.

Rubber Wellington-style boots that reach nearly to the knee are practical (although they give poor ankle protection) when you're in and out of water or mud all day. They will keep you dry and are easy to clean up at day's end. In Kansas one time, we hunted in the rain off and on for nearly a week. By the third day, when all my footwear was soaked, I finally went into a WallMart and bought a pair of 18-inch-high rubber Red Balls. The boots are high enough to tuck pant cuffs inside without worrying about getting wet feet or adding weeds and other trash to the boots.

A good comfort tip is to change boots daily and socks at noon each day.

Pants and Jackets

A word about pants. A dozen or more American companies now make top-quality clothing for upland bird hunters. You can choose from cotton Army duck, cotton twill, wool, Cordura, and a half-dozen other synthetic blends. I like trousers that have rubberized inside waistbands so shirts stay put, back pockets with flaps, and buttons for suspenders. Facings come in everything from brushed pigskin to Naugahyde to 1000-denier Cordura. Whatever you choose, make sure it's tough enough to stop cholla cactus spines if your quail hunting adventures take you into the desert.

You'll appreciate trouser facing as tough as linoleum when you encounter multiflora rose, too. Multiflora rose is the scourge of many Midwestern farms. The first time I tackled a hedgerow of this nasty stuff, I was wearing light pants faced with nylon. In the shower that evening, my legs looked like they had been sandblasted with red pepper. Quail love to duck into multiflora rose, perhaps because they know you and your dogs are fools to follow.

Farmers began planting these "living fences" about the time of World War II. One night in a motel room, my legs on fire from puncture wounds, I had trouble falling asleep. My mind wandered to an especially thorny patch of multiflora rose: There was a farmer, clad only in a pair of Big Mac bibs, charging through the tangle under threat of a cattle prod for planting the stuff in the first place.

Jackets should also be made of tough material with heavy-duty buttons and zippers, plenty of roomy pockets, and little extras like wrist protectors, soft collar, and protective shell loops.

Serious quail hunters are never fussy in their clothing demands.

Chaps are helpful for hunting in contrary cover, especially hedges of multiflora rose and desert cacti.

As for appearance, we simply don't want to make mothers snatch their children off sidewalks when we come into town for lunch. All we want is trousers faced with material strong enough to turn aside a suture needle fired through a blow gun. Jackets that don't bind when we chase a contrary dog or swing fast on a goodbye covey. Detachable, cleanable game vests so we don't have to hang our jackets in the garage after hunting season. Boots that actually fit and last through the season. Easy-to-care-for fabrics that don't require our having to send them to New Zealand for cleaning. Costs that don't preclude our having to hide price tags from a nervous wife.

Such garments exist and you can learn all about them, by brand name and price, in the fall issues of the major outdoor magazines.

The Importance of Conditioning

As I have said elsewhere, the only quail hunting in America today that can still be called "gentleman's sport" occurs on shooting preserves or Southern plantations professionally managed for bobwhites. If you want to shoot wild birds in their natural environment, you will have to work hard. Being in good physical shape goes a long way toward smoothing your experience and making it successful.

A few years ago I mapped out a quail/pheasant hunting trip for a man whose daughter and mine were friends at school. Tom had been reading my magazine articles on upland bird hunting and wanted to try the sport in Iowa or Kansas. I didn't know Tom very well, and I had never met his hunting partners. One was a senior sportsman who would probably do a lot of blocking while the others drove birds past his post. Another was a boy who had yet to prick his first rooster spur. Tom and a third partner apparently had some bird hunting experience and seemed to be in shape.

On the other hand, the only exercise their one dog had received was in his kennel. On a map of Kansas, I circled some good areas for them to try. I also emphasized that they would have to hunt hungry. That meant knocking on doors to get permission, sizing up the habitat, and putting in long days of hard walking.

In four days of hunting, they never shot a bird, and I found myself apologizing for sending them there in the first place. In my opinion, their physical inability to hunt hard — to push themselves — led a list of some half-dozen reasons why this *bird hunt of a lifetime*, as they put it, failed.

Quail hunters should take a cue from their big-game brethren. The more serious a sheep, moose, bear, or deer hunter is about his sport, the more he concentrates on being in good physical condition. A regular exercise program, then, is good advice. And there are many to choose from — jogging, swimming, biking, weight lifting, practicing aerobics, among others.

I highly recommend such activities, though I am hardly an expert on physical conditioning. In fact, I don't participate in any of them. The reason is simple: I hate to work out. Sure, I took up jogging for awhile but deliberately ran on the pavement, hoping to get shin splints so I could quit. My interest in aerobics ends with what the girls are wearing for body suits. The only weights I lift are 50-pound bags of dog food. I don't mean to sound facetious, especially on a subject as important as physical health. But I *am* healthy and that is because I cut and stack the wood I burn to heat my farmhouse. I walk a dog at heel to the post office, and often enough I ride a bike to my office two miles from home.

And I hunt birds every chance I get. Like most everyone else, it takes a day or two for me to get the kinks out, but the kinks do come out. Most bird hunters love to walk. And — as Thomas Jefferson said — while walking you might as well carry a gun.

On that long trip across America to hunt quail, I saved the mountain and valley species for last. Everything I had read about mountain

A bulky game bag that fits over other clothing is ideal for carrying birds and extra clothing.

quail in particular said that they were tough customers to bag. Mountain quail like the high country, and, like most species of Western quail, they are runners. The difference was that they run uphill. If you get lucky enough to flush them, they fly uphill. This means you may have to scale another peak to find them again. I found mountain quail in Nevada at 6,500 to 7,000 feet.

As I related earlier, I shot only two birds in four days of hunting. If I had not been in good physical shape, I would not have shot any, and quite likely would not have ever seen a mountain quail. Fortunately I was acclimated to the altitude, having hunted Mearns quail in southern Arizona hills along the Mexican border a couple of weeks earlier. There is no way to make the body produce more red blood cells, which is what it does at higher altitudes, than to go there. Some hunters experience no difficulty. Others suffer from nosebleeds, fatigue, headaches, even hyperventilation. It took me several days to get fully used to it.

Day's End

Hunting in comfort means having a warm place to clean birds, a hot shower, a good meal, a bed where the quilts are soft and the mattress is firm. Nor is there a better feeling than reliving the day's highlights over a motel drink with your hunting partners. Sometimes in the late afternoon, as you swing back toward the car, the dog bells even sound like ice tinkling in a tumbler of whiskey.

I like to think about that, along with a little talcum powder. And I so reward myself. But only when the birds are dressed, the dogs fed, the guns cleaned, and the electric boot dryers are working overtime to make me comfortable again tomorrow.

Epilogue

Out through the fields and the woods
And over the walls I have wended . . .
I have come by the highway home,
And lo, it is ended.

Robert Frost

There is more to hunting quail than reducing the bird to a game-bag statistic. People and places are just a couple of items that contribute to the making of *The Hunt*. The following impressions were gleaned from the journal I kept daily during my trips across America to hunt quail.

The Hunters. You were a Kansas schoolboy who carried your .410 on the trapline just in case you and Blue happened to bump that gumbo-ground covey. Sometimes you were a factory worker with a long weekend on your hands. A retired financier who hunted bobwhites by the banker's hours you knew so well.

I saw you in faded Carhartt coveralls, in Levis with a permanent Skoal ring on the right rear pocket, in a new Beaufort Shooting Jacket imported from England. Sometimes you owned signed-and-re-marqued shooting prints on your living-room walls. I noticed, too, that your bedroom was adorned with rock-concert posters.

The Landowners. You politely turned down my request to hunt because you said that bobwhites eat chintz bugs and therefore should not be shot. In Kansas, I helped you jump start your grain truck with the vintage 1948 license plate so you could sell your milo for $1.50 per bushel, the same price your father received in 1955. You were 32, your wife only 26, and your six kids looked like a stairstep family.

The Dogs. Some had ancestors with names like Bourgeois of Belvidere. The parentage of others was unknown and questionable at best. In Kansas, I saw you tear a sandwich in half to share with your four-legged partner. In New Mexico, you booted your Britt so she wouldn't have sore paws. In Iowa, your pointer was as shocked as we were when the "bobwhite" he was holding for us turned into a "wild turkey." *We grow big quail in the Hawkeye State,* you said.

In Missouri during a pouring rain, Macbeth picked up a cottontail and brought it back to us. I wasn't impressed and told her to let it go. When she opened her mouth, the rabbit hopped away as though nothing had happened.

The Guns. You took pride in your shotgun, no matter the name, age, or condition. You showed me the .410 you had gotten for your birthday. Another time, hoping you might be in the market to sell, I feigned ignorance when you brought out the 1871 Parker long enough to let me swing through on an imaginary bird or two.

At that motel in Iowa, you cleaned my gun along with yours because you thought I just might not get to it. When I hunted with you in Nevada, I observed that your double-barrel needed new blueing. You observed that new glasses might correct my poor shooting.

The Vehicles. In Georgia, you drove a 1973 Jeep with Lord-knows-how-many-miles. It was jammed with hunting paraphernalia. *You might find anything from a ham sandwich to a string of pearls in here,* you laughed. In Arizona, your Jeep Grand Wagoneer sported a $23,000 sticker. In Oklahoma, you owned a one-ton pickup with a flat bed of boiler plate and oil-drilling equipment. Red dust had settled in the wheel wells.

The brakes were out on the beat-up orange pickup you drove in New Mexico. Chevy Scottsdale pickups were your choice in Missouri: Two in a row each had 128,000 miles. There were gun racks across the rear window, and I smelled the wintergreen flavor of your favorite chew.

The Places. In southern Iowa, the towns are laid out around a square with park statues and county government buildings in the center. Traffic is routed in a one-way pattern. In Corydon was a neon

Lady Macbeth with mixed bag of scaled and bobwhite quail from Kansas. Scaled quail frustrated both her and her owner.

sign that said *DeSoto Plymouth*. In Leon, the church bulletin read, *Emily Spreight is improving!*

In Kansas, the farmers hustled to fetch in their crops. Driving past Clay Center, I saw combines working in the dark. They looked like alien insects with headlights sticking out to each side of the cab and another one over the cutter bar. A street leading to the full grain elevator in Marysville was barricaded. That was because farmers were making a milo mountain by dumping their crop in the road.

In Nevada, the motorhome, parked at the road end far below, looked like a Tonka toy vehicle when viewed from a mountain canyon.

The Stories.   There were enough for another book. In Oklahoma, you talked about how that gutsy pointer fought off two coyotes that tried to drag him from the pickup bed. In Kansas, I could just imagine the look on a motel owner's face when he caught you cleaning birds in the bathtub. In Georgia, we walked the wartime beaches in the Pacific with you and General McArthur.

In Hume, Missouri, population 315, you spoke of Gerald Bogan with unusual reverence for a man yet living. *Eighteen seconds around the town square*, you said. *Back then he drove a '59 Ford and took the corners on two wheels. Nobody could beat 'em. Not even the 409s. Ain't been broke to this day.*

The Weather.   The wettest fall on record in the Midwest. According to the *Indianapolis Star*, it rained every day but three in November. There is nothing more treacherous than an ice-rimed road. In Illinois, it claimed a Jartran rental truck, lying alongside the highway like some overturned African animal. A red-orange sunset in Arizona made one wonder if God was making pizza for supper.

On I-80 in Nebraska, the diesel long-haulers inching past each other in twilight mist reminded me of stream salmon nosing to the weir. Sitting in the car after a fine hunt, we felt the moist heat of Georgia springtime. The engine ticked in the stillness, and I could hear your dogs panting in their wire cages.

There is more to hunting quail than reducing the bird to a game-bag statistic.

Appendix I:
Shooting Preserves Open
to the Public

The following shooting preserves feature quail and are open to the public for fee hunting. List courtesy of North American Gamebird Association, Inc.

Alabama

Wood's Gamebird Farm
Rt. 1, P.O. Box 181
Titus, AL 36080
(205) 567-7771

Selwood Farm & Hunting
  Preserve
Rt. 1, P.O. Box 230
Alpine, AL 35014
(205) 362-7595

Arizona

Salt Cedar Shooting Preserve,
  Inc.
P.O. Box 1001
Buckeye, AZ 85326
(602) 386-6625

Arkansas

Point Remove WMA
P.O. Box 133
Hattieville, AR 72063
(501) 354-0136

217

Crowley Ridge Shooting Resort
Rt. 1, P.O. Box 350
Forrest City, AR 72335
(501) 633-3352

Covey Rise Hunt Club
Stuttgart, AR 72160
(501) 673-6611

Nevada County Game Birds,
  Inc.
Rt. 1, P.O. Box 171
Buckner, AR 71827
(501) 899-2902

California

Raahauge's Hunting Club
5800 Bluff Street
Norco, CA 91760
(714) 735-2361

Red Bank Ale & Quail Game
  Bird Club
P.O. Box 627
Red Bluff, CA 96080
(916) 527-7432

Wildlife Game Birds
8100 Phillip Road
Pleasant Grove, CA 95668
(916) 655-3915

Colorado

Western Wildlife Adventures
31209 W.C.R. 17
Windsor, CO 80550
(303) 686-2621, 686-5210

Florida

Thundering Wings Hunting
  Preserve (preserve)
Rt. 2, P.O. Box 20C
Caryville, FL 32427
(904) 623-0725, 547-9520

Thundering Wings Hunting
  Preserve (office)
969 Lakeside Drive
Milton, FL 32570
(904) 547-9520, 623-0725

Georgia

Babcock Plantation & Quail
  Preserve
Rt. 2, P.O. Box 143
Babcock, GA 31737
(912) 758-5454

Covey Rise Farm
Rt. 3
Mayfield, GA 31087
(404) 444-6739

Callaway Gardens Hunting
  Preserve
Hwy. 18 West
Pine Mountain, GA 31822
(404) 663-2281, ext. 129

D&B Plantation
Adams Road, P.O. Box 119-6
Chula, GA 31733
(404) 252-9989 or (912) 567-2518

Riverview Plantation
Rt. 2, P.O. Box 515
Camilla, GA 31730
(912) 294-4904

Tallawahee Plantation
Rt. 5, P.O. Box 204
Dawson, GA 31742
(912) 995-2265

Turkey Oak Lodge
416 Northside Drive
Valdosta, GA 31602
(912) 247-0225 or (912) 242-4782

Turkey Oak Lodge Quail
   Hunting Preserve
2210 Glyndale Drive
Valdosta, GA 31602
(912) 247-0225 (day) or 242-4782
   (eves)

Hawaii

West Beach Game Preserve
P.O. Box 88537
Honolulu, HI 96815
(808) 395-4309

Illinois

Great Tey Chase
P.O. Box 758
Union Road
Harmon, IL 61042
(815) 359-7345

Heggemeier Hunting Club
R.R. 2
Nashville, IL 62263
(618) 327-3709

Hopewell Views
Rt. 2
Rockport, IL 62370
(217) 734-9234

Huntley Game Farm
10308 Crystal Lake Rd.
Huntley, IL 60142
(312) 669-5600

Rogers Hunting Club, Inc.
RFD #2
Ohio, IL 61349
(815) 379-2427

Richmond Hunting Club
5016 Rt. 173
Richmond, IL 60071
(815) 678-3271

Seneca Hunt Club
P.O. Box 306
Maywood, IL 60153
(362) 681-3999; office (815)
   357-8080

Indiana

Early Rise Shooting Preserve
R.R. 1, P.O. Box 72
Walkerton, IN 46574
(219) 656-8962

King Farms Inc.
R.R. 1, P.O. Box 12
Parker City, IN 47368
(317) 468-6706

Iowa

Arrowhead Hunting &
   Conservation Club
Rt. 1, P.O. Box 28
Goose Lake, IA 52750
(319) 577-2267

Oakview Hunting Club &
  Kennels
Rt. 2
Prairie City, IA 50228
(515) 994-2094

Kansas

Blue Line Club
Rt. 1, P.O. Box 139A
Solomon, KS 67480
(913) 488-3785

Flint Oak Ranch
Rt. 1
Fall River, KS 67047
(316) 658-4401

Lone Pine Shooting Preserve
Rt. 1, P.O. Box 79
Toronto, KS 66777
(316) 637-2967

McDonald Game Farm
107 S. Franklin
Ness City, KS 67560
(913) 798-2541

Maike Hunting Club
R.R. #2, P.O. Box 152
Alma, KS 66401
(913) 765-3820 or (913) 765-3339

Kentucky

Hunter's Paradise #2
Larry Allen
Harper, KY 41440
(606) 349-5977, 743-1560

Keira Hill Hunting Preserve
Rt. 3, P.O. Box 97
Clinton, KY 42031
(502) 653-2161

Watson Pheasant Farm
Rt. 5, P.O. Box 144
Morganfield, KY 42437
(502) 389-3085

Whistling Quail
R.R. 1
Bagdad, KY 40003
(502) 747-8786

Maryland

Hopkins Game Farm
Kennedyville, MD 21645
(301) 348-5287

Native Shore Hunting Preserve
Rt. 6, P.O. Box 486
Easton, MD 21601
(301) 758-0133 or (301) 822-2502

Pheasantfield Shooting
  Preserve
Rt. 3, P.O. Box 21620
Chestertown, MD 21620
(301) 758-1824

Michigan

Rolling Hills Shooting Preserve
17025 McKenzie Street
Marcellas, MI 49067
(616) 646-9164

Minnesota

Pleasant Acres Hunting Club
R.R. #3, P.O. Box 144
New Ulm, MN 56073
(507) 359-4166

Wild Wings of Oneka Hunting
  Club
9491 –152 Street N.
Hugo, MN 55038
(612) 439-4287

Mississippi

Wilderness West Game
  Preserve
R.R. 1, P.O. Box 182
West, MS 39192

Missouri

Baier's Den Kennels & Shooting
  Preserve
Peculiar, MO 64078
(816) 758-5234

Blue Creek Game Ranch
R.R. 1, P.O. Box 167
Mokane, MO 65059
(314) 676-3245

McLaughlin Ranch & Hunting
  Preserve
Rt. 1, P.O. Box 133A
Koshkonong, MO 65692
(417) 264-3260

Snow White Enterprises
Rt. 1, P.O. Box 40
Carrollton, MO 64633
(816) 542-3037

Sorenson Kennel & Shooting
  Preserve
10102 Hwy. DD
Wentzville, MO 63385
(314) 828-5149

Tall Oaks Club
Rt. 3, P.O. Box 202
Warrenton, MO 63383
(314) 456-3564

Nebraska

Hunt Nebraska Inc.
P.O. Box 317
Araphoe, NE 68522
(308) 962-8469

Swanson Hunting Acres Inc.
P.O. Box 99
Niobrara, NE 68760
(402) 857-3514

New Hampshire

Skat Upland Game Preserve
P.O. Box 137
New Ipswich, NH 03071
(603) 878-1257

New Jersey

B. & B. Pheasantry & Shooting
  Preserve
"Main Farm" R.D. 3,
P.O. Box 11
Pittstown, NJ 08867
(201) 735-6501

Belleplain Farms Shooting
  Preserve
P.O. Box 222, Handsmill Road
Belleplain, NJ 08270

Game Creek Hunting Farms
112 N. DuPond Road
Carneys Point, NJ 08069
(609) 299-6313

Oak Ridge Hunting Preserve
R.D. 3, P.O. Box 362
Phillipsburg, NJ 08865
(201) 859-3393

M & M Hunting Preserve
Hook & Winston Roads
Pennsville, NJ 08070
(609) 935-1230 or 1-(800)
   441-8484

New Mexico

New Mexico Game Bird
   Hunting Preserve
P.O. Dr. 3
Nara Visa, NM 88430
(505) 633-2284

New York

Stonegate Hunting Preserve
262 Beattie Road
Rock Tavern, NY 12575
(914) 427-2115, 782-4746

T-M-T Hunting Preserve Inc.
R.R. #1, P.O. Box 297
Schoolhouse Road
Staatsburg, NY 12580
(914) 266-5108

Whaleback Farm Shooting
   Preserve
South Hill Road
Middlesex, NY 14507
(716) 461-0775/385-1595

North Carolina

Derby Hunting Preserve
Rt. 1, P.O. Box 469
Jackson Springs, NC 27281
(919) 652-5752

George Hi Plantation
P.O. Box 1068
Roseboro, NC 28382
(919) 525-4524

Lowe's Shooting Preserve
Rt. 2, P.O. Box 13
Lawndale, NC 28090
(704) 538-7254

Ohio

Beaver Creek Hunt Club
48430 Foster Pike Road
Amherst, OH 44001
(216) 988-8884

Cherrybend Pheasant Farm
2326 Cherrybend Road
Wilmington, OH 45177
(513) 584-4269

Elkhorn Lake Hunt Club
4146 Klopfenstein Road
Bucyrus, OH 44820
(419) 562-6131, 562-1471

Hidden Haven Shooting
   Preserve Inc.
9291 Buckeye Road
Sugar Grove, OH 43155
(614) 746-8568

Oklahoma

Crossed Arrows Ranch Inc.
Rt. 1, P.O. Box 69
Marland, OK 74644
(405) 268-3244

Double W Ranch Kennels &
Preserve
Rt. 1, P.O. Box 511
Beggs, OK 74421
(918) 827-3188

Pennsylvania

Angus Conservation and
Hunting Farm
R.D. 1, P.O. Box 260
Latrobe, PA 15650
(412) 423-4022

The Flying Feather Shooting
Preserve
R.D. 2, P.O. Box 343
Guys Mills, PA 16327

La-Da-Jo Pines Hunting &
Cons. Club
218 N. 25th Street
Mt. Penn., PA 19606
(215) 779-3343

Marshbrook Game Preserve
R.D. 2, P.O. Box 109
Factoryville, PA 18419
(717) 222-4469

T.N.T. Shooting Grounds
R.D. 1, P.O. Box 147A
Smock, PA 15480
(412) 677-4620, 677-2609

Tohicken Hunting Preserve
Rt. 611
Revere, PA
(215) 847-8253

Rhode Island

Addieville East Farm
P.O. Box 157
Mapleville, RI 02839
(401) 568-3185

South Carolina

Rolling Hills Hunting Preserve
Rt. 1, P.O. Box 180
Calhoun Falls, SC 29628
(803) 391-2901

River Bend Sportsman's Resort
P.O. Box 625
Inman, SC 29349
(803) 583-2048

Sassafras Preserve
P.O. Box 8044
Greenville, SC 29604
(803) 232-1050

Santee Cooper Shooting
Preserve
P.O. Box 187
Elloree, SC 29047
(803) 854-2495, 897-2731

Single Tree Shooting Preserve
Rt. 1, P.O. Box 564
Clinton, SC 29325
(803) 833-5477

South Dakota

James Valley Hunting Preserve
R.R. 1, P.O. Box 39
Utica, SD 57067
(605) 364-7468

K. & M. Hunting
Plankinton, SD 57368
(605) 942-7516

Wells Shooting Preserve
Rt. 1, P.O. Box 44
Oldham, SD 57051
(605) 854-3284

Tennessee

Rocky Top Hunting Preserve
Rt. 1
Belvidere, TN 37919
(615) 759-4216

Texas

Central Texas Hunting
P.O. Box 154
Llano, TX 78643
(915) 247-4797

C & J Hunting Farm
Carolyn Johns
Route 1, P.O. Box 100-A
Carmine, TX 78932

Firelake Farms Shooting &
  Game Preserve
Rt. 8, P.O. Box 175
Kemp, TX 75143
(214) 498-8610/498-7993

Landrum Creek Hunting Resort
Hwy. 149, Rt. 7
P.O. Box 40
Montgomery, TX 77356
(409) 597-4267

Running High Hunting Club
P.O. Box 1831
Bowie, TX 76230
(817) 934-6300

Texas Rice Belt Hunting Club
5522 Sanford
Houston, TX 77096
(713) 729-7259

Utah

Pheasant Valley
P.O. Box 86
Howell, UT 84316
(801) 471-2245

Vermont

Tinmouth Hunting Preserve
East Road
P.O. Box 556 Tinmouth
Wallingford, VT 05773
(802) 446-2337

Virginia

Magnolia Shooting Preserve
101 Philhower Drive
Suffolk, VA 23434
(804) 539-6296

Merrimac Farm Hunting
  Preserve
14710 Deepwood Lane
Nokesville, VA 22123
(703) 594-2276

Washington

Triple B Hunting & Cons. Club
Rt. 1, P.O. Box 1855
Selah, WA 98942
(509) 697-7675

West Virginia

Foxy Pheasant Hunting
  Preserve
Rt. 1, P.O. Box 437
Kearneysville, WV 25430
(304) 725-4963

Wisconsin

Hawe Hunting Preserve
Rt. 1A
Waldo, WI 53093
(414) 528-8388

Madeline Island Gun Club
P.O. Box 13
LaPointe, WI 54850
(715) 747-3381

Martin Fish & Game Farm
R.F.D. 3, Hwy. 127
Portage, WI 53901
(608) 742-7205

Pheasant City Hunting
  Preserve
Rt. 1
Markesan, WI 53946
(414) 324-5813

Wern Valley Sportsmens Club
S. 36 W. 29903 Wernway
Waukesha, WI 53188
(414) 968-2400

Wisconsin Pheasant Hunting
  Club
N. Rd. Off of Hwy.
  16 – preserve
623 Park St. – office
Watertown, WI 53094
(414) 261-4686

Wyoming

Clear Creek Hunting Preserve
3004 U.S. Hwy. 14–16E
Clearmont, WY 82835
(307) 737-2237

The Covey
P.O. Box 8
Buffalo, WY 82834
(307) 684-2271

Appendix II: United States, Canada, and Mexico

Alabama

Although populations have declined in recent years, due to habitat loss, Alabama continues to offer good bobwhite quail hunting. Harvest records over the past six years varied from 930,000 to 1.6 million birds, or a range of 20–23 quail per hunter.

The latest estimate shows a statewide population of 1.7 million bobwhites; however, biologists believe the figure to be closer to 2.5 or 3.0 million. The highest number of quail per acre occurs in the southeast, with the Black Belt region and the Sand Mountain area of the northeast rating second and third respectively.

The Alabama Game and Fish Division controls nearly 650,000 acres of land on 29 management areas throughout the state. Quail are an important gamebird on many of the areas. Shooting preserves are another possibility. The best wild-bird hunting, however, generally occurs on farms with small fields and a diversity of habitat.

Current regulations call for an opener in early November and a long season lasting through February in nine counties along the southern border and in the southeast. Elsewhere, the season usually

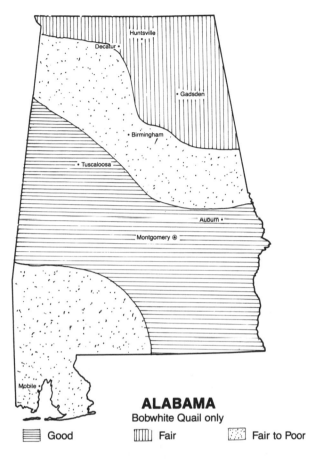

ALABAMA
Bobwhite Quail only

▤ Good   ▥ Fair   ▦ Fair to Poor

begins about November 20 and ends February 28. Recent bag limits are 12 quail daily and 12 in possession.

For more information, contact the Alabama Game & Fish Division, 64 N. Union St., Montgomery, AL 36130 (205) 832-6357.

Alaska

There are no quail in Alaska.

Arizona

Arizona hosts four Western species of huntable quail as well as small populations of mountain quail and the endangered masked

ALASKA
No Quail

bobwhite. Each year an average of about 80,000 hunters seek Gambel, scaled, Mearns, and—to a very limited extent—valley quail.

Gambels make up about two-thirds of the annual kill of 1.3 to 2.9 million quail. The desert quail are found in the southern and western two-thirds of the state in densely vegetated arroyos, washes, and scrubby hillsides ranging from 150 feet to 5,000 feet elevation. Stock watering tanks and other surface water attract the Gambels. In recent years, hunter harvests have ranged from 1.1 to 2.6 million Gambels or a range of 13–27 birds per gun. Recent quail call-count surveys indicate that numbers are holding or improving.

Scaled quail live in arid grasslands and plains of the southeastern and east-central portions of Arizona with a few birds showing up north of the Gila River. The annual kill of scalies varies from 52,000 to 125,000.

Mearns quail live in oak grasslands at 3,000- to 4,000-foot elevations in southeastern and east-central Arizona. Some hunters have reported scattered sightings along the Mogollon Rim and in the Williams area. Hunters annually kill 30,000–80,000 Mearns.

Valley quail, from a private-land release 20 years ago in the Springerville area of east-central Arizona, have spread for a few miles up and down the Little Colorado River. They provide limited hunting opportunities. The game and fish department has stocked mountain quail into the Hualapai Mountains near Kingman. Federal and state biologists are also watching a small band of reintroduced masked bobwhites at the Buenos Aires National Wildlife Refuge near Sasabe.

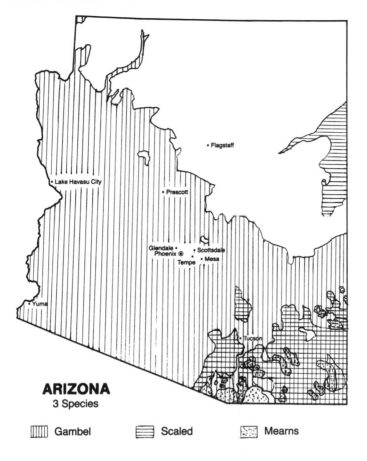

ARIZONA
3 Species

||||| Gambel   ☰ Scaled   ░░ Mearns

Huge areas in Arizona are open to hunting. They include most of the 13 percent of the land base managed by the state along with 44 percent controlled by the U.S. Forest Service (there are six national forests in Arizona) and the Bureau of Land Management. Indian reservations comprise another 28 percent, and portions of these lands are open to hunting through tribal permit. The statewide season for Gambel, scaled, and valley quail usually runs four months, from mid-October to mid-February. The Mearns quail season begins about November 20 and ends February 10. Daily bag and possession limits are 15 and 30 quail.

For more information, contact the Arizona Game and Fish Department, 2222 West Greenway Rd., Phoenix, AZ 85023 (602) 942-3000.

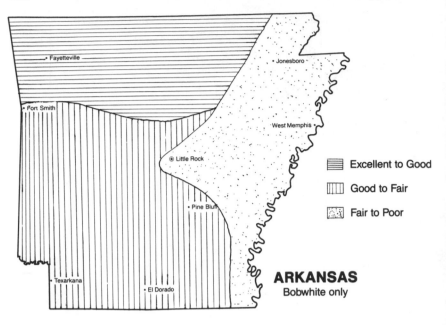

Arkansas

Each year close to 100,000 hunters take to Arkansas' woods and fields in quest of bobwhite quail. On the average, they harvest 1.5 to 2.0 million birds for an average seasonal bag of 26 quail per hunter. However, a short-term but intensive decline since 1982 has occurred because of poor nesting and brood-rearing weather. Research biologists expect a change for the better.

Bobwhites are found throughout the state's four management regions. Pre-hunt fall densities approach one bobwhite per two acres in better areas. That would be the Ozark Mountain region in the northern part of the state, closely followed by the Gulf Coastal Plain in the southern region. The Quachita Mountain (western) area is also good. The Delta region (eastern) generally rates poor to fair.

Hunters can roam most of the 2 million acres of public land in Arkansas' three national forests and 52 state wildlife management areas. Preserve hunting for pen-reared birds is also an option.

The statewide quail hunting season begins about November 20 and ends in early February. Daily limits are currently 10 quail with a possession limit of 16. Hunter-orange clothing is required when small game seasons coincide with firearm deer seasons.

For more information, contact the Arkansas Game & Fish Commission, 2 Natural Resources Dr., Little Rock, AR 72205 (501) 223-6300.

California

About one-third of California's licensed hunters seek valley, Gambel, and mountain quail. The most recent harvest showed slightly more than a million birds, down nearly 29 percent from the previous year and considerably off the most recent five-year average of 1.8 million birds. Despite the downturn in harvest, quail rank third (behind doves and ducks) in the number of birds taken.

Valley quail make up 75 percent of the annual bag. The birds live throughout the state except in high mountain areas and desert regions and in the extreme southeast. The once-good Sacramento and San Joaquin valleys have succumbed to farming, grazing, and urban devel-

CALIFORNIA
3 Species

Valley

Gambel

Mountain

opment. Best areas of production today include interior and coastal foothill brushlands and sagebrush areas east of the Sierra Nevadas. Top counties overall are Fresno, Riverside, Kern, San Diego, and San Bernardino.

Gambel quail constitute about 20 percent of the yearly kill or about 200,000–400,000 birds. Highest numbers occur in the southeast along the Colorado River, in the Imperial and Coachella valleys, and in the eastern San Bernardino desert mountains.

Mountain quail are distributed over roughly 45 percent of the state in mountainous habitat from Mexico to Oregon. Most of the 50,000 to 90,000 birds shot annually are taken incidentally to other upland game although some hunters specifically seek the mountain quail.

Nearly half of the 100 million acres of land in California is publicly owned. Large portions, where quail are among game species being managed, are open to hunting. These include nearly 30 state fish and game hunting areas, state forests, Bureau of Land Management lands, several military installations, and 18 national forests.

The season generally opens first in six counties north of San Francisco on the last Saturday in September. Elsewhere it typically opens on the third Saturday in October. Seasons usually close on either the last Sunday in December or January. A special mountain quail season may open as early as mid-September and run for 35 days. Overall daily bag and possession limits are 10 and 20 quail respectively.

For more information, contact the California Department of Fish and Game, 1416 Ninth St., Sacramento, CA 95814, (916) 445-7613.

Colorado

Colorado is largely a fringe area for bobwhites, Gambel, and scaled quail. The scaled is most plentiful, occupying about 22,000 square miles of sand-sage and yucca grasslands and areas of thick cholla cactus and pinyon-juniper in the southeastern corner of the state. The best counties are Baca, Prowers, Crowley, and southern El Paso. In a good year, 5,000 hunters will kill 40,000 birds.

Bobwhites occur less frequently in limited habitat along the Arkansas and South Platte rivers, from east of Greeley to the northeastern corner, and in east-central and southeastern Baca County. In a good year, 3,000 hunters will kill 12,000 bobwhites. Limited numbers of Gambel quail live in southwestern Colorado, but there is no harvest information available.

The best public hunting occurs in the southeast on portions of the

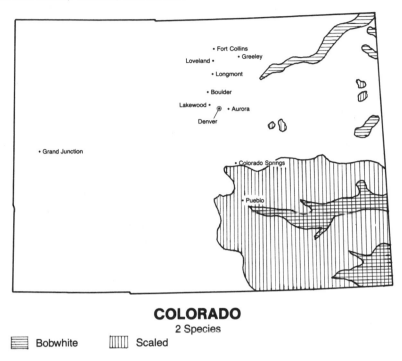

COLORADO
2 Species

▤ Bobwhite ▥ Scaled

Comanche National Grassland. Private ranches are also good if you can get permission to hunt them.

Seasons usually begin in early to mid-November and end as early as mid-December or as late as early January. Daily bag and possession limits for each species are eight and 16 respectively.

For more information, contact the Colorado Division of Wildlife, 6060 Broadway, Denver, CO 80216 (303) 297-1192.

Connecticut

Scattered populations of wild bobwhites live in New London and Windham counties in southeastern and northeastern Connecticut. Together with pen-reared birds released by private hunting clubs, the annual harvest is about 2,000 quail. Also, working cooperatively with sportsmen's clubs, the state raises about 7,000 bobwhites for non-shooting field trials on designated grounds. Some of these quail are eventually reduced to harvest.

Hunters have limited opportunities for wild birds on the Lebanon

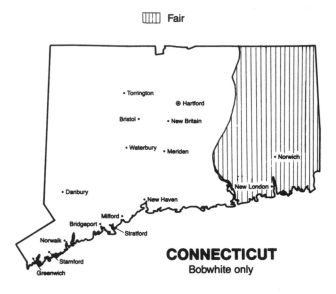

and Franklin state-leased hunting grounds in New London County and at Franklin and Barn Island wildlife management areas and Woodstock Permit Required Hunting Area in the northeast. The season runs for about two weeks in late October. Bag limits are two birds daily and 10 for the season.

For more information, contact the Connecticut Department of Environmental Protection, Wildlife Bureau, 165 Capitol Ave., Room 252, Hartford, CT 06106 (203) 566-4683.

Delaware

Delaware has good hunting opportunities for bobwhite quail although populations can fluctuate widely from year to year. Over the past 10 years, the best season saw a harvest of 96,353 birds; the lowest was 26,879. During the most recent season for which records are available, 4,657 hunters bagged 36,293 bobwhites for an average of about eight birds each.

The best hunting occurs west of Highway 113 in the southern half of the state and in the west-central region, west of a line between Felton and Smyrna. The poorest hunting is in the far northern area, north of a line between Chesapeake City and Delaware City. The rest of the state—for the most part, the eastern region fronting Delaware Bay—has fair to good quail hunting.

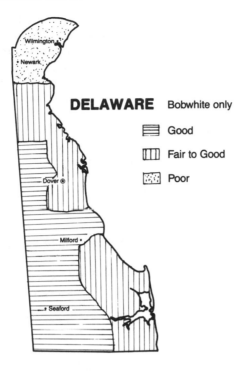

Private lands provide the best sport. However, there are some opportunities on public hunting areas where quail are managed. Eleven public hunting areas total about 30,000 acres, and there are three state forests (about 6,000 acres in all) open to hunting.

Most recently, the quail hunting season opened in mid-November and closed in mid-January for a few days, then opened again until the end of February. The daily bag was eight quail.

For more information, contact the Delaware Division of Fish & Wildlife, PO Box 1401, Dover, DE 19903 (302) 736-5297.

Florida

Florida is an important state for bobwhite quail hunters, even though the long-term trend shows reduced harvests. In the 1970s, the statewide bag never dropped below a million birds. In the most recent season for which records are available, it fell to 457,000. Reasons for the decline include farming and forestry practices and urban-suburban growth.

Bobwhites are found throughout Florida, but the northwestern region (approximately from Tallahassee west, bordering southwestern Georgia and southern Alabama) has the best opportunities. Hunters there averaged 20 birds each during the latest season for which kill figures are available. The south (15 quail per hunter), northeast (13), Everglades (11), and central (10) are the other management areas in the state.

Some five million acres of the state are open to hunting for various species including quail. Bobwhites are managed on several of the 60 wildlife management areas scattered throughout the state. Several state and national forests are also open to hunting. In addition, 17 of the 67 commercial preserves in Florida are open to the public for quail hunting.

The season for wild birds opens statewide in mid-November and runs through early March. Bag limits are 12 daily and 24 in possession with no season limit.

For more information, contact the Florida Game and Fresh Water Commission, 620 S. Meridian St., Tallahassee, FL 32301 (904) 488-1960.

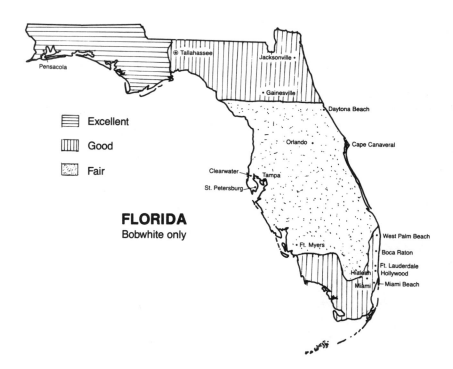

Excellent

Good

Fair

FLORIDA
Bobwhite only

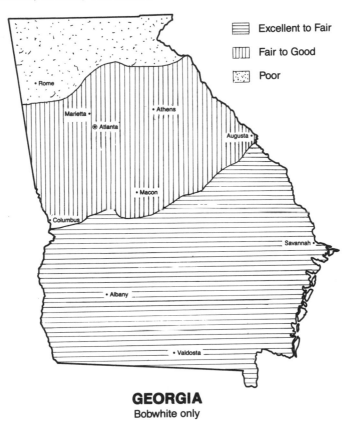

GEORGIA
Bobwhite only

Excellent to Fair

Fair to Good

Poor

Georgia

After tumbling from a harvest high of more than four million bobwhites in the early 1960s to a low of 1.1 million in 1981–82, Georgia quail have been rebounding. The number of hunters during that period fell by half. Today, less than 60,000 quail hunters go afield, and, on the average, they pocket about 20 birds each during the season.

The best opportunities occur in the upper and lower coastal plain regions (southern half of the state) where bobwhite populations range from fair to excellent. This southern area hosts a large number of privately owned plantations whose owners manage the land for wild birds. Hunting in the Piedmont Plateau region (north-central portion of the state) rates fair to good. The mountainous northern part of the state yields poor quail populations.

From three to five million acres of public land in Georgia is open to hunting for quail although most do not provide prime habitat. These include most of the 55 state wildlife management areas, state forests, national forestlands in the northern half of the state, and military installations. In addition, several major timber companies allow public hunting on corporate lands for a small annual fee. Further, there has been a tremendous growth of commercial shooting preserves where hunters pay for released birds.

The statewide quail hunting season generally opens about November 20. In southern Georgia (roughly south of a line from Columbus to Augusta), it closes at the end of February because plantation owners begin prescribed burning in early March, and in some southernmost counties bobwhites begin nesting about that time. In the northern region, the season usually runs until mid-March. The daily limit is 12 birds.

For more information, contact the Georgia Department of Natural Resources, 270 Washington St., SW, Atlanta, GA 30334 (404) 656-3530).

Hawaii

There are no quail native to Hawaii; however, three species that have been introduced now furnish sport hunting. But most upland

HAWAII
3 Species

bird hunters shoot them incidentally to pheasants, francolins, chukars, and other game. Valley quail, introduced from California about 100 years ago, are most abundant on Molokai and Hawaii but are also found on Maui, Lanai, and Kauai. They prefer open parkland forests or pasturelands on the leeward sides of these islands from sea level to 11,000 feet. During a recent season, Hawaii Island hunters shot 2,489 valley quail.

Japanese quail first appeared on Maui and Lanai where they were released in 1921. Sparse populations occur on all the islands, mostly on pasturelands below 7,000 feet. Island of Hawaii hunters shot 182 during a recent season.

Gambel quail, stocked on all the islands except Molokai, today inhabit Hawaii, Lanai, and Kahoolawe. Hunters on Hawaii shot 107 during a recent season.

The state manages public hunting lands on all the major islands except Kahoolawe, which the Navy uses for bomb testing and where hunting is not allowed. Quail seasons usually begin on the first Saturday in November and run through the third Sunday in January with hunting permitted only on weekends and state holidays. The daily bag limit has been 15 birds, singly or in combination. Hunter-orange clothing is required.

For more information, contact the Hawaii Department of Land and Natural Resources, 1151 Punchbowl St., Honolulu, HI 96813 (808) 548-2861).

Idaho

Valley quail are the most populous of four species found in Idaho. They are most abundant and may be legally hunted from Clearwater and Latah counties south along the western and south-central regions. Wooded bottomlands along the Snake River and other streams offer the best opportunities for the 45,000 to 90,000 shot each year during recent seasons. Numbers of valley quail have fallen off in recent years due to tough winters and wet nesting weather.

Bobwhite quail are also legal targets in the same areas, but sharply limited numbers mean few birds in the bag. They are restricted to southwestern Idaho. A few Gambel quail live in the southern desert region, mostly along the Lemhi River bottomlands, but they may not be hunted. Mountain quail used to be an important gamebird in Idaho, but the birds, which live at higher elevations in south-central and southwestern regions, have also suffered population losses. Currently, there is no hunting season for mountain quail.

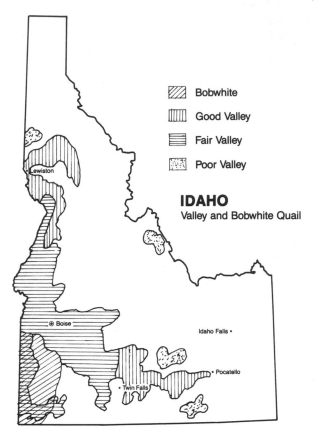

IDAHO
Valley and Bobwhite Quail

Bobwhite

Good Valley

Fair Valley

Poor Valley

Lewiston

Boise

Idaho Falls •

• Pocatello

• Twin Falls

Bureau of Land Management, U.S. Forest Service, and state lands total nearly two-thirds of Idaho real estate. Large portions are open to hunting, and some state wildlife areas that are managed for quail furnish good hunting opportunities. Private lands, assuming you can get permission to hunt, are also a good bet.

The season opens in specified counties about September 20 and ends December 31. Bag limits are 10 quail daily and 20 in possession, no more than two of which may be bobwhites.

For more information, contact the Idaho Department of Fish and Game, PO Box 25, Boise, ID 83707 (208) 334-3700.

Illinois

Bobwhite quail are an important upland gamebird for Illinois hunters. Over the past decade, harvest figures have varied from a low of 393,000 birds to a high of nearly 1.5 million. Quail have been slowly rebounding from a population low in 1979.

Best hunting is in the southern third of the state, which still provides habitat diversity on a large scale. South-central and west-central counties are rated fair, and the northern half of the state is poor.

There are more than 100 public hunting areas scattered throughout Illinois. They vary in size from a few hundred acres to the sprawling 262,000-acre Shawnee National Forest, which spills into 10 counties. The department of conservation manages bobwhites on several of the lands.

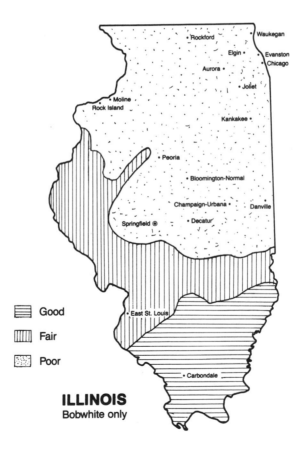

Good

Fair

Poor

ILLINOIS
Bobwhite only

U.S. Route 50 divides Illinois into two zones with slightly different seasons for upland game. Generally they begin in early to mid-November and last about two months each. Limits are six quail daily and 12 in possession.

For more information, contact the Illinois Department of Conservation, Division of Information and Education, 515 Lincoln Tower Plaza, 524 S. Second St., Springfield, IL 62706 (217) 782-6384.

Indiana

Bobwhites are found throughout Indiana but are most plentiful in the southern half of the state below I-74. Since 1978, quail populations have remained unchanged in the central part of the state. However, they have declined drastically in northern Indiana and show little signs of recovery.

Over that period, the annual statewide harvest has ranged from

INDIANA
Bobwhite only

50,000 to 250,000 birds. During the most recent season for which records are available, the southwestern region produced the most quail with 45 percent of the statewide kill. The south-central region furnished 27 percent, and the southeastern region produced 11 percent.

Hunters have more than 700,000 acres of land to hunt, a large share of which is in the southern third of the state. The Hoosier National Forest, which covers portions of nine southern counties, contains 430,000 acres.

The season begins in early November and lasts through the year with an extension to mid-January in some areas. The daily bag limit is five bobwhites, and hunter-orange clothing is required.

For more information, contact the Indiana Department of Natural Resources, Division of Fish and Wildlife, 607 State Office Bldg., Indianapolis, IN 46204 (317) 232-4080.

Iowa

Over the past 20 years, Iowa quail hunters have harvested an average of about 700,000 bobwhites annually. In 1985, the statewide population index was up 135 percent over 1984 but was still 18 percent below the 10-year mean. Quail are found throughout the state, but

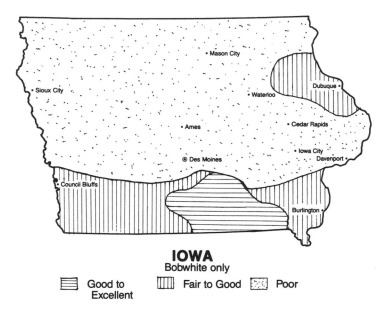

IOWA
Bobwhite only

▤ Good to Excellent   ▥ Fair to Good   ▨ Poor

numbers are lowest in the northern cash-grain belt and highest in the southern pasture region.

Best counties are Clarke, Lucas, Monroe, eastern Decature, Wayne, Appanoose, Davis, and western Van Buren. These are all located in south-central Iowa. Fair to good numbers of quail are found across the lower two tiers of counties. There are also fair numbers of bobs in the northeastern dairy region of Dubuque, Clayton, northeastern Delaware, and eastern Fayette counties.

The Iowa Conservation Commission manages portions of its public hunting lands for quail, but the best hunting usually occurs on private land.

The season traditionally opens statewide on the first Saturday in November and runs through January. The normal daily bag limit is eight quail with a possession limit of 16 allowed.

For more information, contact the Iowa Conservation Commission, Wallace State Office Bldg., Des Moines, IA 50319 (515) 281-5918.

Kansas

As recently as 1982, hunters shot just over 3 million birds. Two years later, the take slid to 920,000, the lowest harvest in more than 20 years. As is true elsewhere, however, populations can fluctuate 50

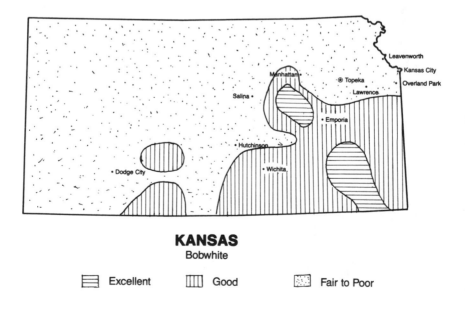

KANSAS
Bobwhite

Excellent   Good   Fair to Poor

percent in a single year, and so Kansas biologists expect quail to rebound.

Bobwhites are found pretty much throughout the state but have the healthiest numbers in the southeastern corner. Wilson, northeastern Montgomery, Labette, and southeastern Neosho rate tops. So do most of Morris and northwestern Lyons counties in the Flint Hills region. In south-central Kansas, Commanche and Edwards counties are good.

In the southwestern corner of the state, in the Cimmaron National Grassland, bobwhites and scaled quail live side by side. Most of the 100,000 acres of public land here are open to hunting, and another 140,000 acres of state-managed wildlife areas—all open to hunting—are scattered throughout the state. Even so, 98 percent of Kansas is privately owned.

The quail season usually opens on the second Saturday in November (third Saturday in western Kansas) and runs until the end of January. The daily bag limit is eight birds with two and three-day possession limits of 16 and 24 respectively.

For more information, contact the Kansas Fish & Game Commission, Rte. 2, PO Box 54A, Pratt, KS 67124 (316) 672-5911.

Kentucky

Bobwhite hunters in Kentucky have been shooting an average of 800,000 birds each fall in recent years. The state is divided into four

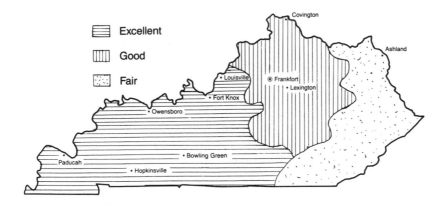

Excellent

Good

Fair

KENTUCKY
Bobwhite

general regions, and quail are found in each. Typically, about 60 percent of the harvest occurs in the western third of the state. The central region accounts for another 20 percent. The bluegrass and eastern areas combine to yield the remaining 20 percent.

Biologists label bobwhite distribution this way: western and central—excellent; bluegrass—good; eastern—fair.

The department of fish and wildlife resources manages quail, along with other game birds and animals, on more than 50 public hunting areas. Scattered throughout the state, these areas range in size from the L. B. Davidson Area in Ohio County at 150 acres to the Daniel Boone National Forest at 618,000 acres in the east-central area. There are also about 25 licensed hunting preserves in the state.

The quail hunting season begins about November 20 and runs to mid-February. Daily limits are eight birds and 16 in possession.

For more information, contact the Kentucky Department of Fish and Wildlife Resources, No. 1 Game Farm Rd., Frankfort, KY 40601 (502) 564-4336.

Louisiana

Each fall 30,000–40,000 hunters shoot an average of about a half-million bobwhites in Louisiana. Highest numbers are found in cutover

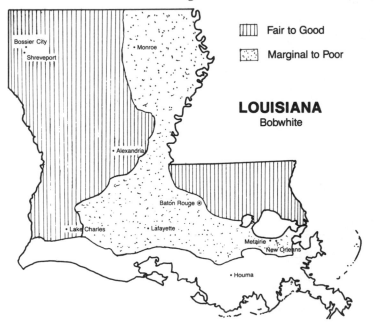

piney woods areas. The state is divided into five regions of varying habitat types with quail living in all except the marsh belt along the ocean. Longleaf pine-covered terraces and hills of the west-central region rate fair to good. So does the shortleaf loblolly pine and hardwood region of the northwest. Bobwhites are also found in fair to good numbers in what is known as the Florida Parish loblolly region. It is located above Lake Pontchartrain. The south-central and northeastern areas of Louisiana rate only poor to fair for quail.

The state manages 38 widely scattered wildlife areas that total more than a million acres. Public hunting is allowed throughout with opportunities for quail ranging from non-existent to good.

The quail season usually begins around November 20 and lasts through February. Daily bag and possession limits are 10 and 20 birds respectively. Hunter-orange clothing is required.

For more information, contact the Louisiana Department of Wildlife and Fisheries, Information & Education Division, PO Box 15570, Baton Rouge, LA 70895 (504) 342-5868.

Maine

There are no native populations of quail in Maine.

Maryland

Maryland has fair to good hunting opportunities for bobwhite quail. The annual kill has averaged about 150,000 over the past 10 years. Today, about 22,000 hunters go afield in search of bobwhites.

Birds are found throughout the state, but heaviest concentrations live along eastern counties bordering Delaware and in the southern counties of Wicomico, Somerset, Worcester, St. Mary's, Charles, and Calvert. Garrett, Allegheny, and Fulton counties in the far western part of the state have the fewest numbers.

The department of natural resources manages many of the nearly 60 wildlife areas in Maryland for quail, along with other game animals and birds. They are open to hunting. The season usually runs from November 15 to January 31, and bag and possession limits are four and eight quail respectively.

For more information, contact the Maryland Forest, Park and Wildlife Service, Tawes State Office Bldg., Annapolis, MD 21401 (301) 269-3195.

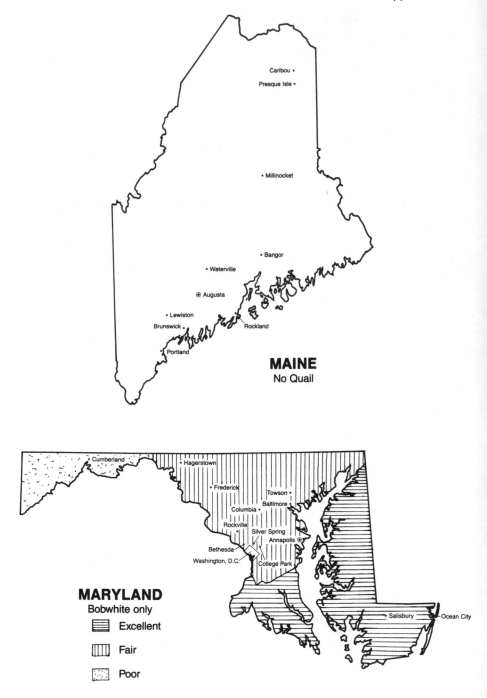

MAINE
No Quail

MARYLAND
Bobwhite only

Excellent

Fair

Poor

MASSACHUSETTS
Bobwhite only

||||| Good to Fair   [⋯] Poor

Massachusetts

Huntable populations of bobwhites are found only in the five southeastern towns of Barnstable, Bristol, Dukes, Nantucket and Plymouth. Quail are present, but reasonably scarce, in other areas of eastern and central Massachusetts and are absent—or nearly so—from the western part of the state.

The division of fisheries and wildlife has no accurate data on hunter harvest, but during a recent season, quail ranked seventh out of nine in preference among small game species and ninth out of nine in harvest. The division has a limited stocking program using pen-reared birds at Crane Wildlife Management Area at Falmouth and in the Myles Standish State Forest. Hunter-orange is required clothing on management areas.

The quail season begins about October 20 and lasts until the end of November. The five towns listed above are the only ones open to hunting. The daily bag limit is five quail. Possession and season limits are 10 and 25 respectively.

For more information, contact the Massachusetts Division of Fisheries and Wildlife, 100 Cambridge St., Boston, MA 02202 (617) 727-3151.

IIIII Fair to Poor

MICHIGAN
Bobwhite only

• Saginaw

• Flint

• Grand Rapids

⊛ Lansing

Warren •

Battle Creek

Detroit
Dearborn

Kalamazoo

Jackson

Ann Arbor

Sault Ste. Marie

Michigan

Bobwhite quail are at the limits of their northern range in southern Michigan, yet small, isolated pockets live in the 33 counties in this
region. After a hunting closure from 1912 to 1965, the department of
natural resources allowed a season for a dozen years. In 1977, the last
season on record, hunters shot 46,000 birds. Bad winters have since
knocked populations down so badly that they have not recovered to
huntable numbers and are not expected to do so in the near future.

Minnesota

Until 1959, Minnesota wingshooters enjoyed a limited bobwhite
quail season from two to three weeks long with bag limits varying
from five to 10 birds daily. The season has been closed since. Biologists
estimate that fall populations number 2,000 to 5,000 birds. They are

MINNESOTA
Bobwhite only

limited to the extreme southeastern portion of the state and are most plentiful in southern Houston and southeastern Fillmore counties.

Mississippi

Bobwhites are the only native quail in Mississippi. Their distribution is statewide, but population levels vary, depending on land-use practices. Generally, good numbers are found in the eastern two-thirds of the state. Numbers are lowest in counties fronting the Gulf of Mexico and in western counties along the Arkansas and Louisiana borders.

During a recent season, hunters shot more than 1.2 million bobwhites for an average seasonal harvest of nearly 25 birds per gun.

The department of wildlife conservation manages 31 wildlife areas scattered throughout the state. When coupled with seven national

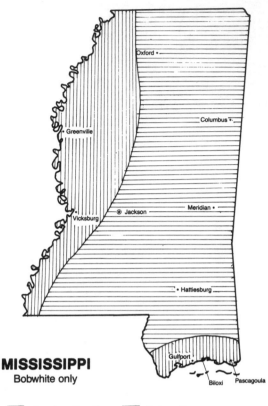

MISSISSIPPI
Bobwhite only

▤ Good to Excellent   ▥ Fair to Poor

wildlife refuges, there are more than a million acres of public land for hunters to roam. Quail are one of several huntable species of wildlife managed on the public lands. In addition, there are more than 30 shooting preserves in Mississippi, many of which are open to the public for fees.

The three-month season begins in late November and runs through February. Bag limits are 12 daily and 24 in possession.

For more information, contact the Mississippi Department of Wildlife Conservation, PO Box 451, Jackson, MS 39205-0451 (601) 961-5300.

Missouri

Bobwhites live throughout the state, but west-central Missouri in the Western Prairie Region has the most birds. Populations are lowest

MISSOURI
Bobwhite only

Excellent

Fair

Poor

in the three Ozark regions in the south where biologists rate numbers as poor to fair. Generally good populations are found north of the Missouri River.

During each of the past 20 years, Missouri hunters have shot between 1.2 and 3.9 million bobwhites for a seasonal average of 11 to 21 birds per hunter. The most recent "good" year on record was in 1982 when they pocketed 2.4 million quail.

Public hunting lands in the form of wildlife management areas and state and national forests are scattered throughout Missouri. The best quail hunting, however, is on private farmland with a good mix of habitat.

Recently, Missouri went to a northern and southern zone system, using the Missouri River as a boundary. In the northern zone, the quail hunting season opened November 1 and closed January 1. The bag limits were eight daily and 16 in possesssion. The southern zone hunting season was November 10 to January 10, and respective bag limits were six and 12.

For more information, contact the Missouri Department of Conservation, PO Box 180, Jefferson City, MO 65102 (314) 751-4115.

MONTANA
No quail

Montana

There are no quail hunting opportunities.

Nebraska

Bobwhite quail were completely protected in Nebraska from 1917 through 1943. In 1944, a 10-day season was allowed in four southeastern counties. Now the entire state is open to hunting.

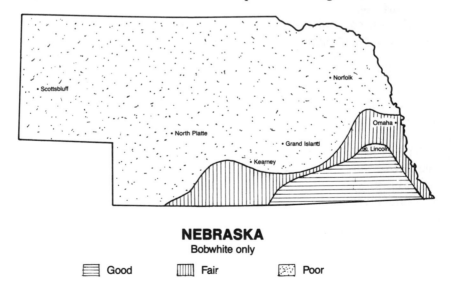

NEBRASKA
Bobwhite only

▤ Good   ▥ Fair   ▦ Poor

Most of the birds are found south of I-80 with the southeastern region providing the best hunting. Rating best are the counties of western Richardson, Otoe, and Nemaha; southern Lancaster; all of Johnson, Pawnee, Gage, Jefferson, Thayer, and Nuckolls; and southeastern Webster.

Annual harvest in recent years has been running from 500,000 to 800,000 birds. Best hunting opportunities occur on private land with mixed habitat, but the game and parks commission also manages portions of several public lands that are open to hunting for quail.

The season usually begins on the first Saturday in November and ends in mid-January. Bag limits are four daily and 12 in possession.

For more information, contact the Nebraska Game and Parks Commission, PO Box 30370, Lincoln, NE 68503 (402) 464-0641.

Nevada

Four species of quail live in Nevada. Valley quail are most abundant and thrive mostly on farmlands in the northern half of the state. Harvests in recent years have ranged from a low of 20,000 to a high of 82,000. Numbers are fairly consistent in northwestern Nevada. In northeastern Nevada, they tend to fluctuate due to winter severity.

Gambel quail live in the desert shrub country of southern Nevada. Hunter harvests range from about 3,300 to 8,500 birds each year.

Mountain quail reside along brushy streams in scattered mountainous areas of western Nevada. Small populations live in the Silver Peak, Wassuk, Carson, and Pah Rah ranges and the White, Pine Nut, and Virginia mountains. Their numbers have declined considerably in recent years. Harvest figures are not known.

Scaled quail have been released at various places throughout the state. Currently they are found along the White River Valley from a few miles south of Sunnyside to Ruth and in the Buffalo Valley region below Battle Mountain. Small, isolated pockets live north and west of Gerlach. Their contribution to the overall quail kill is very small.

Most of the land area in Nevada is publicly owned and open to hunting. However, some of the best hunting, especially for valley quail, occurs on private land.

The hunting season usually begins in mid-October and lasts through January, statewide, except for fenced and cultivated lands of the Lovelock Valley in Pershing County. Recently, a two-day season there was November 9 and 10. Daily and possession limits are 10 and 20 birds, either single species or in aggregate.

For more information, contact the Nevada Department of Wildlife, PO Box 10678, Reno, NV 89520 (702) 789-0500.

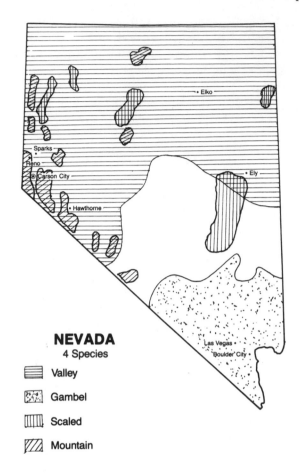

NEVADA
4 Species

▤ Valley

▦ Gambel

▥ Scaled

▨ Mountain

New Hampshire

Historically, bobwhites lived throughout southern New Hampshire, but they were all but gone by the early 1900s. The only birds found today are a few field-trial releases that manage to winter over occasionally.

New Jersey

Although bobwhites were once distributed throughout the state, present range is from Mercer and Middlesex counties south. Excellent numbers are found in the southern tier of counties fronting Delaware Bay. Generally speaking, good populations live above this area from

NEW HAMPSHIRE
None

Atlantic City northwest to the New Jersey Turnpike. For the rest of the
quail range, numbers rate poor to fair.

Throughout the 70s, annual harvests averaged a quarter-million
birds. After a population crash in 1979, bobwhites have been inching
back. Recent harvests have fallen between 128,000 and 149,000.

The best hunting occurs on private land; however, many of the
50 wildlife management areas—where quail are among the species
managed—are in the southern better-quail areas. Altogether, there are
about 350,000 acres of public land open to hunting in New Jersey.

Recently, the hunting season began November 9 and closed December 7, then reopened for the period December 16 to February 8.
The limit was seven quail. Hunter-orange clothing is required.

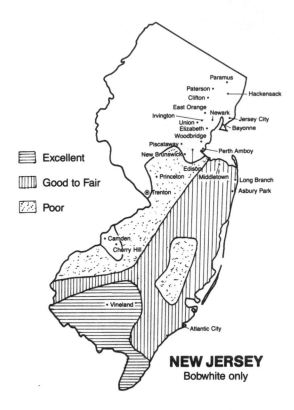

Excellent

Good to Fair

Poor

NEW JERSEY
Bobwhite only

For more information, contact the New Jersey Department of Environmental Protection, Division of Fish, Game and Wildlife, CN-400, Trenton, NJ 08625 (609) 292-2965.

New Mexico

Four species of quail are native to New Mexico with one or more species found throughout the state except for higher mountains of the northern region. Scaled quail are most abundant, ranging from deserts of the Low Sonoran region of 3,000 feet altitude to Upper Sonoran pinyon-juniper woodlands at 7,000 feet. Favored habitats are brushy plains and mesa country, and heaviest concentrations occur in east-central, southeastern and southwestern New Mexico.

Gambel quail are especially plentiful in the tornillo and mesquite thickets of the southwestern and south-central regions. There are also some in the San Juan Valley of the northwest.

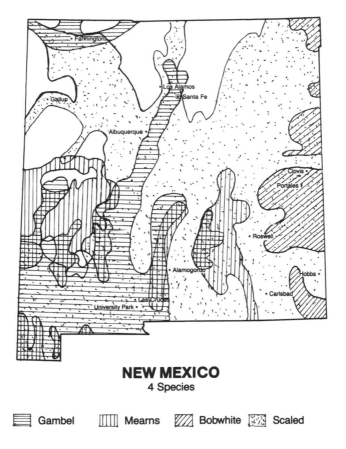

NEW MEXICO
4 Species

▤ Gambel   ‖‖‖ Mearns   ▨ Bobwhite   ▨ Scaled

Small numbers of bobwhites live in eastern New Mexico in prairie habitat and along brushy fencerows containing weeds.

Mearns quail are found only west of the Pecos Valley in the southern half of the state, especially in foothill and mountain habitat above 5,000 feet elevation. The birds show up in small numbers in several of the mountain ranges, and, although they are never really plentiful, hunters sometimes find enough to bag, especially in the Mogollon Mountains and Black Range areas.

New Mexico hunters shoot an average of 200,000 quail each year for a seasonal range of eight to 14 birds per hunter.

Huge portions of the state are publicly owned and open to hunting. Seasons run from about November 9 to February 16 except in Curry, Lea, and Roosevelt counties. There a recent season began November 30 and ended February 16. Limits throughout the state have been 15 quail daily and 30 in possession for all species, singly or in aggregation.

For more information, contact the New Mexico Department of Game and Fish, State Capitol, Villagra Bldg., Santa Fe, NM 87503 (505) 827-7882.

New York

Bobwhite hunting is limited exclusively to Long Island on state-administered cooperative hunting areas. Although the fish and wildlife division does not keep harvest statistics, biologists report that populations are stable and subject to only minimal hunting pressures. Extensive development on Long Island has limited both hunter access and, to a lesser extent, habitat.

Seasons typically begin November 1 and end December 31 with a daily bag of six quail and a season bag of 40 allowed.

For more information, contact the New York Department of Environmental Conservation, Fish and Wildlife Division, 50 Wolf Rd., Albany, NY 12233 (518) 457-5400.

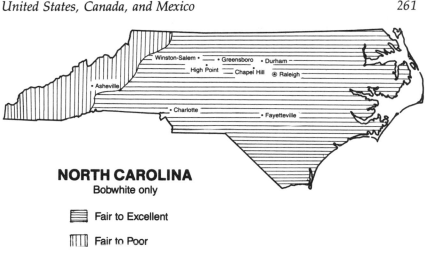

NORTH CAROLINA
Bobwhite only

▤ Fair to Excellent

▥ Fair to Poor

North Carolina

The distribution of bobwhite quail is statewide except that in the mountains populations are scattered and generally quite low. Most of the hunting occurs east of a line from eastern Allegheny County to Transylvania County.

During a recent season, hunters shot 816,204 bobwhites. About 60 percent came from the Coastal region. The Piedmont region yielded most of the rest, with the Mountains region contributing about 20,000 birds. The average number of quail bagged per hunter per trip was 1.73 compared to 1.56 in 1976–77, the last time the state conducted harvest surveys.

Bobwhites are among the primary species hunted on about 40 of the 70 state game lands scattered throughout the state. Private lands, however, support the best hunting. There are a large number of hunting preserves in North Carolina.

A recent season began November 23 and ended February 28 with bag limits of 10 quail daily, 20 in possession, and 100 for the season.

For more information, contact the North Carolina Wildlife Resources Commission, 512 N. Salisbury St., Raleigh, NC 27611 (919) 733-3391.

North Dakota

There is no quail hunting in North Dakota.

NORTH DAKOTA
No quail

Ohio

In 1969, wildlife biologists estimated there were 7.3 million bob-white quail in Ohio. Hunters that year shot 467,000 birds. The terrible winter of 1977–78 knocked numbers down by 90 percent or more to an estimated 430,000 statewide, and the state closed the season.

Bobwhites are making a slow comeback, thanks in part to a division of wildlife stocking program that, since 1979, has released over 30,000 first-generation adult birds from wild stock in 61 of Ohio's 88 counties.

The division of wildlife reopened the season in 1985 in 12 south-western counties, and hunters responded with a small harvest of birds, mostly on state-managed lands open to hunting. Biologists are hopeful that recovery, with their help, can continue.

A three-week season is held in November with a bag limit of three quail daily and six in possession. For more information, contact the Ohio Department of Natural Resources, Division of Wildlife, Fountain Square, Columbus, OH 43224 (614) 265-6789.

Oklahoma

Oklahoma has some of the finest bobwhite quail hunting in the country. Annual harvest figures for the most recent five years available ranged from 1.4 million to 3.6 million birds. Average seasonal kill per hunter during the survey period varied from 17 to 30 quail.

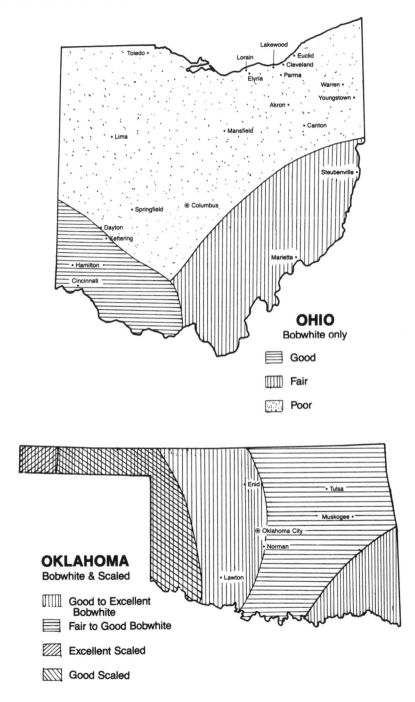

OHIO
Bobwhite only

Good

Fair

Poor

OKLAHOMA
Bobwhite & Scaled

Good to Excellent
Bobwhite

Fair to Good Bobwhite

Excellent Scaled

Good Scaled

Bobwhites are found throughout the state, but the best hunting usually occurs in central and western prairie areas along field edges and shelter belts. Clear cuts in southeastern forest lands also produce excellent shooting. Scaled quail live in southwestern counties and in the Panhandle with best hunting opportunities occurring in rugged uplands of Cimarron County.

Public land is scarce in Oklahoma, and so the best hunting is found on private lands. Some sportsmen and a few professional guides who have landowner leasing arrangements enjoy tremendous wild-bird shooting for themselves and clients.

The hunting season traditionally opens on November 20. East of I-35, it has been closing on February 15. West of I-35, it usually ends on February 1. Hunting on private lands is prohibited on Sundays, Wednesdays, and legal holidays. The bag limit is 10 quail daily and 20 in possession.

For more information, contact the Oklahoma Department of Wild-life Conservation, 1801 N. Lincoln Blvd., Oklahoma City, OK 73105 (405) 521-3851.

Oregon

Huntable numbers of valley and mountain quail are found in Oregon. Valley quail live throughout the state but are most plentiful in the southeastern region. Good populations are found in Jackson and Josephine counties, and the Umpqua and Williamette valleys have fair densities. Valley quail seem to be holding their own in numbers or improving slightly. During the last two years for which harvest records are available, hunters shot 125,000 and 150,000 respectively.

Mountain quail are most plentiful in western Oregon where populations are currently on an upswing. In eastern Oregon the birds are sparsely distributed and remain at low levels. Best places to try for this challenging gamebird are the Coast, Cascade, Blue, and Wallowa mountains. During the most recent year for which harvest records are available, hunters shot 52,500 birds.

Bobwhites are scattered throughout farming areas with highest numbers reported in Umatilla and Malheur counties and portions of the Williamette Valley. There are no kill figures to report.

A recent hunting season in western Oregon began October 12 and ended November 10 for valley quail, and ran from August 31 to November 6 and November 23 to January 12 for mountain quail. Limits for both birds were 10 daily and 20 in possession. In eastern Oregon (except for Columbia Basin counties) the season for both species

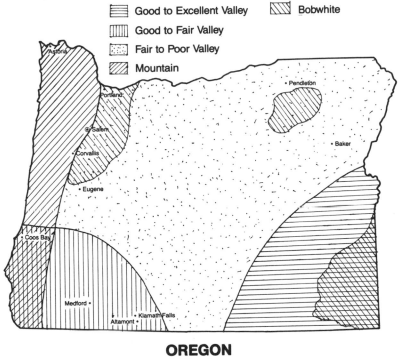

OREGON
3 Species

began October 12 and ended November 24. Valley quail limits were 10 and 20 respectively; for mountain quail they were two daily and two in possession. In the counties of the Columbia Basin, the season was October 12 to December 15 with bag limits identical to the eastern region. Check a current copy of state hunting laws to be sure you are legal.

For more information, contact the Oregon Department of Fish and Wildlife, PO Box 3503, Portland, OR 97208 (503) 229-5551.

Pennsylvania

There is very little, if any at all, hunting for wild bobwhite quail in Pennsylvania. Populations have been extremely low for the past 15 years, and the hunting season is closed in 13 southern counties comprising the birds' historical range. The game commission no longer monitors populations or harvests.

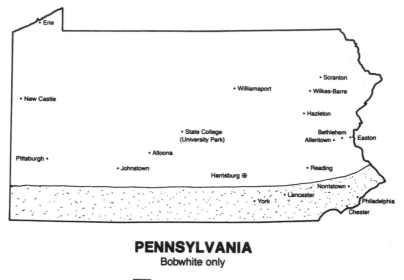

PENNSYLVANIA
Bobwhite only

 Fair to Poor

Many sportsmen's clubs around the state, however, are active with releasing pen-reared birds for the purpose of hunting them. Further, the game commission is attempting to secure wild-trapped bobwhites for release in an area under intensive habitat management for them. Once releases are made, researchers will monitor the results.

In Pennsylvania's other 54 counties, hunters usually observe a three-week hunting season in November with limits of four quail daily and eight in possession. The shooting preserve season begins September 1 and ends April 30.

For more information, contact the Pennsylvania Game Commission, PO Box 1567, Harrisburg, PA 17105-1567 (717) 787-6286.

Rhode Island

Quail hunters have limited opportunities for bobwhites with a few scattered coveys found in the southernmost towns of North and South Kingstown, Charlestown and Westerly. Biologists rate distribution as "fair" but have no recent harvest or population figures.

Hunting season dates are usually mid-October to early December and mid-December through February. The daily bag is five quail. Special regulations apply to Prudence Island.

RHODE ISLAND
Bobwhite only

| Fair

For more information, contact the Rhode Island Department of Environmental Management, Division of Fish and Wildlife, Government Center, Wakefield, RI 02879 (401) 789-3094.

South Carolina

Bobwhite quail are found in all counties of South Carolina, and biologists report excellent distribution in the southern one-third to one-half of the state. Bobwhite numbers are rated "good" elsewhere except in the extreme northwestern region where populations are considered fair.

The most recent quail harvest figures available show that hunters shot an estimated 1.5 million birds. This represents a declining trend from previous mail surveys.

The state manages quail on several game areas scattered throughout South Carolina. Still, the better hunting occurs on private land. In addition, about 20 preserves, most of which offer quail hunting, and all of which are open to the public, are regulated by the wildlife and marine resources department.

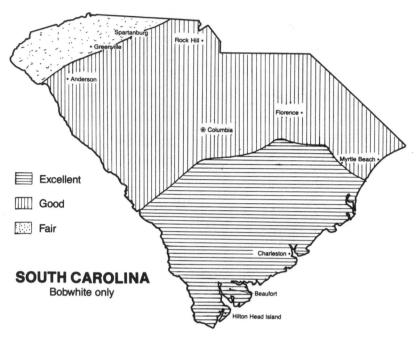

SOUTH CAROLINA
Bobwhite only

The hunting season typically begins in late November and runs until March 1. The daily limit is 10 or 15 quail, depending upon hunting zone.

For more information, contact the South Carolina Wildlife and Marine Resources Department, PO Box 167, Columbia, SC 29202 (803) 758-0001.

South Dakota

Upland bird hunters have available a limited amount of bobwhite hunting in extreme southeastern South Dakota. Quail are found in scattered portions of the southern tier of counties above Nebraska from Tripp County east to the Iowa border. Best opportunities occur along timbered riverbottoms and on private farmland with cover. Quail also live on some of the more than 50 state game production areas in this region.

South Dakota is at the extreme northern limits of bobwhite habitat, and so birds are always at the mercy of the weather. Harvests in recent years have fallen between 1,900 and 3,700 birds. The hunting

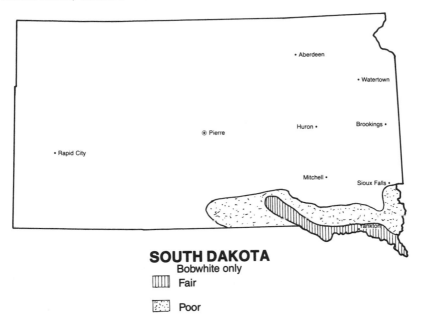

SOUTH DAKOTA
Bobwhite only

▥ Fair

▨ Poor

season usually spans the month of November and is typically limited to seven southeastern counties. The daily limit is five quail.

For more information, contact the South Dakota Department of Game, Fish and Parks, Anderson Building, Pierre, SD 57501 (605) 773-3485.

Tennessee

Bobwhite quail live throughout the state and are reported to be in good supply in all areas except these three: western Shelby county in extreme southwestern Tennessee; Davidson county in north-central Tennessee; and the eastern tier of counties bordering North Carolina. Biologists consider bobwhite populations in these areas to be only "fair."

The 32-year harvest average is for about .75 quail per hunter per hour. Occasional "poor" hunting years over that span included 1981 when the kill dipped to .65 quail per hunter per hour. During each of the three years since for which records are available, it rose above the average. In a recent season, 71,500 hunters shot 1.2 million bobwhites for an excellent kill per trip ratio averaging 3.25 birds for each hunter.

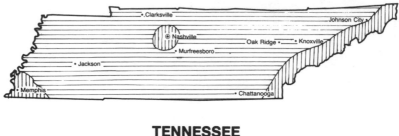

TENNESSEE
Bobwhite only

▤ Good

▥ Fair

The season begins in early November and runs through February with a daily bag of 15 quail permitted.

For more information, contact the Tennessee Wildlife Resources Agency, Ellington Agricultural Center, PO Box 40747, Nashville, TN 37204 (615) 360-0500.

Texas

Texas is home to four species of quail—bobwhites, Gambel, scaled and Mearns—and all the Mearns quail may be hunted. Bobwhites are most plentiful in that half of the state east of the 101st meridian. They share habitat with scaled quail in the central region of the state. The Panhandle and western counties host mostly scaled quail, and Gambel quail live along the Rio Grande River between Big Bend National Park and El Paso. Gambels do not figure heavily in the harvest.

Differing habitats dictate where quail live in Texas. In sand hills of the Panhandle, principal covers are sagebrush, tall grasses, sumac, and wild plum. In the eastern grasslands region, mesquite, granjeno, guajillo, black brush, white brush, and prickly pear provide woody cover. The Grand Prairie of central Texas is punctuated by many creeks with dry feeder streams that finger out into the grasslands and that offer ideal bobwhite cover—vines, trees, thickets and low bushes.

Quail hunting is big sport in Texas. In 1960, 321,000 hunters shot 9.8 million birds for an average of more than 30 birds per gun. Those figures, however, have dropped sharply. In a recent season, 287,000 hunters shot 3,395,000 quail for a per-gun season average of 12 birds.

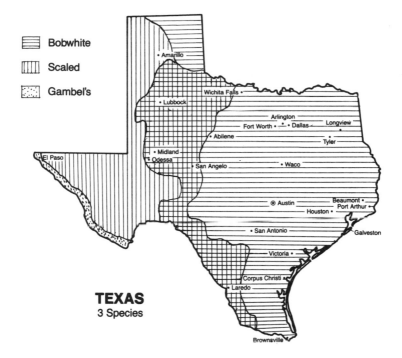

Bobwhite

Scaled

Gambel's

TEXAS
3 Species

Eighty percent of the harvest is typically bobwhites; the rest are mostly scaled quail.

The hunting season begins in early November and ends in late February. Limits have been 12 quail daily and 36 in possession. Hunter-orange clothing is required when hunting on wildlife management areas.

For more information, contact the Texas Parks & Wildlife Department, 4200 Smith School Rd., Austin, TX 78744 (512) 479-4800.

Utah

Although there are huntable numbers of valley and Gambel quail in Utah, there is not a lot of interest among sportsmen. Quail populations are limited by severe winter weather and summer droughts. The 25-year harvest average is 18,876 or less than three birds for each hunter that went afield. During a recent season, 3,654 hunters shot 8,303 quail.

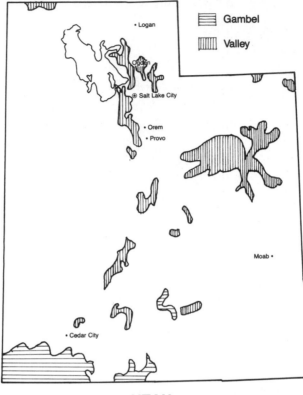

UTAH
2 Species

Valley quail are scattered throughout the state wherever farming is practiced. One area of concentration is south of Highway 191 between Vernal and Duchesne. Other farming pockets occur along Highway 15 from Salt Lake City south to Cedar City. Although the state owns about 3,000 acres of upland game habitat, which is managed for pheasants and quail, the best hunting occurs on private land.

Gambel quail are limited to Washington County in the southwestern corner of Utah. The best shooting is on public lands, which are open to hunting. Preserve hunting for quail is also available.

Hunting periods usually include a nine-day season in early November, open statewide except for five selected counties. In Duchesne and Uintah counties, the November season typically lasts 17 days. Bag limits for these two seasons are five quail daily and 10 in possession.

In Washington County, where the limits are eight and 16 respectively, the season lasts until the end of December.

For more information, contact the Utah Division of Wildlife Resources, 1596 West North Temple, Salt Lake City, UT 84116 (801) 533-9333.

Vermont

Vermont currently has no populations of wild quail in the state. Any scattered bobwhites that may exist are only the remnants of sportsmen's club or individual releases for put-and-take purposes.

Quail hunting is permitted from the last Saturday in September through the last Thursday before the deer season, which usually opens in mid-November. Limits are four quail daily and eight in possession.

VERMONT
None

For more information, contact the Vermont Fish and Wildlife Department, Montpelier, VT 05602 (802) 828-3371.

Virginia

In 1980, Virginia ranked 17th in total quail harvested out of 40 states that have quail populations. There are about 40,000 quail hunters in Virginia, and during a recent season they shot 346,354 bobwhites.

Eastern Virginia, namely the Tidewater and east Piedmont areas, has been the most productive. Quail distribution in these regions, roughly the eastern third of the state, is rated "good." "Fair" numbers are found in the west Piedmont and northern areas, or what is roughly the central portion of Virginia. The central and southwest mountain divisions are regarded as marginal range with only scattered bobwhite populations, mainly in valley agricultural areas.

The best hunting occurs on private lands although some wildlife management areas are also productive. In general, those areas east of the Blue Ridge Mountains provide some quail hunting; those west do not. Some timber company property also yields good quail populations for several years following clearcutting.

The season west of the Blue Ridge opens on the first Monday in November and runs through January. West of the Blue Ridge, the season begins on the Monday preceding Thanksgiving and lasts

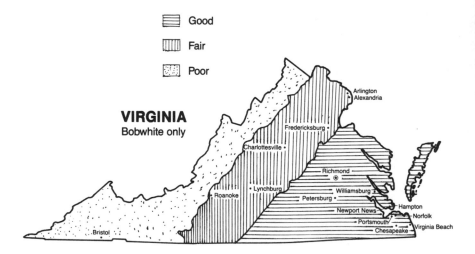

through February. Bag limits are eight quail daily and 125 per year. It is not legal to hunt quail in the snow in Virginia.

For more information, contact the Virginia Commission of Game and Inland Fisheries, Box 11104, Richmond, VA 23230-1104 (804) 257-1000.

Washington

Washington has fair to good numbers of valley quail and small, scattered populations of mountain quail. Although both species have fluctuated in numbers from year to year, they have not suffered the populations crashes and peaks experienced by some other states. In fact, valley quail in particular are currently increasing. Favorable spring nesting weather is one reason; a winter feeding program by the department of game is another.

Valley quail live mostly in eastern Washington along draws and river bottoms and are usually associated with farms. Some of the best hunting occurs on such private lands, but there are also some noteworthy opportunities on public lands where quail are among the spe-

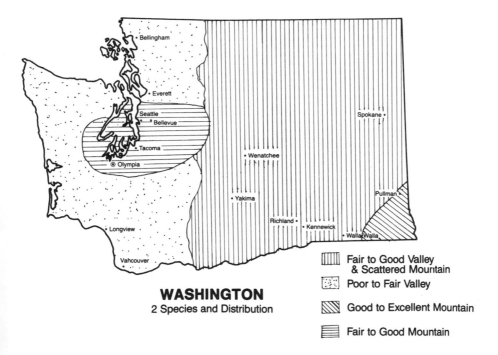

WASHINGTON
2 Species and Distribution

Fair to Good Valley & Scattered Mountain

Poor to Fair Valley

Good to Excellent Mountain

Fair to Good Mountain

cies managed. During the period 1980 through 1984, hunters shot an average of 204,000 quail each year, and most were valley species. The best places to try for mountain quail are in the Blue Mountains of southeastern Washington and in Pierce, King, and Mason counties in the South Puget Sound area.

The statewide season begins in mid-October. In western Washington, it usually ends on December 1; in eastern Washington, it runs until the end of the year. During a recent season, limits were five quail daily and 15 in possession in the western area and 10 and 30 quail respectively in the eastern unit.

For more information, contact the Washington Department of Game, 600 N. Capitol Way, Olympia, WA 98504 (206) 753-5700.

West Virginia

There are small pockets of bobwhite quail and quail habitat scattered throughout West Virginia. However, the state is more than 80 percent forested, and the potential for an increase in quail is therefore sharply limited. The department of natural resources does not conduct population surveys and has no harvest figures on record.

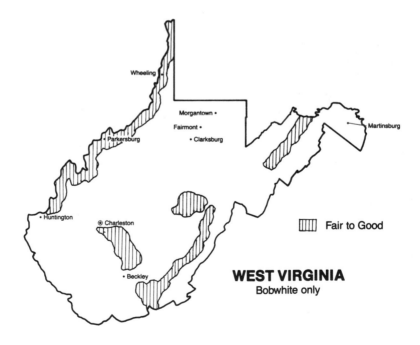

IIIII Fair to Good

WEST VIRGINIA
Bobwhite only

The best areas to find bobwhites are the Ohio, Lower Kanawha, Greenbrier, South Branch, and Potomac River valleys on private farmlands featuring a mixture of habitat. Other good hunting possibilities exist on those public lands which the state intensively manages for quail. Better ones include Kumbrabow State Forest, McClintic Wildlife Station, and Pleasants Creek, Lewis Wetzel, Chief Cornstalk, Hilbert, and Bluestone public hunting and fishing areas.

The hunting season usually begins in early November and runs through February. The limit has been seven quail daily and 21 in possession. For more information, contact the West Virginia Department of Natural Resources, Wildlife Resources Division, 1800 Washington St. E., Charlestown, WV 25305 (304) 348-2771.

Wisconsin

There are limited hunting opportunities for bobwhites in about 20 south-central and southwestern counties. Highest populations are currently found in three areas: southern Waushara, western Green Lake, and most of Marquette counties; southeastern Green and

WISCONSIN
Bobwhites only

southwestern Rock counties; and northern Iowa, northeastern tip of Grant, most of Richland, extreme eastern Crawford, and eastern Vernon counties.

Populations rise and fall with winter severity levels. The department of natural resources has kept harvest data for more than 50 years, and annual hunter bags have been as high as 52,000 in 1957 and as low as 4,200 in 1982.

The best hunting occurs on private land although the state also manages public lands for quail, along with other game species. Further, many commercial preserves in Wisconsin offer quail hunting and are open to the public.

The hunting season usually begins about October 20 and ends in mid-December. Limits are five quail daily and 10 in possession. For more information, contact the Wisconsin Department of Natural Resources, PO Box 7921, Madison, WI 53707 (608) 266-1877.

Wyoming

There are so few quail in Wyoming that there is no open season, and the game and fish department has no management practices to benefit them.

WYOMING
None

CANADA

||||| Bobwhite Quail

≡ Valley Quail

YUKON

NORTHWEST TERRITORIES

NEWFOUNDLAND

QUÉBEC

ALBERTA

SASKATCHEWAN

MANITOBA

BRITISH COLUMBIA

ONTARIO

NEW BRUNSWICK

NOVA SCOTIA

Canada

Most quail hunting in Canada occurs on shooting preserves in the southern provinces. In Ontario, for example, there are seven commercial preserves that offer bobwhite or coturnix (Japanese) quail hunting.

The only hunting for wild bobwhites occurs in Wildlife Management Unit 92 in southern Ontario west of London and in Wildlife Management Unit 65 in eastern Ontario near Cornwall. A recent hunting season began October 30 and ended November 7 in the western unit and ran from September 20 to December 15 in the eastern unit. Bag limits in each were three quail daily and six in possession. Privately owned farmlands produce the best sport.

For more information, contact the Ontario Ministry of Natural Resources, Outdoor Recreation/Wildlife Information, Parliament Bldg., Toronto, Ontario M7A IW3 Canada (416) 965-4251.

The Okanagan Valley in south-central British Columbia contains fairly good populations of valley quail although the overall trend is for a population decrease. This is mainly due to urban expansion and a shift from orchard fruit growing to vineyard operations. There is also a small valley quail population on Vancouver Island. Biologists estimate that 150,000 to 200,000 valley quail live in the province.

In the Okanagan Valley, hunting seasons begin in early October and end about the third week in November with generous bag limits of 10 birds daily and 30 in possession. On Vancouver Island, the season is a little shorter with bag limits cut in half.

There is also a small remnant population of mountain quail— estimated at 300 to 800 birds—living on Vancouver Island, but the birds may not be hunted. For more information, contact the British Columbia Ministry of Environment, Wildlife Branch, Parliament Buildings, Victoria, BC Canada V8V 1X4 (604) 387-4573.

Various species in 28 of Mexico's states

Mexico

In 1984–85, hunting for quail was allowed in 28 of Mexico's 32 states. Bobwhites are the main attraction in most although some states offer scaled, Gambel, Montezuma (Mearns), Yucatan, Barred, valley, mountain, and Douglas quail. Depending upon the state and species of quail, daily limits vary from two to 15, possession limits from four to 30. Seasons open as early as late September and run as long as March 10.

For information on current seasons and regulations, contact Wildlife Advisory Services, PO Box 76132, Los Angeles, CA 90076 (213) 385-9311.

The company will also provide hunters with appropriate licenses and permits.

Tom Huggler with Lady Macbeth and Chaucer during a rest break while hunting in Arizona. *(Tony Mandile photo)*

Index